To: Bob,

We hope to see a section about You, in the next edition of this Book.

Ian, Judy & Charlotte,

xxx

CHRISTMAS 1987

The Innovators

The Essential Guide to Business Thinkers, Achievers and Entrepreneurs

OTHER BOOKS
by William Davis

Three Years Hard Labour

Merger Mania

Money Talks

Have Expenses, Will Travel

It's No Sin to Be Rich

The Best of Everything *(editor)*

Money in the 1980s

The Rich: A Study of the Species

Fantasy: A Practical Guide to Escapism

The Corporate Infighter's Handbook

The World's Best Business Hotels *(editor)*

The Super Salesman's Handbook

The Innovators

The Essential Guide to Business Thinkers, Achievers and Entrepreneurs

William Davis

EBURY PRESS
LONDON

Published by Ebury Press
Division of The National Magazine Company Ltd
Colquhoun House
27-37 Broadwick Street
London W1V 1FR

First impression 1987

ISBN 0 85223 537 2

Designed and produced by
Genesis Productions Limited
30 Great Portland Street, London W1

Printed and bound in Great Britain by
Butler Tanner Ltd, Frome and London

Contents

List of Illustrations

Picture research by Anne-Marie Ehrlich

Acknowledgments

In thirty years of writing about the business world I have had the good fortune to meet many of the people featured in this book. Clearly, though, I have not been able to interview them all. Many made their mark before I was even born. I have, therefore, had to rely to a considerable extent on a wide range of sources, including autobiographies, contemporary press reports, and material supplied by the companies which they created or worked for.

I have done my best to check and cross-check the facts, and I am grateful to Tessa Nicholson, who helped with the research; to Esther Jagger, who provided useful suggestions and edited the book; and to the numerous people who so kindly provided other invaluable assistance.

Main entries are arranged alphabetically. Within those entries names in CAPITALS are sometimes followed by a short account of the achievements of another, associated, innovator. If there is no such account, the name in capitals is a cross-reference to another main entry.

Introduction

Innovation is surely the most exciting part of business life. It can also be one of the most frustrating, but there is nothing to compare with the thrill of finding a new idea and turning it into concrete reality. This book is about people who have done just that. It covers a wide range of activities, because innovation is clearly not confined to any particular field.

The past century and a half has seen advances in technology which are without parallel in history. As a result, it has become commonplace to associate the word 'innovation' with technological change; but it has a much wider application. We live in what Peter Drucker has called 'The age of discontinuity'. People everywhere are constantly looking not only for new products but for new ways of doing things – in manufacturing, in finance, in services, in management, in the arts, in economics. Some innovations, such as instalment buying and the supermarket, have made as much of an impact on our lives as the great advances in technology.

Perhaps, at the outset, a distinction should be made between the two terms 'inventor' and 'innovator', because they are so widely confused. The inventor produces ideas; the innovator makes new things happen. Many talented people do both, but someone who is good at inventing is not necessarily good at turning his concept into a viable commercial proposition. Many inventors are more interested in the idea as such, and in the challenge it represents, than in the business of making it into a marketable – and profitable – product or service, with all the difficulties and hazards which that involves.

The successful innovator is a *doer* – someone with imagination who can visualize the possibilities of an idea and who has a strong desire to see it realized in concrete form. He or she usually encounters considerable scepticism and even determined opposition. There may be discouraging setbacks. It takes a lot of nerve to press on despite all the doubts and uncertainties.

Sometimes, of course, the sceptics turn out to be right. Ideas which look brilliant on paper may prove unworkable, or too costly to implement, or too limited in their appeal. There may come a point at which it is plain that to press on would be a foolish waste of time and money. But one of the most noteworthy characteristics of the many people featured in *The Innovators* is that they are not the kind of men and women who give up easily.

King C. Gillette had the idea for a safety razor while he was shaving one morning in 1895. 'In a moment', he later recalled, 'I saw it all.' He wrote to his wife: 'I've got it! Our fortune is made!' The jubilation was decidedly premature. He made many experiments with steel blades, but the 'experts' whom he consulted advised him to forget it; they insisted that he would never succeed in putting an edge on sheet steel that would shave. He persisted, but the venture did not get off the ground until 1903 – after a young graduate from the Massachusetts Institute of Technology, William E. Nickerson, had found the answer to the technical problem.

Sir Alastair Pilkington, who developed the 'float' method of glassmaking, struggled for seven years to prove that his theories had practical value. People, he says, used to ask him: 'When will you succeed?' All he could say was: 'We will know the answer to that only when we have succeeded.' His process eventually made all the existing ways of manufacturing plate glass obsolete, and the company earned millions from licensing fees. But there must have been many times when his board of directors wondered whether to go on supporting him.

This situation occurs more often than is generally realized, and not everyone gets the chance to see things through. The man with a new idea is frequently regarded as a crank until the idea succeeds. Then, of course, people are only too eager to claim at least part of the credit.

Ironically, some of the strongest resistance to innovation sometimes comes from people who have played a major role in the previous innovation. They not only dislike the suggestion that there might be a better way, but may have a vested interest in defending the status quo. One of the most famous examples is Edison's rejection of the argument that alternating electrical current had advantages over direct current. To accept it would have meant that he was wrong and his great rival George Westinghouse was right; it would also have meant that the plant which Edison's firm already had in operation was obsolete.

This reluctance to abandon familiar concepts is by no means confined to individuals. Many corporations reject innovative ideas, which they regard as disruptive and risky; they prefer to defend their existing business. The same is often true of entire countries. Britain, for example, has been much slower to accept the need for change in the last few decades than competitors like Japan.

It would clearly be unfair to suggest that large companies cannot innovate. They can, and do. In some fields they are the only ones who can afford the massive outlay on research and development, or on capital equipment, which is required to convert an idea into successful reality. But there is no doubt that the bureaucratic structure of some big organizations presents a formidable obstacle to innovation.

Employees are generally expected to follow established procedures; conformity is valued more highly than initiative. The individual who attempts to do things differently can easily get into trouble. This is why so many outsiders who try to sell ideas to large firms find it hard to make any headway. The executive who listens to the proposal (if anyone listens at all) has to weigh up the personal risks involved in supporting it. There is bound to be internal opposition. Do the potential rewards of success outweigh what he or she can lose if the idea fails? It is much safer to say 'No' than 'Yes', and that is what usually happens. The outsider is told that it can't be done because it hasn't been done before, or that 'It isn't right for us', or because the risks are too great. Sometimes it is adopted at a later stage – *after* a competitor has made it work so well that the company's position in the marketplace is threatened.

If one works for a large and apparently solid corporation it is all too easy to assume that tomorrow will be more or less like today. The emphasis tends to be on making the operation even more cost-effective, rather than on innovation. But tomorrow may *not* be like today; indeed, in a rapidly changing world it is very likely that it won't be. Innovation is risky, but it may be even more risky *not* to innovate.

Henry Ford was one of the business leaders who acknowledged this back in the 1920s. In *My Life and Work* he wrote:

> If to petrify is success, all one has to do is to humor the lazy side of the mind; but if to grow is success, then one must wake up anew each morning and keep awake all day. I saw great businesses become but the ghost of a name because someone thought they could be managed just as they were always managed, and though the management may have been the most excellent in its day, its excellence consisted in its alertness to its day, and not in slavish following of its yesterdays. Life, as I see it, is not a location but a journey. Even the man who most feels himself 'settled' is not settled – he is probably sagging back. Everything is in flux, and was meant to be. Life flows. We may live at the same number of the street, but it is never the same man who lives there.

And later in the same book:

> It could almost be written down as a formula that when a man begins to think that he at last has found his method, he had better begin a most searching examination of himself to see whether some part of his brain has not gone to sleep.

Ford was a great innovator, but even he fell into the trap. He made the classic mistake of the production man: he failed to keep pace with the changing demands of the market, contemptuously dismissing fashion and style, which allowed his competitors to exploit what he had begun.

The attitude of senior management is of vital importance: if it gives low priority to innovation, little will be done. The most innovative companies tend to put in influential positions people who, although they may come up with few original ideas of their own, possess an emotional commitment to creative work and do their best to encourage it. It also helps to have two separate budgets: an operating budget and an innovation budget. The first contains everything that is being done at the moment; the second contains the things that could be done differently and the different things to be worked on.

Small and medium-sized companies tend to be more innovative than entrenched large ones. They are more flexible, more willing to try new ideas and approaches. New product development is a crucial factor in determining their financial success, and they have the attacker's advantage. Management–employee relationships are better because people feel more closely involved, have a greater sense of achievement and spend less time on corporate in-fighting. Communication resembles consultation rather than command. The leaders of such companies usually have considerable entrepreneurial flair.

Bright, creative people tend to perform well in that kind of environment. Some large companies, recognizing this, have adopted various ways of instilling entrepreneurial attitudes into their employees. One is the setting up of independent task forces – groups which operate outside mainstream management with the maximum possible freedom to carry out specific tasks. IBM created such a force to develop a personal computer and catch up with Apple. Another method is to encourage team competition within the company. The prototype is Hewlett-Packard, in whose early days autonomous teams competed with each other to develop products and sell them to the sales forces. In many cases, these people take over the running of a new subsidiary set up to exploit the ideas.

At 3M, one of the most innovative of the big US corporations, senior management has long believed in the concept of the 'champion' – the man or woman with a fanatical faith in the specific product that he or she has in mind. The product champion is protected by an 'executive champion' (someone who knows how to deal with the corporate staff) and supported by a new venture team, which consists of people with expertise in various areas, including manufacturing and sales. If anyone wants to stop a project aimed at developing a new product, the burden of proof is on the one who wants to stop it, not the one who proposes it. Paperwork is kept down to a minimum. Many experiments fail, but failure is forgiven. The management at 3M wants its people to keep on trying. Each division is required to ensure that at least 25 per cent of its sales is derived from products that did not exist five years ago. The system seems to work: 3M has introduced more than fifty thousand new products to date.

The risk, of course, is that real champions may eventually take the plunge into starting on their own. Having developed a taste for independence and adventure they may decide, perhaps in partnership with others, that they want to be free to make the most of their endeavours.

The desire for independence, for doing one's own thing, has always been a strong driving force in business. It is often regarded as more important than money, though naturally most entrepreneurial people would like to get rich. A vast number of new companies are launched each year. Management buy-outs have become a familiar feature of the business scene. Many of these enterprises run into trouble and go bust, but the high failure rate among small companies clearly does not deter others from having a go.

Independent entrepreneurs are mavericks. There is something about them that sets them apart from the crowd. They love to make things happen. They are not content with reacting to events; they want to control them. They are opportunists who are constantly on the look-out for new worlds to conquer. They are innovators.

The men and women featured in this book come from widely different backgrounds. Some were born into poor families and there is no doubt that the urge to acquire wealth – and the sense of security that it provides – has been a powerful factor in their behaviour. Some, like Andrew Carnegie and

Helena Rubinstein, were immigrants, fiercely determined to succeed in their adopted countries. Many did not complete their formal education. Soichiro Honda, the Japanese mechanical genius who created the company that bears his name, was dismissed from technical high school. Steven Jobs, the founder of Apple, dropped out of college. So did Jeno Paulucci, who built up a large food distribution business. Britain's Sir Clive Sinclair left school at seventeen 'because I can only concentrate when I can do what I want'. Cornelius Vanderbilt, the most astonishing of the *parvenus* who made great fortunes in America during the nineteenth century, never went to school at all.

There is, however, one common factor: a great enthusiasm for new challenges. Carnegie, the steel magnate, coined the much-quoted phrase 'Pioneering don't pay.' But his subsequent career showed that he simply couldn't resist it: he became one of the most successful pioneers in the US steel industry, not only in the technological area but also in the organization and management of resources.

Carnegie started small and went on to build a giant corporation. Many others have done the same: some of the biggest enterprises in the world today, including IBM and ITT, were launched by independent entrepreneurs. But it is an interesting (though not altogether surprising) fact of business life that creative people often find it difficult to adjust themselves to new disciplines when the company they have started grows big and successful.

Steven Jobs is a much-publicized example. His innovative talents made him a genuine American business hero while he was still in his twenties. His personality, however, didn't fit easily into a large organization. He was enthusiastic, hard-working and full of ideas; but he was also restless, easily bored and blunt to the point of tactlessness. In 1985 the board of directors decided that he would have to leave. The power struggle was bitter and very public, and it ended in defeat for the man who had created the business. He was worth \$150 million or so, and could easily have opted for a life of leisure.

He tried it for a while, but he missed the challenge which Apple had provided. So he put up $7 million of his own money, hired people who had worked for him and who had left when he did, and launched a new company. 'We are going to take the technology to the next level,' he told the press.

H. Ross Perot, founder of Electronic Data Systems, is another innovator who ran into problems. A brashly unconventional Texan, Perot left the US Navy as a young man because he was frustrated by the slow system of promotion. 'I have no patience for red tape and inactivity,' he later said. He joined IBM, where he quickly became one of their star salesmen. While in that job, he proposed that IBM should create a service organization that would design, install and operate electronic data processing systems on a fixed contract basis. IBM's senior management thought the idea was absurdly impractical, so he left and started EDS with $1000 of savings. Six years later he went public, and the shares received a warm welcome on Wall Street. In 1984 General Motors made him an offer which he felt he couldn't refuse: it bought EDS for $2.5 billion.

GM's chairman, Roger Smith, wanted EDS primarily because of its computer expertise, but he also expressed the view that Perot's drive and 'entrepreneurial spirit' would be good for the vast organization. Whether he meant it or not, it soon transpired that Perot's attitudes and tactics were far from welcome. He chastised General Motors for its volume of rules and for not seeing that car-making is the economic equivalent of war. He also made it clear that he wanted to break down the corporate hierarchy.

Inevitably, it made him a lot of highly placed enemies. But what really upset Roger Smith and the other directors was Perot's insistence on breaking one of GM's most fundamental rules: never go public with criticism. Perot told workers that the management was out of touch with its employees. At a meeting of car dealers, he said that GM wasn't making the cars that customers wanted. Interviewers were told that changing GM's corporate culture was like 'teaching an elephant to tap-dance'.

In December 1986 the board decided that enough was enough. In an extraordinary move it voted to pay him about $700 million to shut up and get out. The experiment was probably doomed from the start. Men like Perot flourish in an entrepreneurial format and need to be in charge. The remarkable thing is that apparently GM did not recognize this obvious fact when they took him on.

Jobs and Perot are typical mavericks: opinionated, aggressive, opportunistic, in a hurry. They made their reputations and fortunes in the computer industry, but the same kind of people can be found everywhere.

One of the great growth areas is what is loosely called the 'service sector', a term which encompasses everything from airlines, hotels, stores and supermarkets to health care, entertainment, communications and financial services. It attracts more newcomers than any other area because in many cases less capital is needed since there is no manufacturing element, and because it offers so much scope for the development of new ideas.

Franchising, itself a splendid innovation, has given many people an opportunity to share in the success of clever marketing concepts like McDonald's and Kentucky Fried Chicken. The entertainment business has grown at an impressive rate, and communications has become a vast, worldwide industry, aided by new technology. The range of financial services on offer today is staggering, and travel has become a far bigger business than pioneers like Thomas Cook could have foreseen. It has not only led to the creation of international hotel chains like Hiltons and Holiday Inns, and made fortunes for imaginative tour operators and others, but it has also made it easier for innovations to cross national frontiers.

Not so very long ago, people thought themselves lucky if an idea made money in their own country. Many still do. But, increasingly, innovators think in terms of world markets. Ray Kroc, the founder of McDonald's, started with the dream of building a chain of hamburger franchises in the USA. It was a lofty ambition. How pleased he must have been when he discovered that his concept also appealed to the British, the Italians, the Japanese and even the French.

They, in turn, picked up ideas on visits to America. Masaru Ibuka of Sony went to the USA to enquire into American uses of the tape recorder; instead, he found out about transistor technology. He got a licence from Bell and, with his partner Akio Morita, went on to develop a highly successful range of consumer products. Alan Sainsbury 'discovered' the supermarket on a trip to the USA, recognized the potential and introduced the concept to Britain. The charge card, too, was an innovation which originated in America. A Chicago businessman, Frank McNamara, found that he couldn't pay for dinner in a New York restaurant because he had forgotten his wallet. That embarrassing evening led him to create the Diners Club, a simple idea which has spawned a multi-national industry.

Travel has been of benefit to many others. Helena Rubinstein got into the cosmetics business because, on a visit to Australia, she was shocked by the dry, rough skins of Australian women and reckoned – correctly – that they would welcome the creams her mother made in her native Poland. Anita Roddick, founder of the Body Shop, had the idea for her business during a year-long trip around the world at the age of twenty-five. She learned how women in unsophisticated societies cleaned and cared for their skin and hair, and thought that products made from their natural recipes might also go down well in Britain. The scope turned out to be greater than she had expected, and today there are more than 250 Body Shops all over the world.

For many innovators in Europe and Japan, America has long been the Promised Land – the country which, if it likes a concept, will happily help them to make a lot of money. It worked for Masaru Ibuka and Soichiro Honda. It also worked for Britain's Mary Quant, who exported the mini-skirt and other London fashion ideas to the USA in the 1960s, and for Laura Ashley, who re-created the style of the Victorian era and found that Americans, too, were fond of the past.

The market is so huge that success can bring immense rewards. The Japanese, as we all know, have shown an exceptional talent for making the most of their opportunities. They have also been good at developing the inventions of others or finding new uses for them. This, too, is part of the innovative process.

Americans who complain about the 'invasion' by foreign companies should remember that it was they who showed the way: US corporations have been 'invading' other markets for years. Their impact on the international scene has been enormous: IBM, Ford, ITT and others are vast multi-national corporations whose influence is felt everywhere.

The Innovators is not about companies, or teams, or projects, but about *individuals* – their ideas, their hopes and dreams, their struggles, their successes and failures. Some departed long ago for the great boardroom in the sky, but their careers seemed sufficiently interesting to merit inclusion. Many are still with us, and may well continue to surprise the world in the years to come. I cannot claim that I have managed to deal with *all* the people who have made things happen over the last century or so; that clearly would have been an impossible task. I have selected the innovators whose lives struck me as particularly fascinating, and whose thoughts and actions seemed to me to hold valuable lessons for the rest of us.

Gianni Agnelli

b. 1921

'A monarch surrounded by managers'

A joke every Italian schoolboy delights to tell has a small boy attending mass in St Peter's Square and turning to his father to ask: 'Who is the man in the skull cap standing next to Signore Agnelli?' Once one of Italy's most flamboyant playboys, Gianni Agnelli is the country's most powerful industrial baron, a business superstar. For Italian sensibilities, it is hard to imagine a more dashing combination for a national hero than a man who runs a car company in a country infatuated by cars, is married to the embodiment of a seductive Italian princess, has lived *la dolce vita* with indefatigable gusto and actually owns, as well as roots for, one of Italy's most passionately favoured soccer clubs.

Agnelli's business clout is estimated to contribute about a twentieth of Italy's entire domestic gross product. Besides Fiat cars, his interests include defence systems, aerospace, parts of Zanussi and Cinzano, insurance, fibres, department stores, newspapers, bio-engineering, financial services, cement-making, communications, robotics and the Juventus football club.

He was born in Turin, where his grandfather had started Fiat, and the family was already very rich. For a time it seemed that Gianni was determined to devote himself to the pursuit of pleasure rather than to business success. In the 1960s he was constantly seen in the company of the most beautiful young actresses in Italy. He still says that he had 'a better time before thirty than afterwards'.

In 1966 he was asked to take over as head of Fiat and

decided that the time had come to take life more seriously. The years that followed, however, were by no means easy. By 1979 Fiat was in deep trouble, beset by industrial strife, the Red Brigades, terrorism and a huge debt burden. Agnelli decided that his top team needed a shake-up: he persuaded his brother Umberto, then managing director, to give up his job and hired some tough-minded professional managers. Together they turned the company round and embarked on a bold, innovative programme of expansion, including major diversification into hi-tech activities.

Agnelli's associates say that he gets easily bored and, despite razor-sharp business acumen, does not follow transactions in detail. His impatience is formidable: there is apparently nobody at Fiat who can remember when Gianni Agnelli last sat still for the duration of a board meeting. He sees himself primarily as a leader, a man who sets the course for others to follow. John Kenneth Galbraith has said of him that he is unique among industrialists in that he thinks for himself instead of repeating fashionable clichés.

To his friends, he is a man of wit and charm, and he still seems to be popular with the ladies: in a wide-ranging national

John Kenneth Galbraith has said of him that he is unique among industrialists in that he thinks for himself instead of repeating fashionable clichés.

opinion poll held in 1986, women readers of the Italian paper *La Repubblica* nominated him as their number one heart-throb. On a more serious level, the Academy of International Business named him International Executive of the Year.

His biggest coup in 1986 was a $3 billion buy-out, arranged by him in talks with the controversial Colonel Gadaffi, of Libya's shareholding in Fiat. He arranged for two-thirds of the holding to be sold internationally by Deutsche Bank, in the largest secondary share placing that the world's stock markets had ever seen. Agnelli's family kept the rest, raising its stake in Fiat to more than 40 per cent.

It was a deal which brought smiles in the White House and cleared the way for Fiat to take a stake in Strategic Defence Initiative (SDI) contracts. Agnelli is a Star Wars enthusiast and Fiat is on stream for projects worth $2 billion. Defence contracts and their associated hi-tech spin-offs are nowadays high on his list of priorities: he makes no secret of his belief that, while cars may come and go, the world's demands for weaponry never falters. Agnelli also found time to snap up the Alfa-Romeo company, seeing off rival bidders Ford. With Lancia already in the stable, Fiat is well placed to take on the luxury car market.

Agnelli readily concedes that he is not a professional manager, but he seems to be good at picking those who are. The two key appointments he made when brother Umberto stepped down have paid off handsomely. Cesare Romiti, formerly head of Alitalia, came in as managing director and another workaholic, Vittorio Ghidella, was chosen to head the car division.

It was Romiti who, under Agnelli's careful supervision, pushed through the expansion programme. He also engineered, again at his master's urging, a crucial showdown with the unions. In 1980, at a politically sensitive time when mass lay-offs seemed more than usually risky, he sacked more than twenty-three thousand Fiat workers and precipitated a general strike. To the astonishment of many, the gamble paid off. The management stood its ground and within weeks the unions were forced to capitulate. Now less than a quarter of the workforce is unionized. The factories were rapidly automated with robots as far as the eye could see. Production and sales went up and up and up.

Rivals have described Agnelli as a 'monarch surrounded by managers' and some claim that it 'isn't healthy for the Italian economy to have so much power concentrated in the hands of one man'. Agnelli clearly isn't bothered by such comments.

But ultimately things will have to change, because he has no obvious heir. His only son, Eduardo, imitated his father's example of an action-packed adolescence and has since demonstrated an urge to spend his time managing the Juventus football team. Big business does not seem to be his forte.

The great unknown is whether Fiat will still be a major force in the car business by the end of the century, when according to most estimates the industry will be confined to half a dozen giants at most. Agnelli certainly intends to hang in there, but he and his successors may well decide that it makes more sense to concentrate on the 'other Fiat', with hi-tech aerospace the front runner.

Horatio Alger

1834–99

Creator of the American Dream

Horatio Alger had a tremendous influence on young Americans in his day – and for a long time afterwards. Many who later won fame and fortune in the business world publicly acknowledged that they were initially inspired by his books. More than 200 million copies were sold between the end of the Civil War and the end of the century.

Born in Revere, Massachusetts, Alger was the son of a pious Unitarian Minister. He went to divinity school and was ordained at the age of thirty; two years later he quit the ministry, went to New York and tried to earn a living as a journalist. He sold a serial story called 'Ragged Dicto' to a boys' magazine, and it was such a success that a Boston publisher asked him to write several books about the same character. In the years that followed Alger produced numerous volumes with one basic theme: that the American Dream could, and did, come true in real life.

Each told essentially the same story, and the message was always that, to succeed, you had to be a man of character. The villain was a failure because he deceived and embezzled. Critics called it 'literary tripe', but it is easy to see why the books had such an impact on impressionable young minds. Many boys from humble backgrounds desperately wanted to believe that they too could achieve success if they tried hard enough. Alger's books assured them that, yes, they could make it. Ironically, when Alger died he was flat broke.

One of the young men who years later avidly read all his work was W. CLEMENT STONE (b. 1902), who went on to make more than $400 million in insurance and then wrote some highly successful inspirational books of his own. In one of them, Stone recalled how he first came across Alger's stories when he was twelve: 'I'll never forget the first day I went upstairs to the attic . . . at least fifty of his books, dusty and weather-worn, were piled in the corner. I took one down to the hammock in the front yard and started to read. I read through them all that summer.'

'I'll never forget the first day I went upstairs to the attic . . . at least fifty of his books, dusty and weather-worn, were piled in the corner. . . . I read through them all that summer.'

Stone, who had been born in a poor, run-down Chicago neighbourhood, became an insurance salesman while still in his teens. The Alger books, it seems, gave him confidence. At the age of twenty he set up his own one-man insurance business with capital of $100 and desk space rented for $25 a month. The firm prospered, and by the late twenties he had more than a thousand salesmen operating from coast to coast. By the end of the 1930s he was a millionaire, as Alger had said he could be. He subsequently bought the Commercial Credit Company of Baltimore. By 1956 it had grown into the largest accident and health insurance company of its kind in the United States.

Stone intended his own inspirational books to be primarily of help to his employees. Many were already familiar with Alger's volumes, and had also read other writers like Samuel Smiles and Dale Carnegie. But Stone was different: he was not only the boss but he had actually made several hundred million dollars in the insurance business. His advice was based on practical experience, not just theory. He was an authentic Horatio Alger hero.

His books had inviting titles like *Success Through a Positive Mental Attitude* (written jointly with Napoleon Hill) and *The Success System That Never Fails*. They were a peculiar and often confusing mixture of folksy platitudes and chamber-of-commerce exhortations, but like the Alger and Carnegie books they appealed to a lot of people. Stone's message was essentially the same: anyone can make it in the land of opportunity.

I once interviewed him at length about his formula for PMA – a Positive Mental Attitude. It was he said, a type of auto-suggestion. You start on the road to success by telling yourself how marvellous you are. Have you ever considered the battles you won before you were even born? Just think: 'Tens of thousands of sperm cells participated in a great struggle and only one of them won – and that one is *you*.' The next step, he said, is to plant a number of 'self-motivators' – simple slogans – in your mind by repeating them every morning and night and at odd hours during the day. When these have taken root you no longer need to think about them, and in the midst of any business situation the correct self-motivator will assert itself and guide you automatically in the direction of success.

The key phrase, he went on, is 'Do It Now!', flashed from your subconscious to your conscious mind. With practice you will develop a reflex response so powerful that you will take action come what may. Most people, said Stone, fail to develop all the useful self-motivators naturally as they grow to adulthood. Confronted with an opportunity that involves some element of risk, they tend to back off. They prevaricate. The opportunity evaporates before their eyes. They then blame a capricious fate for their bad luck. This kind of experience, repeated over and over again, confirms them in the belief that they are born losers. The PMA technique changes all this. It gives them self-confidence and turns them into winners.

Stone distributed millions of inspirational books – his own and others' – to employees, shareholders, schools, hospitals, veterans' organizations and even inmates of correctional institutions. Horatio Alger, I am sure, would have been proud of his disciple.

Elizabeth Arden

1884–1966

The woman who made make-up respectable

Like Helena Rubinstein, her great rival, Elizabeth Arden was a shrewd businesswoman who understood the demand for beauty – and the fortunes that could be made from it. She introduced hundreds of new products and was one of the pioneers of the health farm concept.

The origins of cosmetics reach far back into antiquity. Cleopatra knew all about make-up: she painted her eyebrows and lashes 'a stark black; her upper lids blue-black; and the lower ones as green as the Nile'. She also, of course, liked to bath in asses' milk. The ancient Romans were very keen on beauty aids, and in America the Indians were painting their faces long before people like Arden and Rubinstein came along. But the beauty industry, as we know it today, did not really begin until the nineteenth century. A hundred years ago there were few products within the reach of the average woman, and even if there had been, many women would have declined to use them. Self-declaration was still thought to be against God's will; coloured make-up was widely regarded as the trademark of the harlot.

Elizabeth Arden, we are told, was shocked when she went to Paris and saw women wearing eye shadow and lipstick. If so, she didn't remain shocked for long: she later boasted that she was the first to bring eye shadow to the American market.

Born Florence Nightingale Graham in Ontario, Canada, she was the daughter of an immigrant truck driver. She worked at several jobs before she set off in 1908 for New York, where her first job was as a treatment girl with Eleanor Adair, then a leading light in the small world of cosmetics. A year later she joined Elizabeth Hubbard at a new salon on Fifth Avenue. She soon quarrelled with her employer and set up a rival establishment, with the help of a $6000 loan from one of her cousins.

Miss Graham was bothered by her name: it wasn't glamorous enough. She wanted to personalize her business, but felt that 'Florence Nightingale Graham' conveyed the wrong image. (Such considerations do not appear to have troubled Helena Rubinstein, who became a huge success despite her equally unglamorous name.) She rather liked the name Elizabeth, and apparently took 'Arden' from the title of a Victorian novel.

The new Elizabeth Arden copied Mrs Hubbard's creams and soon had two salons in New York. She went to Europe to study what was happening there and it was on that visit, which included a stay in Paris, that she made up her mind to try a bolder approach when she got back home. On her return journey she also met the man who was to become her first husband, Thomas Jenkins Lewis. He acted as her business manager until their divorce in 1935, and later went to work for her arch-rival, Helena Rubinstein.

Elizabeth Arden spent as much time on packaging and design as on developing her ever-growing range of products. One of her more interesting innovations was the 'Vienna Youth Mask', which involved the application of diathermy techniques to the face. Diathermy heats tissues in the body by means of electrical current and has been used to treat arthritis and damaged muscles and nerves. Arden transformed it into a beauty treatment. A device made of papier-mâché and lined with tin foil was fitted to the client's face and connected by conducting cords to a diathermy machine. Arden claimed that electricity applied in this way had the effect of replenishing the cells in a woman's face which, she said, die first under the eyes and next under the chin. There was no medical evidence to support this theory (all that diathermy does is stimulate the circulation), but many beauty-conscious women eagerly tried the new treatment.

Her first 'beauty farm' was opened in 1934, in Maine. Called the Main Chance Farm, it quickly attracted an impressive following among the wealthy citizens of the day. It offered massages, exercises, facials, face masks and wax baths 'to draw out all the poisons'. The food was low-calorie and alcohol was banned. Over the years famous people like Ava Gardner, Pearl Mesta, Clare Boothe Luce and Mamie Eisenhower became regular visitors. A second Main Chance Farm was opened in Phoenix, Arizona, in 1947.

By all accounts Elizabeth Arden was not a nice person. Headstrong and arrogant, she had very few friends. In 1944 she married Prince Michael Evlanoff, but the union lasted barely two years. Apart from business, horses were her main interest. In 1945 she was the top-money winner in US racing; in 1947 her horse Jet Pilot won the Kentucky Derby.

'I treat my women as horses and my horses like women,' she was once quoted as saying. Her stable lads found out what she meant when she objected to the smell of the liniment they used to rub down the horses, and ordered that the fragrantly scented Ardenia skin tonic should be applied instead. A trainer who protested that this treatment might not suit horses was promptly replaced.

Arden died in 1966, leaving a large personal fortune. There was some dispute at the time about how old she was when she departed for that great salon in the sky, because she had given different dates for her birth. Some sources said she had lived to

'I treat my women as horses and my horses like women,' she was once quoted as saying. Her stable lads found out what she meant when she objected to the smell of the liniment they used to rub down the horses, and ordered that the fragrantly scented Ardenia skin tonic should be applied instead.

the age of eighty-one; others said she was eighty-eight. It has since been established that the latter was correct.

Her one big business mistake, it seems, was not to have set up a foundation during her lifetime, as Helena Rubinstein did. After her death the estate had to find $37 million in taxes. The company was bought by a conglomerate, Eli Lilly & Co., in 1971.

Laura Ashley

1930–85

Inspiration from the past

Laura Ashley was an unusual innovator: she prospered by turning the clock *back*. When she launched her business in 1954, she used a design concept which attempted to re-create the style of products from a bygone era. She reasoned, correctly, that there was a substantial market for clothes and other items which reminded people of English country life in Victorian times. She designed, for a target consumer image, products with a mood and style that she felt met an unfulfilled need – a core image which remains unwaveringly in place in the 1980s.

What really made the business a huge success, however, was that her clothes were not only attractive but also highly practical, adaptable, easy-to-wear and relatively inexpensive. Women who could not afford high fashion, and did not care for the ostentatious products sold in trendy boutiques, liked her designs and felt comfortable in her dresses.

She was also fortunate to have the support of a husband who had an aptitude for engineering and a good head for finance. The story of the Laura Ashley business is essentially one of a highly effective husband-and-wife partnership. Bernard Ashley is still the chairman of what is now a large multi-national enterprise. A Laura Ashley shop is opening somewhere in the world at least once a week.

The beginning was modest: they had little capital and, using simple silk screens, printed tablemats and scarves on an old kitchen table in the living room of their attic apartment in London's Pimlico district. They sold them to small shops and department stores. Bernard Ashley later developed a continuous textile printing machine, which was a great help. But the first three years were tough: money was always short, credit even shorter, and several times the firm's future was touch and go. Laura also had to cope with two babies, and they decided that a move to the country was essential. So the family left London for Surrey, to live in an idyllic country cottage set in an orchard and facing open farmlands. Bernard Ashley says that it was here that the first seeds of Laura's design philosophy were sown:

> In the quiet and in the perspectives of this rural setting, with her young family and the exchange of news about the business when I came home at weekends, ideas began to grow which were to develop and form, gaining more speed later in Wales, into the firm's design philosophy. It is really this quiet home and family background, the essential part of Laura's character, that made the long-run business partnership which eventually became Laura Ashley worldwide.

They moved the factory to Brasted in Kent, a few miles from the cottage, using an old coach shed and building a larger

She designed, for a target consumer image, products with a mood and style that she felt met an unfulfilled need – a core image which remains unwaveringly in place in the 1980s.

printing machine. Business was expanded to international markets, with products shipped to customers in Paris, Amsterdam, the United States and Australia. They also opened a showroom in London.

As the fifties ended, they decided to move again – this time to a small town in Laura's native Wales. But sales continued to be handled in London. Bernard acquired a shop in South Kensington and in the late 1960s they embarked on an ambitious expansion programme, putting the profits back into more factories, more shops and more research. The factory in Wales was enlarged and new manufacturing facilities were built elsewhere, including the Netherlands, Dublin and Kentucky in the USA. Warehouses were opened in London, Paris, New Jersey, and Helmond in the Netherlands, and the shop network was extended.

The 1970s and early 1980s saw further rapid growth. Separate divisions were set up to control the various activities. The design department continued to be guided by Laura, but her younger son, Nick, joined the company as design director. In 1985 the business was successfully floated on the stock market. Sadly, Laura Ashley died that year.

Bernard Ashley says that the principles of the business have remained unchanged. They are:

1. A clear design image, which is carefully maintained and actively enhanced.

2. Vertical integration whenever it is the most practicable and effective approach.

3. Multi-national activity of production, marketing and retail.

4. Strategic and long-term planning for the group's autonomous operating companies.

The Laura Ashley business is unique in being the only significant UK-based multi-national group which designs and manufactures its own products, and successfully retails them in four continents. Bernard is optimistic about the future: the company, he says, has identified major opportunities for expansion in each of these markets.

New products are developed in response to briefs by the retail divisions. Clothes collections are 'themed' to provide a balanced and carefully co-ordinated range from which a customer may choose. Inspiration for such designs is, nowadays, drawn from many sources – a reflection of the international nature of the group. Cultures, arts, and even politics provide the basis from which designers may work. 'In this way', the company says, 'Laura Ashley's design portfolio is a mixture of contemporary and historical designs which can reflect both current moods and changing attitudes.'

The remarkable woman who laid the foundation for all this lives on in the name of the company she and her husband started in that attic apartment over thirty years ago. Her great achievement was to introduce a mood and fashion that millions of people could identify with – a factor still present today.

Warren Avis

b. 1917

'We're number two, we try harder'

Warren Avis developed the airport car rental concept while still in his twenties. It was one of those ideas which, with the benefit of hindsight, seems all too obvious but at the time – the late 1940s – nobody had tried it and the sceptics, including Hertz, thought it was crazy. As Avis himself has recalled: 'The objections ran the gamut of negative thinking. I was told that a national car-rental system of this type would be impossible to control. There would not be enough demand from business travellers. The cost of buying and maintaining the cars would undermine any profitability. You name it, and the naysayers threw it at me.'

The concept first came to him while he was an air force combat flying officer during World War II. During that period, he travelled around the United States and overseas. He found that, wherever he went, he could never find any decent ground transportation. He often had to take a taxi to a town that might be fifty miles away. 'Sometimes', he says, 'we even carried motorcycles in the bomb bays of our planes so that we'd be able to get around after we landed.'

The Hertz system had moved into many cities around the country, but not into the airports. Avis felt that there was a crying need for this kind of service, but recognized that, if it was to work, it had to be established on a national basis. Passengers travelling to any part of the country had to know that a car would be available for them at any major airport where they might land. It was a tall order for a young ex-officer who didn't have much capital.

Avis decided to start with the Detroit Willow airport, and then Miami. He put $10,000 of his own hard-earned money into the venture and managed to borrow another $75,000, for which he signed personally. He set up his car rental counters near the airport baggage pick-up area, where people had to wait twenty minutes or so for their luggage. Nobody else wanted this location for business, but it was ideal for his kind of operation. Many people didn't know how to rent a car in those days, so his employees took advantage of the baggage delay to explain the system.

At the beginning, Avis only had about half a dozen people working for him at his airport locations. But the business grew so quickly that he had to hire more staff and set up a central office. He also decided that, wherever appropriate, he would make licensing arrangements with local operators who would take day-to-day responsibility for business in the many cities necessary to make up a national and international company. If he could find good operators already in place in the cities where he signed up the airports, he would bring them in to run the airport business. Otherwise he would get everything started and then have his own company take care of the operation.

Within seven years, Avis became the world's second largest international rent-a-car system. There was no competition from Hertz at airports for the first three years because Hertz still thought that the idea had little merit and would fail; they changed their minds when it became obvious that it was a success.

During those early years, Avis also originated the rent-a-car credit card concept. To attract the most credit-worthy customers, the company convinced the airlines that they should mail out its card with their airline travel card, adding a flyer which explained how the system worked. He later persuaded them to insert his pamphlets in aircraft seat pockets (there were no in-flight magazines then) and to publish co-operative ads. All this helped to tie Avis to the airlines in the public eye –

'The objections ran the gamut of negative thinking. . . . You name it, and the nay-sayers threw it at me.'

a good example of how to project an image of a national nature with a comparatively modest amount of money. Avis followed it up by getting the airlines to give the company a free teletype service to take reservations.

Another innovative move was to buy *new* cars every year for the rent-a-car operation. The aim was to show business travellers that, if they used Avis, they could rely on being provided with the best possible vehicles and the least possibility of breakdowns. It also meant that he didn't have to set up an expensive garage system that would have to focus on repairs and maintenance.

Warren Avis had established a Ford dealership in the Detroit area – a separate venture – and Ford welcomed his move, especially after he pointed out to them that a good car rental experience would go a long way towards convincing businesspeople to buy a Ford for their own use. People would, in effect, be 'test-riding' a Ford.

At that time there was a shortage of cars, and the federal government had set prices for the sale of automobiles to the public. Avis found that if he bought them new for the rent-a-car business, used them for six months and then sold them through his Ford dealership, they would be worth more than he had paid. The government price-control system didn't last for long, but it gave the company extra funds at a crucial stage of its development.

Warren Avis sold out in 1954, for several million dollars, so that he could move on to other ventures. He saw himself primarily as an originator and builder – an entrepreneur – rather than as a manager. He also wanted to enjoy life, which didn't include sixteen-hour work days. He later regretted his decision and said that he would like to buy the company back. It has had several owners since then and some colourful characters have run it, including Robert Townsend, who was responsible for the famous cheeky advertising campaign proclaiming that 'We're number two, we try harder' and who later wrote an irreverent book about the business world, *Up the Organization*.

Warren Avis's story underlines a basic rule of the entrepreneurial game: the big idea is likely to arise from some big public need. Avis saw the need for car rentals at airports and he rushed in to satisfy it. It took courage, determination and a flair for marketing as well as creative financing. The licensing arrangements undoubtedly helped, though Avis later discovered that some of the licensees had cheated by reporting lower revenues than they were actually turning in. (The people who took over the company had the good sense to send in auditors.) Tying in with the airlines was a clever ploy, and his decision to buy new cars every year turned out to be not only financially sound but also earned valuable goodwill from those who ultimately counted most of all – the customers. There were anxious moments – there always are – but his optimism and persistence paid off handsomely. His great mistake was to sell out too soon, but that is not unusual among restless entrepreneurial types. The millions are always tempting; so is the prospect of new challenges.

Jim Bakker

b. 1940

Founder of the 'Electronic Church'

Jim Bakker is one of the American evangelists who have built up a multi-billion dollar industry known as the 'Electronic Church'. Early in 1987, he became the central figure of an extraordinary drama which rocked the business to its very foundations. The US media christened it Godscam and Pearly-gate. Bakker admitted to having committed adultery with a Church secretary six years before; worse, it emerged that she had been paid $250,000 to keep quiet about it.

Until then, he had enjoyed astonishing success. His religious recreational empire, called PTL (Praise the Lord), had earned $129 million in 1986. Half came from individual donations, but it also had a vast income from a theme park in South Carolina called Heritage USA, which had become the third most popular in the country after Disneyland and Disney-world. Bakker was planning to add a full-size replica of London's Crystal Palace at a cost of $100 million.

Religion has been a useful source of revenue ever since the medieval popes hit on the idea of selling indulgences, a practice which caused Martin Luther to make his historic break with the Catholic Church. But no one has ever matched the innovative skill of America's twentieth-century TV evangelists.

Bakker, the son of a piston-ring machinist from Muskegon Heights, Michigan, got his start in the TV Ministry working for the Christian Broadcasting Network founded by Pat Robertson. In 1974 he began to build his own network and the complex of enterprises that would become Heritage USA. By 1986 his daily show, which features Jim and his singing wife

Tammy Faye, was reaching 14 million households via its own satellite system to 178 stations. On the hour-long show, Jim continually pleaded for funds to support his various projects.

Unlike rivals such as Jim Swaggart, who offer a vision of hell and a rocky road to redemption, Bakker espoused an affluent style of life for Christians as a reward for their belief. He evolved what some have called a 'health and wealth' theology, which holds that Christians will enjoy prosperity because of their faith and makes no apologies for luxuries or instant gratification.

According to Professor Martin E. Marty, an expert on modern Christianity at the University of Chicago, Bakker's ideas followed the growth of charismatic religion among the affluent that began in the 1960s. People were encouraged to give money and gain more in return. Instant gratification replaced self-denial. Where once religious women did not wear make-up, fancy clothes or revealing swimsuits, Bakker and his wife not only encouraged beauty contests but even marketed their own line of cosmetics. Their approach, essentially, amounted to a rationalization of upward mobility. It also, of course, served to justify their own lavish lifestyle.

Heritage USA is a 2300-acre 'inspirational park' visited by

There are shops with names like Noah's Toy Shoppe and the Heavenly Fudge Shop. . . .

six million people every year. It employs 1600 people, and the TV studios are there. The hotel and shopping complex in the centre of the park is also the headquarters of the PTL organization. There are shops with names like Noah's Toy Shoppe and the Heavenly Fudge Shop; other attractions include tours of Billy Graham's childhood home (which has been moved from Charlotte and rebuilt in the park); bible seminars; counselling sessions; camp fire singalongs; and meetings in the

Upper Room, which is said to be a copy of the building in Jerusalem where the Last Supper was held. There is also a Heritage Island Water Park, which cost $10 million and contains the world's longest water slide and the world's largest wave pool. It was built, so it is claimed, to keep children happy while their parents are seeking spiritual refreshment.

Most of the visitors to Heritage USA are 'partners' in PTL, the privileged status accorded to those who make regular donations. The public relations director says that the park is designed to meet the tastes and interests of the average evangelical family in America. Here, he maintains, it is just like home, an idealized home where conservative values are secure against the pagan world and where pain, conflict and responsibility are absent.

The news of the founder's confession, and his subsequent resignation, must have come as a terrible shock. On his TV show Bakker insisted that he had relinquished the reins not because of that one afternoon of sin in 1980, but because he wanted to stop a 'diabolical plot' to destroy his ministry and take over his Church. He put much of the blame on Swaggart, who denied the plot but admitted spreading the story of Bakker's indiscretion. Swaggart had earlier been dropped from Bakker's twenty-four-hour religious cable television network, which was thought to be one of the reasons for the feud between the two men.

The other big media names all took sides with Baker or against him. One of his supporters included another famous evangelist who has built up a formidable personal empire, ORAL ROBERTS of Tulsa, Oklahoma. Roberts, a Pentecostal preacher who has claimed the spiritual power to heal by the laying on of hands, has been active in broadcasting since the mid-1950s. His syndicated thirty-minute programme, carried by 210 stations, reaches more than a million people and gathered contributions of $55 million in 1986. The empire includes the 4500-student Oral Roberts University and a City of Faith medical complex that offers physical as well as spiritual healing.

Roberts has sometimes resorted to extreme measures to

boost flagging donations. In 1980 he described a visitation to his bedside by a 900-foot-tall Jesus, who, he claimed, asked him to build the City of Faith. Funds immediately started to pour in. Early in 1987 he came up with an even more bizarre gambit. He told his followers that God would 'call him home' if he did not raise $8 million by 1 April. He entered the 200-foot-high glass and steel 'praying tower' at his university on 22 March, vowing to fast until he had the money. The faithful obliged just in time. The following week, the tower was struck by lightning. Even before that ominous signal, however, many Christians had expressed dismay at what they perceived to be implicit spiritual blackmail.

The evangelists say that they are doing 'God's work', and there is no doubt that their efforts have given help and comfort to many people. It would be unfair to suggest that they are only out to enrich themselves. The Vatican, too, is deeply involved in financial affairs and no one accuses the Pope of manipulating the Church for personal gain. But there are limits – as Martin Luther proved all those years ago.

The Duke of Bedford

b. 1917

The maverick aristocrat

Britain's snobs were appalled when the 13th Duke of Bedford, known to his family and friends as Ian, decided to turn his splendid ancestral home, Woburn Abbey, into a tourist attraction. But Ian, the maverick among the dukes of the realm, was unperturbed. He needed money to pay for the upkeep of Woburn Abbey and he felt that the best way to get it was to attract paying customers.

The Dukes of Bedford used to own elegant mansions and lucrative parcels of land in the better part of central London (the family connection is still commemorated in over seventy street names), but unlike some members of Britain's nobility, notably the Dukes of Westminster, they have not managed to keep them. Death duties are one of the principal reasons: the deaths within fifteen years of the 11th and 12th Dukes, neither of whom had taken adequate steps to protect the estates, decimated the family fortunes. In his youth Ian worked as a reporter, and for a while lived in South Africa where he learned farming. He returned to Britain when he inherited the title in 1953.

Woburn, an elegant masterpiece, had been the scene of some of the most gracious living in the eighteenth and nineteenth centuries. It was, a diarist noted in 1825, 'a house abounding in every sort of luxury and comfort, with inexhaustible resources for every taste . . . the house, place, establishment, and manner of living are the most magnificent I have ever seen. There is no place which gives so splendid an example of a Great English Lord as this.'

Some of this style of living continued until the death of the 11th Duke, Herbrand, in 1940. He maintained a staff of over two hundred, including fifty footmen with powdered hair, one of whom would stand behind the chair of each guest at dinner. Although he visited London barely once a year, he kept two fully staffed establishments in Belgrave Square and eight chauffeurs. There were gardeners to look after the 3000-acre park, and servants whose sole task was to polish the vast collection of silver. Duke Herbrand did not regard his way of life as ostentatious; it would simply be silly, he thought, for a nobleman to live in any other fashion. But by the time the 13th Duke came into his inheritance, it was all over. Even Woburn no longer belonged to him; as a result of arrangements made by his father and grandfather, who did their best from preventing him from setting foot in the place, the owners were the Bedford Estates, whose trustees had absolute discretion over what should be done with it and who should live there. They wanted to give the house and park to the National Trust, but they met with such fierce opposition from the Duke that they allowed themselves to be persuaded to give him a limited tenancy while he tried to rescue Woburn from neglect and took steps to see that it paid for itself.

'No one lives like a proper lord these days: it's a question of getting the poor to feed the rich.'

He and his wife cleared the junk which had accumulated while his father was Duke. They personally cleaned, scrubbed, polished, and rearranged the rooms to make them worth visiting. He was the first Duke to take in paying guests – mostly American tourists, who paid large sums for the privilege of dining with the Duke and Duchess – and he introduced all kinds of showbiz gimmicks. There was no end to the tricks and inventions he would entertain in order to lure people to the house and park. If a farmhouse was derelict and needed to be demolished, he would advertise the fact and charge a fee for watching it go up in flames. He even joined Equity, the actors' union, so that he could appear in films and on television shows, and made regular appearances on chat programmes in Britain and America, plugging Woburn Abbey with all the skill and determination of a thorough professional.

Visitors to Woburn would receive the Duke's autograph whether they asked for it or not, and were often allowed, not to say encouraged, to shake the ducal hand. 'Having been brought up with servants,' he once said, 'I have a servant's mind.' His efforts made it the most popular stately home in the country, with an average of nearly 1,600,000 visitors a year, many on second or third visits. He was so successful that the

Israeli government is said to have sought his advice on how to increase their tourist trade.

His ideas were copied by other aristocrats, and today tourists have a wide choice of diversions, including game parks and motor museums. A peers' co-operative was formed in 1975 to publicize Britain's stately homes abroad. Calling themselves the Magnificent Seven, they included the Duke of Argyll and the Duke of Marlborough, whose ancestral home, Blenheim Palace, was given to his illustrious ancestor by a 'grateful nation' for his victories against the French. Another member of the co-operative, the Marquess of Bath, told reporters: 'We have no alternative. No one lives like a proper lord these days: it's a question of getting the poor to feed the rich.'

Having shown the way, the Duke of Bedford handed Woburn over to his son, so that he could get to know the stately home business. The Duke went to live in a modest apartment in Paris with his French wife Nicole, who used to be a television producer. He continues to appear on shows and to collect handsome fees for speaking at conventions.

James Gordon Bennett Sr

1795–1872

First of the press barons

Bennett was a pioneer in popular capitalism – an editor, journalist, entrepreneur and innovator. A dour Scot, he emigrated to the United States at the age of twenty-four – 'to see the place where that wondrous man Ben Franklin was born' – and after working as a journalist on various publications he founded a paper of his own, the *New York Herald*, which appeared daily at a mere one cent per copy. Combining an exciting, even salacious, reporting style and highly energetic news-gathering techniques, it rapidly became the city's largest-selling paper. To Bennett also goes the more dubious credit of introducing so-called 'yellow journalism' to the United States, through his encouragement of sensationalized reporting of political intrigue, violent crime and passionate love affairs among the great of the land. His many innovative techniques included the use of the telegraph as a news-gathering device, and the setting up of a highly organized network of newsboys to guarantee the efficient distribution of his paper.

Bennett has often been called 'the first of the press barons'. His son, James Gordon Bennett Jr, carried on his father's work. It was he who sent the journalist and explorer Henry Morton Stanley to Africa to find the missionary David Livingstone.

Another early press baron was ALFRED HARMSWORTH (1865–1922), who later became Lord Northcliffe. Pulitzer invited him to edit the New York paper, the *World*, for the first day of the new century. Harmsworth printed it as a ten-page tabloid, about half its normal size. On the front page he announced that his slogan 'All the news in sixty seconds' was the right approach for 'the Twentieth or Time-Saving Century'. But Harmsworth made his biggest impact in Britain. His key observation of the trade in the 1880s was devastatingly simple: 'Most of the English newspapers were edited for what might be termed the high-brow classes and were not interesting to the masses.' He embarked on the self-imposed task of filling the gap by launching, in 1888, a weekly paper called *Answers*, which reached a circulation of one million within a few years. It promised – and delivered – 'Information on Every Subject Under the Sun'. If you wanted to know that in 1795 it had been calculated that all the flour used by British hairdressers in a year would have made 5,314,280 loaves, *Answers* was the place to look.

The methods he used to reach his audience was adventurous: copies were given away to spread the word (Harmsworth claimed to have invented this device) and valuable publicity came from an *Answers* pipe, *Answers* prize dogs and toothache cures. New magazines followed, several a year, with titles like *Comic Cuts* ('Amusing without being vulgar'), *Halfpenny Marvel* and *Pluck Library*. Later *Answers* was used to boost his first venture into daily journalism, the *London* Evening News, which had been doing so badly that he managed to buy it for a mere £25,000. In 1896 he launched the *Daily Mail*, priced at a halfpenny, and made it into the kind of paper that ordinary people wanted to read. Like Bennett before him, he made constant successful attempts to ensure that the paper itself was news – by offering a £10,000 prize, for instance, for the first flight by aeroplane from London to Manchester. He later had the satisfaction of buying the staid *Times*, but had the good sense not to make drastic changes.

If you wanted to know that in 1795 it had been calculated that all the flour used by British hairdressers in a year would have made 5,314,280 loaves, Answers *was the place to look.*

Success brought Harmsworth a peerage as well as great wealth, but it also destroyed him. The more power he had, the more possibilities presented themselves, and megalomania turned into madness. His descendants, though, have kept control of what is now a formidable business enterprise.

In America, WILLIAM RANDOLPH HEARST (1863–1951) took Bennett's idea for a penny newspaper and expanded it into a vast publishing empire over which he ruled as a supreme autocrat. At the time of his death, he owned eighteen newspapers, nine magazines and a clutch of related news-gathering enterprises.

Hearst, who had a painting of Napoleon behind his desk and went to fancy dress balls as the Little Corporal, tried to run for the White House, but got nowhere. He did, however, have an enormous influence on public opinion. In his personal life he was one of the most profligate men of his day. He owned seven castles around the world, including the extraordinary San Simeon, which was more of a private kingdom than an estate. Here he reigned supreme amidst the jumble of art treasures he loved to collect. His weekend parties were legendary. Among the regular guests were movie stars like Charlie Chaplin, Mary Pickford and Clark Gable, and for a time he tried his luck in the movie business – chiefly, it seems, to please his mistress, Marion Davies. But his keen sense of public taste, which had played such an important role in his newspaper ventures, failed him in Hollywood. His movies consistently lost money for Hearst and those associated with him. Ironically, the great picture *Citizen Kane,* made by someone else – Orson Welles – but based on Hearst, stands as his abiding contribution to the cinema. (See also RUPERT MURDOCH.)

Ladislao José Biro

1899–1987

Inventor of the ballpoint pen

Ladislao Biro was a Hungarian journalist who became world-famous not because of what he wrote, but because of what he wrote *with*. He is credited with inventing the modern ballpoint pen. Someone else had earlier invented a ballpoint pen for marking rough surfaces, but Biro is generally reckoned to have been the first to produce a ballpoint pen for handwriting.

While editing a cultural magazine in the 1930s, Biro noticed in the printing shop the advantages of instant-drying ink. This led him to make experiments with a crude ballpoint. He went to Argentina in the 1940s – at the invitation, it is said, of the President of Argentina, who had spotted him using a strange kind of pen at a resort hotel in Yugoslavia. Biro later became an Argentine citizen.

Backers were found to raise the equivalent of $80,000 for a company of which Biro – being a refugee, he was penniless – received one-third of the shares, most of which went on bringing members of his family to safety after the outbreak of World War II. As a result he received much less than one-third of the $2 million paid jointly by Eversharp and Faber for exclusive patent rights in North America in 1944. The pen was first offered for sale in Argentina at $40.

Biro had a naturally inventive mind. In 1938 he had been a member of Hungary's Royal Academy of Sciences, and at the age of seventeen had received payment for his design of a hand-operated clothes washer. He was responsible for more than thirty successful inventions, among them a pick-proof lock, a wrist dial which taped a record of blood pressure and body temperature, and a heatproof tile. But he had little taste for business, and in 1947 he withdrew from the firm in order to concentrate on his favourite hobby – painting. In 1969 he was persuaded to return as an adviser to the company; by then, it was turning out nearly seven million biros a month.

The ballpoint was one of those simple ideas which revolutionized a whole industry. The ancient Egyptians, like the Chinese, used a brush for writing, while the Romans and Greeks used the sharp point of a stylus to scratch their characters on wax tablets. The quill feather was the main pen of the Middle Ages, and indeed of modern times down to the nineteenth century. The first fountain pens appeared in the 1860s, but they were unreliable. The ink flowed irregularly, flooding one minute and non-existent the next. They also had a tendency to leak.

An insurance broker from New York, LEWIS WATERMAN

(1837–1901), eventually found the answer. An embarrassing incident – which also lost him business – persuaded him that there just *had* to be a better way. Waterman had bought one of the new fountain pens to sign an important contract, because he thought that it would be more stylish and convenient than the dip pen and pocket inkwell that he usually carried. The contract was all ready on the table and the client had the pen in hand. But disaster struck. Once, twice and even a third time the pen refused to write – worse, it spilled ink on the document. Waterman rushed back to his office for another contract, but when he returned the customer had signed up with a rival broker.

Waterman eventually came up with a pen that produced a smooth, steady flow of ink. He obtained a patent in 1884, took a workshop at the back of a retail cigar store, and put up a sign: 'Waterman's Ideal Fountain Pen, guaranteed for five years'. The response was encouraging, and the L. E. Waterman Company was incorporated in 1888.

Lewis Waterman died in 1901, but the business continued

Once, twice and even a third time the pen refused to write – worse, it spilled ink on the document. Waterman rushed back to his office for another contract, but when he returned the customer had signed up with a rival broker.

to grow. By the time of his death it was selling 350,000 fountain pens a year. In 1904 gold and silver plating and specialist designs made their first appearance on pens. The customer could have his initials, a date or a posy engraved. Fountain pens became part of the good things in life.

A French associate, JULES FAGARD, secured the right to manufacture Waterman pens in France and produced some especially elaborate models. The cap often had the owner's coat of arms engraved on it. Colours pushed black into the background, and effects such as precious stone imitations – onyx, agate, pearl and turquoise – were popular.

But Waterman had formidable competitors, and in 1954 the management shut down its manufacturing facilities in the USA. The French company fared better under the leadership of Fagard's widow, who showed a remarkable talent for adapting its products to the public's need. When ballpoints became fashionable, MADAME FAGARD was quick to recognize the damage it could do to the company's established trade. They were not fancy, but they were easy to use and it didn't matter if the customer lost them. So she came out with her own ballpoint pens, and added much-publicized refinements: in 1947, for example, Waterman launched a pen with four interchangeable colours, which was a great success. Today the company is the largest manufacturer of writing instruments in Europe. Like others, it still produces elegant fountain pens, but most people nowadays prefer the simpler ballpoints. In recent years, fibre-tipped and felt pens have also become popular.

Ladislao Biro and Lewis Waterman were typical examples of a particular type of inventor: the individual who, on the basis of personal experience, decides to have a go at something for which he or she has no professional training but which is perceived to be *useful*. We all know the feeling. The difference is that *they* took the next step, alone and unaided, and in doing so laid the foundation of a large multi-national enterprise. They were innovators. The same is true of Jules Fagard and his widow, who showed what can be achieved by skilful marketing.

Ivan Boesky

b. 1937

'The Pied Piper of Arbitrage'

Until his misdeeds were exposed in November 1986, Ivan Boesky was widely respected for his mastery of the mysterious financial game known as 'risk arbitrage'. He did not invent it, but he was the first to set up a business devoted purely to arbitrage and the first to bring investors into his operations – pioneering efforts which, because he was so successful, impressed both Wall Street and the media. The financial world was astonished when it was announced that Boesky had agreed to pay penance of $100 million – half of it a fine for violating the Securities and Exchange Commission's insider trading rules, and half for a fund to compensate wronged investors and companies who sued. *Fortune* magazine called him the 'Crook of the Year'.

The son of a Russian immigrant, Boesky was born and brought up in Detroit. He obtained a law degree, and worked for a time as clerk to a federal judge. But he was eager to make money, and was fascinated when a friend explained risk arbitrage to him. He went to New York and found a job with a brokerage firm; he later joined another firm and was put in charge of its arbitrage department.

Risk arbitrage has to do with betting on the outcome of business transactions. The arbitrager puts his money into securities which are the focus of a tender offer, a merger or a liquidation. If he gets it right, he makes a profit from the difference between his purchase price and the selling price at the time the deal is finalized.

In a takeover situation, he has to assess the chances of the deal going through. Various obstacles may emerge – the authorities may veto it, for example, because they think it violates anti-trust legislation; or the acquiring company may be unable to raise the finance needed to complete the transaction. If this happens, the price of the stock is liable to drop sharply. Many investors are unwilling to take the risk, and sell out at an early stage. The arbitrager may or may not decide to get involved. If he thinks the deal *will* go through, he starts buying shares. He often builds up a substantial holding – perhaps a quarter or more of a takeover target's shares – which may give him the clout to influence the nature of the outcome.

To most people, this sounds like gambling on a grand scale. But Boesky always insisted that arbitrage was a discipline, 'a very judgmental, artistic process'. He taught a course in the subject at two universities, and wrote a book called *Merger Mania; Arbitrage; Wall Street's: Best Kept Money-Making Secret.*

Boesky started his own company in 1975, after the brokerage house he worked for had gone bankrupt. He is said to have accepted $700,000 from his in-laws to open Ivan Boesky & Co., located in two small rooms which had belonged to his previous employers. He decided to split his profits with his investors so that he would receive 55 per cent of the profits while they would have to absorb 95 per cent of the losses. He and his family kept almost all the stock in the business. It was an arrangement which many people seemed happy to go along with, because they believed that Boesky played the game with exceptional skill.

His first great coup came in 1977, when he made an estimated $7 million from a takeover battle. By early 1980 he had turned his $700,000 stake in the firm into $90 million of capital. But 1980 turned out to be a bad year for him – he lost $45 million in the first quarter – and he sold his interest in the business to six senior employees. But in 1981 he was back in action, with a new company called the Ivan F. Boesky Corporation.

The timing was good: a new wave of mergers was under way

and the next few years would see hectic activity, offering people like Boesky the opportunity to make big profits. In the mid-1970s Wall Street had only about a dozen major arbitragers. By the mid-1980s there were more than fifty, with another hundred or so lesser players. As head of the largest firm, Boesky was the undisputed king. He risked vast sums and made staggering gains. He is reported to have made $40 million when Du Pont bought Conoco in the summer of 1981;

The financial world was astonished when it was announced that Boesky had agreed to pay penance of $100 million. . . . Fortune *magazine called him the 'Crook of the Year'.*

$100 million when Texaco acquired Getty Oil in January 1984; and $80 million when Chevron won control of Gulf in March 1984. There were big losses too ($70 million in the struggle for control of Phillips Petroleum), but he did well enough to be able to diversify into real estate and other businesses. In the spring of 1986, when he reorganized his main investment pool as a private limited partnership, he was worth an estimated $280 million.

Boesky made all the firm's major investment decisions. The $3 billion partnership, heavily financed with debt plus $220 million in equity from partners, held seventy-five to a hundred stocks. He set up the pool so that he could take an outsize 50 per cent of the profits as general partner, plus a management fee. Money came ahead of everything else; he would start work at 7 a.m. and spend the whole day – often until midnight – on the telephone, delving into deals. Investors were constantly reminded of the phenomenal returns possible from buying takeover stocks before the takeovers were publicly known. *Business Week* dubbed him 'The Pied Piper of Arbitrage', and financial journalists wrote admiringly about his legendary list of contacts. The Securities and Exchange Commission, though, was not so easy to impress. It started an investigation into his methods and eventually charged him with insider trading. Insider trading is, essentially, trading in shares on the basis of confidential information not available to investors generally. An obvious example is that of the director who knows that his company is about to make an offer for another company and uses that knowledge to buy the takeover

Money came ahead of everything else; he would start work at 7 a.m. and spend the whole day – often until midnight – on the telephone, delving into deals.

target's stocks for himself or his relatives before a public announcement is made. Such transactions are illegal; it is also against the law to share such information with friends or contacts who are likely to use it for their benefit, and for them to buy or sell shares knowing what is about to happen.

The purpose of the law is to prevent investors from being defrauded of their rightful profits. It is one thing to exercise one's judgment; it is quite another to make use of insider tips. The SEC charged Boesky with doing just that between February 1985 and February 1986. Others were subsequently accused of the same crime, but Boesky's case got the most publicity because of the scale of his deals. The tip-offs to the SEC that were his undoing came from another trader, Dennis B. Levine, who hoped that it would secure him more lenient treatment. Once charged, Boesky himself agreed to co-operate in the government's continuing probe of insider rings.

The public's reaction to the news was curious. Many people had clearly never heard of insider trading, and were unaware that taking advantage of confidential information was illegal. Surely, some argued, it was all part of the game? Where did one draw the line? Others were appalled by the greed of Wall

Street operators like Boesky: why did they have to chase more and more millions? Opinion was divided between those who wanted to see him punished and those who thought his only mistake was to get caught.

The real puzzle, though, is why it took the SEC so long to act. There had long been rumours that Boesky was using insider information in his trades. Two years earlier, *Fortune* had questioned him about these rumours. His reply was: 'We do not violate the rules. Period.' But the SEC had already become suspicious, and it surely should have been possible to step in before November 1986.

Perhaps the best thing that can be said about this sorry affair is that it has brought the issue of insider trading out into the open as never before; the small investor should, as a result, enjoy greater protection in future.

Alan Bond

b. 1938

The signwriter who made it to the top

Alan Bond is the brash Australian who turned an ornate piece of silverware into a major business asset and made his adopted city world-famous in the process. He was born in Ealing, London, where his father was a builder. The family emigrated to Perth in Australia when Alan was thirteen. Two years later he left school and became an apprentice signwriter. At eighteen he got married and bought a plot of land in suburban Perth. It was the start of a remarkable business career.

Bond reasoned that there were thousands of young couples like him and his wife, Eileen, and that they all needed cheap parcels of land. His father-in-law, a prosperous businessman, guaranteed a short-term finance company loan to enable Alan to buy several acres of former state government land a few miles out of town. Bond subdivided it and sold it with all the flair and sales hype usually associated with second-hand car salesmen. He went on to develop housing estates as fast as he could find the land, and branched out into the construction business, tendering for contracts to build airstrips in the remote north-west. By the age of twenty-one he had made his first million.

A year later he embarked on high-rise development in the heart of Perth itself. The first move was to secure a prime site. The Australia and New Zealand Bank in the city's main street was due to move elsewhere. The old building was put up for auction, and the audacious young man put in the highest bid. Bond recalls the old President of the Real Estate Institute shaking his head and saying: 'The boy's gone too far. Doesn't understand the values.' He eventually built on the site the thirteen-storey stock exchange building, and while doing so got to know a lot of stockbrokers with whom he would later do business.

At this point Alan Bond was merely another imaginative property developer. He might have remained just that if he had not grasped the sales potential of the America's Cup, the silver yachting trophy which the United States had first won from Britain in 1851 and kept ever since. Few people outside the sailing fraternity had ever heard of it, but Bond knew that the idea of beating the Americans at anything would have popular appeal in sports-mad Australia, and that an attempt to do so would make him a national figure. He had already found that, as he put it, 'You meet an enormous number of banking people through sailing', and he calculated that a winner's aura would make it easy to raise money for bold new ventures. Victory would also do a great deal for Perth, where the next contest would have to be held.

Bond financed an Australian challenge in 1974 and, as expected, got a lot of useful publicity. By this time he had borrowed heavily to finance land deals, and some of his creditors hinted that they might have to call in their loans. His response was typical. He told them that to act at this particular moment would be very unpatriotic. What would Australians think of fellow Australians who stood in the way of his chances of beating the Yanks? But Bond also owed money to the *American* banks. For them he painted the other side of the picture. If they called in their loans the whole world would consider them unsporting; it would look as if they were afraid that his challenge would succeed. It worked. His creditors waited.

But winning the Cup was by no means easy. His first attempt ended in failure. His business situation, too, got worse rather than better. But Bond has an enviable capacity for bouncing back from setbacks which would shatter lesser men. 'Bond's corporate life', one Australian commentator wrote during the seventies, 'has been one long cavalry charge. Just in the nick of time he turns up with cheques, a A$100 million line of credit . . . and complex deals to save his exposed front from the circling creditors.' He eventually recovered sufficiently to pay them off, and promptly plunged A$36 million – most of which he did not have – into an oil and gas venture, which he subsequently managed to sell for A$190 million.

'Bond's corporate life', one Australian commentator wrote during the seventies, 'has been one long cavalry charge. Just in the nick of time he turns up with . . . complex deals to save his exposed front from the circling creditors.'

His second Cup challenge, in 1977, was also unsuccessful. Undaunted, he tried again in 1981. This time he won and he became a national hero. Australians were ecstatic. One of their own had taken on the might of the USA and come out on top: it was a terrific morale-booster. The Americans, too, were impressed. This fellow Bond was clearly a man to watch.

With his financial position strengthened by the lucrative oil and gas deal, and bankers eager to listen to his ideas, Bond embarked on new conquests. He bought Australian Occidental Petroleum for A$42 million, then spent A$86 million drilling nine exploratory wells and A$25 million constructing a huge production platform and a giant storage facility. A few months later he paid A$1.2 billion for Castlemaine Toohey's brewery, the country's second biggest brewer, surprising corporate Australia and astonishing the Castlemaine board, which had watched him marshalling his resources for the bid with amused condescension, convinced that he would never find the cash. With his Western Australian Swan Brewery, acquired earlier, it gave Bond nearly half of Australia's beer market.

The Cup defence was not due to begin until 1986, so there was plenty of time to prepare for the boom that Perth and nearby Fremantle seemed sure to experience as a result of its new-found status. Every developer got in on the act. A fortune

---

Interviewed after the announcement, Kerry Packer seemed still stunned by what he had done. 'We sat down to negotiate,' he said, 'and I ended up being the seller rather than the buyer.'

---

was invested in new luxury hotels, a yacht marina, a casino, a new international airport terminal and other projects. Bond led the way. His schemes included Observation City, on the beach between Perth and Fremantle: almost every room in the hotel section, he promised, would have a panoramic view of the America's Cup course. He also gave himself a personal treat: a A$10 million luxury vessel with its own helipad, executive sauna and gym.

Some of the local businessmen were dubious about all this activity; if Perth lost the Cup, they warned, the bubble would burst. But the city was used to taking risks – it had grown up in the 1880s as a gold-mining town. Speculation and entrepreneurial flair were well-established elements of the Western Australian psyche.

The defence duly took place, and was shown on television all over the world. Dennis Conner, who had lost the Cup to Bond in 1981, emerged as the undisputed victor. Bond's yacht did not even make it into the final race. But on the day he lost, he amazed Australia with news of yet another remarkable deal: he became Australia's biggest television tycoon by buying Kerry Packer's interests for more than A$1 billion. It gave him twenty-five broadcasting stations with interests in Australia, Britain, the United States, the South Pacific and Hong Kong. Bond, who already had TV stations in Perth and Brisbane, could now lay claim to owning the first nationwide commercial network in the country. Interviewed after the announcement, Kerry Packer seemed still stunned by what he had done. 'We sat down to negotiate,' he said, 'and I ended up being the seller rather than the buyer.' Why? 'I was presented with an offer too good to refuse.'

Bond said that he intended to recoup a substantial part of his outlay, financed by the National Australian Bank, by floating the acquisition together with his other media interests into a new company to be known as Bond Media. The public would be invited to buy shares.

The former signwriter's empire now spans a wide range of activities – electronic media, brewing, oil, gold, coal-mining, property, retail and banking. He also owns British Airship Industries and helped to fund Australia's first private university. At home, he has an expensive art collection, mostly of French Impressionists and early Australian paintings.

At forty-nine he feels that he still has a long way to go. A close associate says that he loves the thrill of competing against his peers and beating them: 'That's what life is all about for him.'

Edwin G. Booz

1887–1951

Father of modern management consulting

Ed Booz was one of the first to recognize that companies would pay good money for advice from outsiders who could help to solve business problems. With a master's degree in psychology, Booz got his first assignment after he went to see the management of his local bank to ask for a loan. When he explained his theories that business problems were mainly people problems, they not only gave him the loan but also hired him to study their bank.

He established a one-man consultancy firm under the name of Edwin G. Booz Engineering Surveys – the term 'management consultants' did not come into general use until much later. Men like Booz were at first known as 'business counsellors', 'management engineers' or, more often, 'efficiency experts'. A good share of the work done by these pioneers did, indeed, revolve around making business more efficient: taking a task involving five minutes' labour and determining how to do it in one minute. Time and motion studies are still an important part of management consultancy, but the scope has been widened to include areas such as marketing, production, executive recruiting, organization, operations research, executive compensation and so on.

Booz sold judgment rather than particular expertise. He was a tough individualist who didn't hesitate to state bluntly what he thought. It wasn't always popular. One story involving his bluntness concerns his relationship with Montgomery Ward & Co. The main order firm had difficulty remaining solvent during the Depression and Booz was called in. When the head of the company asked him what he considered to be the main problem, he replied in his most straightforward manner: 'You!' That reportedly ended his association with Montgomery Ward. But he went on to tackle many other clients, including the US Navy Department. He hired more people, and by the time of his death in 1951 the firm of Booz, Allen & Hamilton was generally regarded as the leader in the field.

World War II gave a tremendous boost to the consultancy business. With so many executives despatched to the front, serious problems developed in many companies; when they looked around for help they found that they could get it from firms like Booz, Allen & Hamilton. They were also used in the armed services, and the work they did during these years greatly helped to establish recognition of the value of management consultancy.

Another pioneer was JAMES O. MCKINSEY (1889–1937), who founded his consulting firm while working as an economics professor at the University of Chicago. Like Booz, he was a strong-minded individual who took a tough line with clients. He had a very analytical mind and great powers of concentration. The trouble with most people, he used to tell associates, was that they were mentally lazy and unwilling to do good, plain, hard thinking about a subject.

Between 1920 and 1929 McKinsey wrote numerous articles and four books, the best known being *Budgetary Control*, published in 1922, which was the first definitive book on budgeting. It helped him to secure accounts when he started his firm in 1926. Much of his early business came from banks and other financial institutions whose defaulted loans arose in many cases from inept management.

In 1934 Marshall Field & Co., the Chicago department store, retained McKinsey's firm to conduct a thorough examination of its business, which in addition to retailing at that time also included manufacturing and wholesaling. McKinsey himself supervised the study and recommended Field's to abandon wholesaling and manufacturing and to concentrate on maintaining retail leadership. The board of directors not only accepted this idea, but asked him to become chairman and chief executive officer. The opportunity to become a doer instead of merely an adviser was apparently too tempting for McKinsey to resist. He accepted. His leadership was, by all accounts, highly successful. But in 1937, at the age of forty-eight, he contracted pneumonia. Taken to hospital on Saturday night, he died on Monday morning. His partners continued to build up the business, which later won worldwide fame.

Management consulting has become a billion-dollar industry, with thousands of firms giving advice to others – not only in the United States but also in Europe and elsewhere. Some are generalists, offering broad analytical skills; some concentrate on one particular discipline; some confine their work to specific industries. The best are much more sophisticated than they were in the days of Booz and McKinsey, but the primary function hasn't really changed. The main reason why companies use management consultants is still that, as

Booz got his first assignment after he went to see the management of his local bank to ask for a loan. When he explained his theories that business problems were mainly people problems, they not only gave him the loan but hired him to study their bank.

outsiders, consultants can offer a fresh point of view, identify problems and recommend practical solutions. The value of their advice to the company depends largely on what the people who pay them substantial fees decide to do about it. Many businessmen resent criticism, especially if they feel that it is directed at them personally, and end up doing nothing. They have demonstrated their willingness to listen but, like the head of Montgomery Ward all those years ago, they don't like what they hear. It takes courage, as well as perception, to recognize that others may have a valid argument.

The management consultant is not there to solve problems in a purely theoretical, abstract and technical sense. If he is any good at all, he is action-oriented: his thinking is directed towards improved managerial performance – and results – for the client. This includes the creation of understanding and commitment towards a particular change and methods by which it can become integral to the client's organization. He must urge and persuade his client and, when necessary, help him towards a sound course of action. Most organizations possess the knowledge to cure many of their problems; the rub is utilization.

The consultant must think not only of his fee, but of what he owes his client in terms of responsibility, of candour, of ability and of willingness to turn down an assignment which either exceeds his competence or, even more important, does not appear to him what the client really needs or should do. Many practitioners, regrettably, fail to meet the standards set by people like Booz and McKinsey. This failure goes a long way towards explaining why many companies have become disenchanted with the management consulting profession.

The term 'consultant' is often used as a euphemism. It may hide activities like business spying, or it may simply be used by an unemployed executive while seeking a job. Sometimes an executive becomes a 'consultant' in the company records even though his salary continues, as a dodge to avoid compulsory retirement policies. Prospective clients should, therefore, always make enquiries about the status of consultants before they ask them for help. (See also PETER DRUCKER.)

Horatio Bottomley

1860–1933

The con man who started the *Financial Times*

Horatio Bottomley was the founder of what is, today, Europe's most highly respected business newspaper, the *Financial Times*. He was also a crook. It was fortunate for the paper that he fell out with his partner, who took it over. Bottomley went on to launch other new ventures and to make much-publicized appearances in court, defending himself against charges of fraud.

Born in London's East End and brought up in an orphanage, Bottomley was successively an errand boy, a solicitor's clerk and a law courts shorthand writer. His first business venture, a suburban weekly paper, went bankrupt and led to his debut in the dock, accused of fraud. He won an acquittal. The judge was so impressed that he suggested the defendant should become a barrister: he warned him, however, against entering the world of business again.

Undaunted, Bottomley started the *Financial Times*. After he split with his partner, he managed to land a contract to print *Hansard*, the official record of English parliamentary proceedings, and merged four established printers and publishers into the Hansard Printing and Publishing Union. The company received a stock market listing in 1899, capitalized at £500,000. All seemed to go well for a time – the company was profitable and paid a reasonably good dividend. The share capital was doubled. But appearances were deceptive: Bottomley was borrowing against assets to pay those dividends, and when the debenture holders eventually got a look at the books they found that £600,000 could not be accounted for and that the company was broke. Bottomley was again declared bankrupt and charged with fraud. The prosecution thought it had a watertight case, but he handled his defence so well that, after a trial which lasted twenty-two days, the jury's verdict was 'Not guilty'.

He now set himself up as a promoter of Australian gold mining shares, which had become fashionable. By 1897 he had amassed a fortune of several million pounds. But his companies failed regularly, and between 1900 and 1905 he was served with numerous petitions of bankruptcy. The shares he sold would look good through the generous first dividend. New investors would come in. Then he would dissolve the company. It worked well until 1906, when Bottomley once more found himself in court on a fraud charge: astonishingly, he won another acquittal.

One would have thought that by now the public would be wary of this glib salesman. But no: the voters of South Hackney elected him as their Member of Parliament! Three years

Bottomley remained the star even in court, demanding and receiving a special 'medicinal' champagne break at 11.30 every morning.

later he went bankrupt *again*, this time for £233,000, and was forced to give up his seat.

Meanwhile he had founded another publication, a jingoistic weekly magazine called *John Bull*. Bottomley portrayed himself as a fervent patriot, and under his editorship the journal acquired a popular following. He wrote hard-hitting editorials about people whom he disapproved of, and even had his own detective agency to seek out 'anything nefarious'. He also gave patriotic recruitment speeches at £50 a time.

The success of *John Bull* enabled him to discharge himself from bankruptcy, and South Hackney re-elected him to Parliament. His reputation as a patriot also enabled him to launch the greatest of his schemes – the Victory Bond Club. The bonds had been issued by the government, but the price was much too high for 'the little man'. The Club was started to solve the problem. Everyone would contribute what they could and Bottomley, the 'Friend of the Poor', would make the investments on behalf of the members.

The public put up more than £500,000. Some did go to the Treasury, but Bottomley himself creamed off some £150,000. In October 1921 the Chancery Court appointed a receiver to investigate the whole network of his affairs. A few months later he was charged on twenty-four counts under the Larceny Act. Bottomley remained the star even in court, demanding and receiving a special 'medicinal' champagne break at 11.30 every morning. But his luck ran out. Found guilty on twenty-three of the charges, he was sentenced, at the age of sixty-two, to seven years in prison. The following year Bottomley was judged personally bankrupt for one last time.

Released on parole in 1926, he started a new paper, *John Blunt*, but it failed. He spent the rest of his days writing his memoirs (which he sold to the Sunday press), contributing articles to various journals, and making pathetic personal appearances on the stage of the Windmill Theatre.

Richard Branson

b. 1950

'From the rock market to the stock market'

The cliché image of the British businessman, much loved by cartoonists (especially those working on the Soviet satirical magazine *Krokodil*), is that of a haughty City gent in a pin-striped suit and bowler hat, carrying a furled umbrella even on the hottest day of the year. It has little to do with reality, these days, and it certainly has nothing to do with Richard Branson, one of the most successful of the country's younger entrepreneurs, who has a penchant for jeans and is liable to turn up at meetings wearing unmatched socks. But it did not prevent this astute promoter from making use of the cliché, in his own way, when he floated his company, the Virgin Group, on the London Stock Exchange in 1986. His television commercials showed a stockbroker in pin-striped suit and bowler disco-dancing in his office as the message 'From the rock market to the stock market' flashed on the screen. Investors, attracted by the much-publicized glamour of the business, responded with enthusiasm. More than eighty-five thousand people applied for the shares. Branson's own holding was valued at £200 million.

Richard Branson was born to a family whose menfolk had for six generations been lawyers; his father was struggling to make his way in the profession. His mother, born Eve Huntley-Flindt, had been a dancer – playing Peter Pan in London – and an air hostess in South America in the 1930s, when you had to wear an oxygen mask to fly over mountains. They lived near Guildford in Surrey, and Richard was sent away to school when he was eight. He seems to have been an indifferent pupil (though good at sports) because he had to be sent to a crammer in Sussex so that he could improve enough academically to qualify for admission to Stowe, one of Britain's public schools.

By the age of sixteen he had flung himself into preparations for a national magazine, first for schoolchildren and then for students. He spent a great deal of time in the phone box outside the school library soliciting ads for the first issue, and inside the library writing letters to names in *Who's Who*, demanding contributions. Then, with £3000 worth of advertising in hand, he left Stowe in the summer of 1967. Six months later he launched *Student*, and the next three years were taken up with constant hustling for ads. In 1969, acting on a hunch, he placed an advertisement for cheap mail-order records in the magazine. The response was excellent – embarrassingly so, because he had no actual records. He could not go direct to the record companies, who were trying to prevent exactly the sort of price-cutting operation he was setting up. Eventually he found a shop-owner in the East End of London who would sell to him. Meanwhile, he had closed the magazine. Mail order seemed more promising.

Branson called his new venture Virgin. He later said it was in acknowledgement of his naïveté in business. Whatever the reason, it was an eye-catching name which he has used in other enterprises, including his own airline, ever since. ('It goes with everything,' he once told an interviewer. 'I've often thought of setting up businesses just for the name – like Virgin Foods or a model agency called Virgin Girls.') But in those early days the company was often short of cash, and when the enterprise was threatened by a postal strike he decided that they needed a shop. One of his colleagues found an empty floor above a shoe shop in Oxford Street and they opened for business in January 1971. It was an instant hit, and Branson went on to open shops all over the country. For £25,000 the company also bought Shipton Manor near Oxford and started converting it into a recording studio. In 1972 the Virgin record label was born with a worldwide success, Mike Oldfield's 'Tubular Bells'.

After hitting a bad patch in the mid-seventies, when its first batch of musicians had fallen from fashion, the label was revised and the signing of the Sex Pistols in 1977 was followed, in the 1980s, by such successes as Culture Club, Phil Collins and Simple Minds. Meanwhile the shops established themselves as more sophisticated mega-stores, selling a wide range of pop-related products, including videos and books. Offices were opened rapidly in twenty countries, the number of employees rose to 2500, and by the time of the stock market flotation in 1986 the group had a turnover of more than £300 million. Branson continued to run it from a houseboat in Little Venice, a quirky touch which puzzled the City but appealed to his many young admirers.

> *'I've often thought of setting up businesses just for the name – like Virgin Foods or a model agency called Virgin Girls.'*

Branson's most spectacular expansion, in 1984, was into the airline business. FREDDIE LAKER had shown, some years earlier, that there was substantial scope for a carrier which offered to fly passengers across the Atlantic at a discount. The Laker venture had ultimately ended in failure, but Branson felt that the basic idea had been good and that he could avoid Laker's mistakes. He leased a jumbo jet, and started regular services between London and Newark, New York. Unlike Laker, he offered a frills service: hot meals, on-board movies, music videos and so on. Passengers sometimes found themselves entertained by live performers, who were given free round-trip tickets in exchange for their acts. Virgin's aim, Branson declared, was to 'put the fun back into flying'.

The media loved it: here, once again, was a British entrepreneur bold enough to take on the big names in the business. Branson gained further publicity by stunts like a record

Atlantic crossing in his *Virgin Challenger* racing boat. By 1986 the airline had two 747s and a smaller jet, and was also flying to Miami and Holland. The financial world, however, was understandably sceptical about its prospects and advised him to keep his fledgling airline out of the stock market offer: it was hived off as a separate company.

Many shrewd investment analysts expressed doubts, at the time of the flotation, about the long-term future of the entire enterprise. The entertainment business, they noted, is notoriously fickle. But Branson had become, at thirty-six, a symbol of what Margaret Thatcher liked to call 'Britain's entrepreneurial revolution'. Restless and energetic, always wanting to go somewhere and to do something, he was the kind of person who, she felt, was needed to make the country great again. In 1986 she put him in charge of an unlikely-sounding project: a campaign to create jobs for the unemployed by tackling the environment. He was typically enthusiastic.

Branson is a genuine entrepreneur, full of ideas and eager to tackle new challenges. He rejects the criticism that, like so many of his breed, he is a one-man band. 'I immerse myself completely in any new venture, and then appoint people to run it and stand back,' he says. But one is still entitled to wonder how the business would fare without him. He is conscious of his responsibility, not only to the company but also to the many young people who are seeking to follow his example. 'A lot of them would like to do well in life,' he says. 'I didn't have anything when I began. Perhaps they say: "If Richard can do it, so can I." That's an awfully big responsibility.' It will be fascinating to see how he handles it in the years to come.

Billy Butlin

1899–1980

Creator of the Holiday World

Billy Butlin was a shrewd, ambitious businessman who created something of a revolution in the holiday habits of the British working class by his establishment of a chain of holiday camps. This was in the days before jet travel made it possible for people from all walks of life to head for the sunnier climes of countries like Spain and Italy. Butlin's innovative move was based on the recognition that the British weather often made holidays a misery: there was nothing to do in the rain. His solution was to establish seaside camps which offered plenty of activity. 'The most important thing', he once said, 'is that no one is left to himself even for a moment.' The concept was later taken up by many others, including GILBERT TRIGANO of Club Med, but when Butlin opened his first camp in 1935 it was a novel idea.

William Edmund Butlin was born in South Africa where his father kept a cycle shop; his mother was the daughter of a Gloucestershire baker who used to sell his own gingerbread at country fairs. As a child of ten, Billy was taken to England for a holiday and spent most of his time with his uncle on the gingerbread stalls. His parents then moved to Canada, and at the age of fourteen he was working in the Toronto branch of Eaton's, the famous department store. He later went to Montreal, but in 1921 he decided to try his luck in England and worked his passage on a cattle boat. When he arrived in Liverpool he was alone, unknown and had only a few pounds in his pocket. He made his way to Bristol, where his uncle was by then running a travelling funfair. Billy helped out at the fair and eventually bought his own hoopla stall for thirty shillings. The experience not only taught him the basic rules of showmanship but also gave him a valuable insight into the leisure habits of the British working class.

Butlin built his first holiday camp at Skegness in Lincolnshire. It had been a potato field – but it was near the sea, a matter of prime importance. When it opened it could accommodate a thousand people, and this number doubled within a year. His next camp was built at Clacton-on-Sea in Essex, and when war broke out in 1939 he was on the point of opening a third, at Filey, in Yorkshire. All the camps were immediately taken over by the Admiralty and Air Ministry, and Butlin became Director General of Hostels to the Ministry of Supply. Soon after the end of the war, in 1946, he was back in business, providing holidays for over four thousand people a week. Further camps were opened and in 1947 his customers totalled in the region of three hundred thousand. By 1955 that number had doubled.

The camps' appeal lay primarily in the fact that they offered a relatively inexpensive way to have a good time. The

'The secret of success in life, and consequently of making money, is to enjoy your work. If you do, nothing is hard work – no matter how many hours you put in.'

accommodation was plain but adequate and there were all kinds of facilities – swimming pools, boating lakes, pleasure gardens, dance halls, child care schemes and so on. Redcoated hosts did their best to keep everyone in a happy mood, organizing a wide range of often bizarre contests: there was, for example, a competition in which prizes were awarded for men who were judged to have the best knobbly knees, and another in which contestants were invited to compete for the dubious distinction of having the shiniest bald head. Billy Butlin also brought dodgem cars to Europe.

He was knighted in 1964 and retired four years later, handing over the direction of the group to his son Robert. In 1972 it was acquired by the Rank Organization. It still bears the founder's name, but the word 'camp' has been dropped, along with the cries of 'Hi-de-Hi!' and knobbly knee contests. People now stay in a Holiday World. The accommodation has been upgraded and Butlin's nowadays tries to cater for a broader market. But the company still believes in giving its customers plenty to do. The range of facilities is impressive, and particularly suitable for people with young children. For large parts of the day entertainments and supervised games (including soccer-coaching lessons) relieve parents of their offspring, and in the evening a child-listening service and security patrols mean that parents can enjoy an anxiety-free evening out at a disco or cabaret while the little horrors recharge their batteries.

Billy Butlin set out to cater for the masses, and he succeeded. He offered them an alternative to the conventional British seaside holiday, at a time when foreign travel was still widely regarded as the prerogative of the rich, and the response was tremendous. The middle classes might sneer, but he gave pleasure to millions. The new Holiday Worlds are still primarily for gregarious people: you have to like crowds and be willing to make new friends.

'What is life', Billy Butlin used to say, 'if you can't enjoy yourself?' Much of his own pleasure came from work. As he put it: 'The secret of success in life, and consequently of making money, is to enjoy your work. If you do, nothing is hard work – no matter how many hours you put in.' But it wrecked his first two marriages and he had a difficult relationship with his children: the man who organized family holidays for millions seldom took his own kids for one. He tried to make up for it after his retirement, but could not resist getting involved in new activities, this time for charitable organizations. Prince Philip said of him: 'Few men have done so much good in secret and out of sheer kindness of heart.'

Andrew Carnegie

1835–1919

The steelmaster philanthropist

It was Carnegie, one of the American 'robber barons', who coined the phrase: 'Pioneering don't pay.' His subsequent career, though, is encouraging proof that the opposite is true. Carnegie became one of the most successful pioneers in the US steel industry, not only in the technological area but also in the organization and management of resources.

Born in Dunfermline, Scotland, he was the son of a poor damask linen weaver who, with other members of the family, was much involved in radical politics. His father's views made a deep impression on young Andrew. 'As a child', he said in later years, 'I could have slain kings, dukes, or lords, and considered their death a service to the state.' Work was hard to come by, and in 1848 his mother persuaded her husband to sell up their possessions and emigrate to the United States, where her two sisters and a brother already lived. They arrived in New York and made their way to Allegheny City, Pennsylvania, which is now part of Philadelphia. Andrew, then thirteen, found a job as a bobbin-boy in a cotton factory, earning $1.20 a week. He later became a messenger in the Pittsburgh telegraph office. At eighteen he was hired by the superintendent of the Pennsylvania Railroad as his private secretary.

While working on the railroad, the young man invested what he had saved, and more that he had borrowed, in a firm that made iron bridges, a healthy business in an era when railroads were expanding rapidly. He also got involved with a German named Kloman, who was making iron axles for rolling stock and owned a well-equipped mill. Kloman was doing very well, but needed more capital. Carnegie found it for him, with the help of his brother Tom and two friends, and became a partner. He resigned from his job with the railroad. Within a few years the brothers acquired a majority interest in Kloman, and Carnegie combined it with his iron bridge firm. He also invested in an iron rail manufacturing business and in another company which made locomotives.

Carnegie was a first-rate salesman, tireless in his search for new orders. He even found time to sell Pennsylvania Railroad bonds on Wall Street. The handsome commissions were ploughed back into the iron trade, and his companies continued to prosper. He moved to New York and put a sign on his office door: 'Andrew Carnegie, Investments'. He thought of himself as a businessman rather than a manufacturer, a salesman rather than an ironmaster. By 1868 he had an income of $50,000 a year – and he was still only thirty-three.

His dream, at that time, was to arrange his affairs in such a way that the $50,000 per annum would be assured for life, and to 'cast off business for ever'. He wrote a memorandum in which he set down his vision for the future. He

'Whatever I engage in I must push inordinately; therefore I should be careful to choose that life which will be the most elevating in its character.'

would go to England, settle in Oxford, and get a thorough education. He would 'make the acquaintance of literary men'. He would then go to London 'and purchase a controlling interest in some newspaper or review, and give the general management of it attention, taking a part in public matters, especially those connected with education and improvement of the poorer classes'. No idol, he wrote, is more debasing than the worship of money. 'Whatever I engage in I must push inordinately; therefore I should be careful to choose that life which will be the most elevating in its character. To continue much longer overwhelmed by business cares and with most of my thoughts wholly upon the way to make more money in the shortest time, must degrade me beyond hope of permanent recovery.'

But Carnegie soon forgot his youthful resolutions; he was much too deeply involved in business to let go. He did get to England, but there was by then no question of settling in Oxford or buying a London newspaper. Instead he made the acquaintance of Henry Bessemer, who had invented a new process of making steel from pig iron. Carnegie had known about it, but had been sceptical. (This was the time when he made his much-quoted remark about pioneering not paying.) In London, though, he changed his mind and, having done so, decided to act at once. Steel, he declared, was the key to an industrial economy and the Bessemer process was ideal. He diverted all his resources into steel, and constructed a huge mill on a site near Pittsburgh. It was a wise move, and by 1881 Carnegie was the foremost iron- and steelmaster in America. He undersold the competition, built more plants, and acquired many other companies.

Carnegie had a large number of protégés who, if they showed promise, were given both quick promotion and shares in the company as a bonus. 'We cannot', he said, 'have too many of the right sort of men interested in the profits.' But he was opposed to organized labour and regarded unions as a divisive intrusion into his private affairs. This inevitably led to a showdown. In 1892, while Carnegie was on holiday in Scotland, a strike broke out at his steel works in Homestead, Pennsylvania. Henry Clay Frick, a partner, was running the company at the time and he took a tough line. The workers were locked out, a high fence was put around the mill, and three hundred guards from the PINKERTON Detective Agency were brought in to protect the place. This led to riots which lasted for several days. State troops eventually moved in to take charge. Fourteen men had been killed, and 163 had been seriously wounded. The Homestead works soon reopened with a wholly non-union workforce, but Carnegie later said that he was deeply hurt by this tragic affair. 'No pangs remain of any wound received in my business career save that of Homestead.'

The 1890s saw further rapid expansion, chiefly under the aggressive management of Frick. But the relationship between Carnegie and his partner deteriorated and Frick eventually

---

'No pangs remain of any wound received in my business career save that of Homestead.'

---

sold his stock and left the company. Carnegie took the helm, but he was once more in a self-questioning mood. He was sixty-five, and he wanted to devote himself to other pursuits. In 1901 he sold the business to the banker J. Pierpont Morgan, who incorporated it into a new creation, United States Steel. Carnegie received more than $300 million and Morgan congratulated him 'on being the richest man in the world'.

But Carnegie had no intention of keeping his millions: with typical energy he set about the task of giving them away. In an article published in the *Pall Mall Gazette*, he argued that the accumulation of wealth was necessary for human progress but that it was the moral obligation of the wealthy to dispense their money for the good of society. His first act was to set up a $5 million pension fund for Carnegie employees. For the next eighteen years his chief interest was to deplete his fortune. He seemed to enjoy doing so as much as he had the making of it; and he was just as successful at giving as he had been in accumulating. At his death, in 1919, only 10 per cent of his $300 million remained.

The best way to improve mankind, Carnegie felt, was to improve understanding. The removal of ignorance could best be accomplished by exposure to books. He and his various trusts therefore provided for 2811 free public libraries (1946 in America, 660 in Britain and Ireland and 205 in the British colonies) at a cost of nearly $60 million. Virtually non-existent before him, the free library, as a result of his philanthropy, became as much a part of both urban and rural America and Britain as the school or the church.

Carnegie made numerous other benefactions – to individual colleges, to the Carnegie Institutes of Pittsburgh and of Washington, to Scottish universities, to the Endowment for International Peace (he was a staunch pacifist) and to his Hero Funds, which he set up 'to compensate those injured in helping their fellow-men'. He also gave $10,000 annuities to President William Howard Taft and Britain's Lloyd George, and $5000 a year to the widows of Presidents Grover Cleveland and Theodore Roosevelt. His one real personal extravagance was an estate in Scotland, where he built a baronial mansion and took pleasure in playing the role of Highland laird.

Carnegie was one of the most interesting of the great nineteenth-century American industrialists. He had immense drive and he was bold and imaginative. But he was also a complex character, with a wider range of interests than most of his contemporaries and an attitude to wealth – and the moral obligation it imposes – which led many people to regard him as an eccentric. He could be ruthless, but he could also be remarkably considerate. He made his fortune in the steel industry, but could probably have been successful in just about any other kind of business.

Coco Chanel

1883–1971

The designer who liberated women

Coco (Gabrielle) Chanel was a remarkably talented designer who, with flair and daring, instigated a revolution in the fashion world: at the height of the Belle Epoque period, she liberated women from their corsets and plumage and introduced a new concept of elegance. Chanel invented sports fashions and the unisex style, pioneered the use of costume jewellery and originated couture perfume. Her stylishly simple but comfortable clothes became immensely popular with the 'new women' of the 1920s and by the late 1930s she was the wealthiest couturier in France, owning four businesses and factories making textiles, jewellery and perfumes. Her fame spread to other countries, notably America, and she remained one of the most influential figures on the international fashion scene until her death in 1971, at the age of eighty-eight.

She was born Gabrielle Chanel, the daughter of a provincial fairground peddler who hawked suspenders and handkerchiefs from a pushcart. Orphaned at an early age and brought up by nuns, she originally wanted to be a singer. She made a stage debut in a concert-café, with a repertoire consisting of two songs, both of which contained the word 'Coco'. Her audiences began calling her by that name, and it stuck. But her voice was limited and work was hard to come by. She eventually got a job as a milliner, and started to design hats – many for the stage stars of the day. Later, young socialites also went to her for help with their wardrobes.

She soon rebelled against the elaborate clothes of the period, which struck her as ridiculous. Because in 1913 women had neither fashionable nor even appropriate clothing for sports, and because her contemporaries, as she phrased it, 'attended sporting events the way women in hennins attended medieval tournaments', she invented a whole new style for relaxation and outdoor living. She opened her first boutique in Deauville and, among other innovative ideas, produced a chaste bathing suit.

After World War I, during which she served as a nurse, she founded a couture house in Paris. She continued to turn her back on the past, and her unconventional approach attracted a lot of attention. She later said of this period: 'I did not go into society because I had to design clothes. I designed clothes precisely because I did go into society, because I was the first to live the life of this century.'

Chanel invented beach pajamas, introduced the chemise dress and the collarless cardigan jacket, and then the bias-cut dress and other trademarks such as floating neck scarves and heavy costume jewellery. in 1920 she launched Chanel No. 5, presented in a spare, minimal bottle – a flagon as clean as a cube – that stood in stark contrast to the frippery then favoured by perfumiers.

'I did not go into society because I had to design clothes. I designed clothes precisely because I did go into society, because I was the first to live the life of this century.'

During the exciting 1920s the Chanel style was widely seen to stand for the whole notion of modernity. Her clothes were extensively copied and worn by young women everywhere. But there were critics, too. Many journalists deplored the suppressions – 'no more bosom, no more stomach, no more rump'. The couturier Paul Poiret said that Chanel had invented 'poverty de luxe'. Formerly, he declared, 'women were architectural like the prows of ships, and very beautiful. Now they resemble little undernourished telegraph clerks.' But women were no longer willing to be told by men what they should wear; they identified with Chanel's simplifying tastes. One of her most publicized innovations was to put women into slacks. She gave this emulation of masculine attire an air of class and adapted it to every occasion.

In 1931, she was asked to design clothes for leading movie stars like Gloria Swanson. She went to California, but she didn't care for Hollywood and soon left. Chanel was by then accustomed to being treated as a celebrity in her own right, and she resented the attitudes of the imperious prima donnas of the screen.

The couturier Paul Poiret said that Chanel had invented 'poverty de luxe'.

World War II, and the defeat of France, inevitably dealt a severe blow to the fashion scene. When Paris was occupied, she dismissed her staff and closed the House of Chanel. During the occupation she had an affair with a German officer, which created a scandal when it was discovered and then brought violent recriminations when the war ended. She did not reopen her salon, but exiled herself to Switzerland and, for a decade, stayed out of the business. A new designer, Christian Dior, began to make his mark during this period. He created what quickly became known as the New Look, emphasizing the 'womanly woman'. Chanel was almost forgotten.

But in 1954 she came out of her voluntary retirement to challenge the young Dior. By now seventy-one, she felt that before long women would want to discard all those waist cinchers, padded bras, heavy skirts and stiffened jackets. She once again threw herself into her work with enthusiasm and presented her collection at a new Chanel salon in the Rue Cambon.

The critics were merciless: the verdict was that after her long absence Coco Chanel had lost her touch. But her clothes sold well, especially in America, and within a year the 'Chanel look' was back in fashion. When asked to comment on her victory, she said that it was based on an approach that was essentially simple: 'A garment must be logical.' In her view, the creations of *ces messieurs* – by which she meant her male competitors – were the very opposite of logical: 'Ah no, definitely no, men were not meant to dress women.'

Chanel did not succeed in destroying Dior, but she regained the primacy of the couture world. Despite her age, she continued to work with a ferocious determination – a solitary figure, respected, proud and always tyrannical.

Coco Chanel was, without doubt, one of the most extraordinary women of her time. She knew and collaborated with all the luminaries of the age: Diaghilev, Cocteau, Picasso, Jean Renoir, Visconti. Though pursued by many rich admirers, she never married. She was a pioneer of the feminist movement – an independent, highly successful female who, from her early days, did things her own way and who had a long and remarkably eventful life.

Liz Claiborne

b. 1929

The executive woman's dress designer

Liz Claiborne has built a highly successful fashion empire by designing clothes for a new class of American woman. She was one of the first to recognize that well-paid working women needed clothes that were fashionable but not faddish, businesslike but not dull, comfortable but not dowdy. In 1986, the company she and her husband founded in 1976 had a turnover of $800 million and moved on to the *Fortune* 500 list of the largest industrial enterprises in the United States, one of the youngest companies ever to achieve that distinction.

Liz Claiborne was born in Brussels to American parents, and spent most of her childhood in Europe. Her mother taught her to sew. She later lived in New Orleans, but returned to Europe without completing high school. Her father, a banker, didn't want her to go into business, so she studied painting in Brussels and Paris. At twenty she won a *Harper's Bazaar* design contest, moved to New York, and picked up work drawing and modelling. She married an art director from the Bonwit Teller store, but the marriage didn't last. In the mid-1950s she met Arthur Ortenberg, who was running the junior dress division of a women's sportswear company, and hired her as a designer. He eventually became her second husband.

Claiborne moved on to a company called Youth Guild, where she was the chief designer. She tried to persuade her employers that they should get out of junior dresses and create quality clothes for professional women, but they didn't much care for the idea. So she and Ortenberg decided to launch their own business. They put up their life savings, about $50,000, and managed to get another $200,000 from family and friends.

The venture was profitable almost from the start. Her clothes were practical and, unlike the dresses and suits worn by models in the high fashion magazines, they were reasonably priced. When Liz Claiborne Inc. went public in 1981, the initial offering raised about $6.5 million. Investors got a bargain; the stock is now worth many times what they paid for it.

The truly remarkable thing is that the company's extraordinary growth has been achieved without building a single factory or putting a sales force on the road. Independent suppliers, located mostly in the Far East, manufacture the clothes under contract. Labour is cheaper there, which helps to keep down prices. And retailers deal directly with the company's headquarters in New York. They don't seem to mind: the Liz Claiborne label has proved to be a winner.

As president, Claiborne no longer has time to do any designing herself. She supervises the work of a team of fourteen designers, choosing fabrics and colours, and 'editing' their work. Ortenberg heads operations. Retailers say that one of the main reasons for their success is that they are very good at responding to customers. Ten Liz Claiborne 'fashion specialists' spend all their time visiting stores, talking with customers and giving seminars to salespeople. A sophisticated computer system records what styles, colours and sizes consumers buy each week in a cross-section of stores. There is a constant flow of new merchandise – six seasons instead of the traditional four.

Liz Claiborne Inc. has nine divisions today. Children's clothes were introduced in 1973, and Liz-Kids shops have been opened in a number of department stores. Men's clothing followed in 1985. The company has also linked up with Avon Products to launch a perfume that could lead to a full line of

---

She was one of the first to recognize that well-paid working women needed clothes that were fashionable but not faddish, businesslike but not dull, comfortable but not dowdy.

---

cosmetics. And there are plans to create the company's own speciality stores. They will sell products with a different label, to avoid antagonizing retailers who already sell her garments.

But Liz Claiborne clothes for working women, the concept that got the business started in the 1970s, continue to provide the bulk of the revenue. As more and more women reach executive positions, sales should go on expanding.

The founders still work long hours, and live in the same

New York apartment they had when they began. But they are grooming their successors and intend to spend more time, in future, at a ranch they have bought in Montana. They can well afford to do so. Claiborne's stock alone is reckoned to be worth $80 million.

Charles Clore

1904–79

The takeover king of the fifties

Charles Clore dominated the British takeover scene in the 1950s: a series of much-publicized deals made his name a household word. No one did more, in his day, to make industry – and shareholders – aware of the value of under-used assets, and he was a pioneer of the sale-and-leaseback method of raising cash. His takeover technique eventually became standard procedure, but in the early fifties it was still novel enough in Britain to take many boards of directors by surprise – and to shake them out of their complacency.

Clore, the son of a Russian-Jewish refugee who built up a small textile business, thought big and took calculated risks. He was all for making audacious bids and he didn't mind too much if they didn't come off. The way he operated meant that there was usually a profit for him if he didn't quite make it. Months before making his move he bought shares in the market, hiding his identity by using a nominee name. It gave him a useful starting base, acquired at a level well below the eventual bid price. And if the offer failed, the efforts of his opponents to justify rejection to their shareholders boosted the value of his holdings to a point where he could sell at a useful profit. It is a common enough approach in the 1980s, but at the time few people saw merit in the concept of the 'successful loser'.

Clore first attracted the financial community's interest when he bought his way into a London issuing house called Investment Registry. Like so many other enterprises of its type, it was mainly concerned with introducing private firms to the stock market and helping established companies to raise fresh capital. Clore used it as a vehicle for his first big deal – a bid for J. Sears & Co., a company which owned more than nine hundred shoe shops (most of them freehold) but made only a modest profit. To Clore, its main attraction lay in the potential of the nine hundred choice properties.

The board put up a valiant fight. It almost trebled the dividend and, as countless other defenders have done since, made all kinds of promises. But Clore's offer held out the prospect of immediate capital gain – then still tax-free – and was accepted by a majority of the stockholders. He went on to show how to turn high-street properties into millions without losing them. He sold most of the shops to the financial institutions, who

No one did more, in his day, to make industry – and shareholders – aware of the value of under-used assets, and he was a pioneer of the sale-and-leaseback method of raising cash.

were always on the look-out for ways of employing their huge incomes, and took them back on long leases. He had, in effect, managed to get control of properties worth more than £8 million – *plus* a well-established business – for a total outlay of £3 million. It laid the foundation for a considerable trading empire and, inevitably, a number of eye-catching takeover deals.

With the benefit of hindsight, of course, it could be argued that the move wasn't all that clever – he would have made a great deal more if he had held on to those assets for a few more years. But he was one of the first to demonstrate how someone with little cash could buy a company with its own money.

Terence Conran

b. 1927

The man who brought taste to the high street

Terence Conran is a talented designer who went into retailing because he felt that Britain's furniture stores were doing a poor job; today he runs a retail empire with interests on both sides of the Atlantic. The British public knows him best as the man who created the Habitat chain.

Conran comes from a middle-class background. He went to Bryanston public school, where he excelled in arts and pottery; while at school he used to make toys and sell them in a local shop. Later he studied textile design at London's Central School of Art. When he left, in 1950, design jobs were hard to get and he became a window dresser at Simpson's in Piccadilly. He went on to launch himself in business with a series of trendy bistro-type Soup Kitchens in Chelsea, but eventually decided to leave catering to others and became a designer and manufacturer of furniture. He says that he didn't think of retailing until the year he took his team around the country to look at the way their furniture was being displayed and sold in shops. He was appalled, and talked scathingly about 'that great dull ditch of buyers, those who totally control taste in the big shops'. It was clear that they needed their own premises. Then they realized that they should sell not just furniture, but everything that went with it, in an ambience of bustle, colour, cheerfulness and light. The original Habitat store opened in the Fulham Road in 1964 and it quickly became apparent that Conran's approach fitted in with the mood of Londoners, particularly the young (these were the days of 'swinging London'). 'Many of the first-time visitors', *The Times* commented, 'thought they must have gone to heaven.'

Conran's aim was twofold: to produce good design for everything that people used in their homes, and to produce it inexpensively. His dream was that quite ordinary families should share his vision of what a home should look like – modern, practical, simple, fresh. He recalls walking down a street and looking in through front windows. 'It was absolutely predictable where people had put their furniture and what they'd got, like peas in a pod. I longed to march in and tell them that you can turn things around. You can have two sofas instead of a three-piece suite, you can take out the centre light.'

By this time, Conran was on his second marriage and busy setting up again himself. His first marriage, to an architect, had lasted only six months. His second wife, Shirley, later became famous as a racy novelist. They had two children, but this union, too, ended in divorce. Conran later married Caroline, a cookery writer, and they now have three children.

The Habitat store was so successful that others soon followed: when the company went public there were more than fifty, of which thirty-two were in Britain, fifteen in France and Belgium, and six on the East Coast of America, trading under the name of Conran. The flotation put a paper value of more than £25 million (then about $50 million) on Conran's shares.

The Habitat concept still arouses conflicting emotions. Those who are for it say that it has raised people's visual consciousness and transformed their homes, as Conran intended. To them, he is a crusader. To others it has become a symbol of design dictatorship, an anodyne spreading of predigested Good Taste. Conran thinks the criticism is absurd: no one, he points out, *forces* customers to buy his wares. 'The Habitat philosophy has always been simple and unpretentious; we haven't made great statements, we have allowed people to do it the way they want. After all, the objects are good enough to speak for themselves and to please in any environment. Nobody has, or had, a Habitat Home.'

In 1981 Conran took control of another innovative chain, the Mothercare stores, which traded under the slogan 'Everything for the mother-to-be and her baby and children under five'. His group has since acquired further retail interests,

---

The original Habitat store opened in the Fulham Road in 1964. . . . 'Many of the first-time visitors', The Times *commented, 'thought they must have gone to heaven.'*

---

including British Home Stores. One of his major ventures, through BHS, is a series of hypermarkets built on the outskirts of towns and operated in partnership with the Sainsbury food chain.

Conran takes an active interest in the design of all the buildings, as well as the products. He likes them to have a happy atmosphere, an approach he has extended to his own homes. His country house in Berkshire is an elegant ten-bedroom mansion, set in parkland, which he and Caroline bought in 1972. It had been a boys' prep school, and for a time there was a demolition order on it. Conran got it cheaply, but spent a lot of money on doing it up over a period of two and a half years. He is particularly keen on the use of plants and has several conservatories; he has even produced a book on them called *Plants at Home*.

Habitat is now so huge that its middle-class image has gone; it is now a mass-market chain. Conran's vision has to some extent come true, and his work has been acknowledged by the award of a knighthood. But there are still millions of homes around the world which fill him with dismay, and which he regards as a challenge. He has made a great deal of money, but says: 'It doesn't make any difference whether you have £10,000 in the bank or £10 million. Money is actually of little importance to me personally. I'm interested in it from a business point of view. That's what is exciting.'

Thomas Cook

1802–92

'Globe-trotting and temperance'

The father of organized mass tourism was an English bookseller by trade and a temperance worker by conviction. In 1841, while on his way to a temperance meeting in Leicester, he was inspired with 'the idea of engaging a special train to carry the friends of temperance from Leicester to Loughborough and back to attend a quarterly delegate meeting'. He persuaded the railway company to give him a special reduced fare in return for his guarantee of five hundred passengers to travel on the newly opened rail extension, which normally carried only one-tenth of that number. Cook was as good as his word, and on 5 July that year 570 teetotallers crowded into the open carriages, 'to crush the monster Intemperance'. Cook saw to it that there were hams, loaves and tea for everybody; later, there was dancing and cricket in between the exhortations.

His first meeting went so well that he was urged to organize others. In 1843 he transported three thousand schoolchildren to Derby for tea so that they would be out of Leicester while the horse races were exerting their pernicious influence on that town. 'We must have railways for the millions,' Cook proclaimed in the name of virtue. Two years later he organized his first pleasure excursions, from Leicester to Liverpool, and became a professional. He also ran tours to the wilds of Scotland, where 'the strongest sensibilities of your natures shall be awakened', and initiated the first tour of a stately home when the Duke of Rutland opened Belvoir Castle to his excursionists. Cook recognized that there were many other possibilities: 'I had become so thoroughly imbued with the tourist spirit that I began to contemplate foreign trips, including the Continent of Europe, the United States and the Eastern lands of the Bible.'

Most of the major obstacles in the way of organized mass tourism in Europe had been removed by the advances in transport technology. A year after Waterloo the first Channel crossing by steamer was made (the site of the battle itself became a major tourist attraction). By 1821 a regular service was operating between Dover and Calais, and in 1844 the first railway tracks were laid in France and Austria. The ground was already well prepared; Cook's great achievement was to give many more people the opportunity to travel.

He saw tourism as a great and beneficial social force, and his work as 'appertaining to the great class of agencies for the advancement of Human Progress'. His trips were conducted on the principle of 'the greatest benefit for the greatest number at the lowest cost'. He spent much time and effort persuading the directors of railways and steamship company that this was not merely altruistic but also good for business. They did not always share his enthusiasm, but in 1856 he succeeded in setting up his first 'grand circular tour of the continent'. The response was so encouraging that he repeated it six weeks later.

His conquest of Europe began in earnest in 1862, when he made arrangements with the London, Brighton and South Coast Railway for passenger traffic to the continent via Newhaven and Dieppe. His Paris excursions were the first true 'package tours'; all the details of transport and accommodation were prearranged and the tourists were generally of modest means. Switzerland was next. In 1864 he wrote: 'France and Switzerland now present to me new and almost unlimited fields of tourist labour. At the moment I am surrounded in Paris with some five or six hundred enterprising tourists and am expecting an addition of four or five hundred more tomorrow night. Already a party of a hundred has started for Switzerland. . . .' The same year, the first guided tour left England for Italy. The 1860s also saw the introduction of Cook's railway and hotel coupons.

His 'tour escorts' led the adventure-minded groups through strange places and gave a running commentary on every town, statue or scene. These briefings were so thorough that the descriptions themselves became famous. Soon, taking any kind of pleasure trip was regarded as the same as saying you were going on a 'Cook's tour', and the phrase became a household word.

Thomas Cook always made a personal survey of the countries and cities he had in mind, in order to familiarize himself with their tourist attractions and facilities. He made his first

'. . . railways and steamboats are the results of the common light of science and are for the people . . . the best of men, and the noblest of minds, rejoice to see the people follow in their foretrod routes of pleasure'.

exploratory trip to America in 1866. He found American Express already in existence, but with no fully developed excursion system. His own excursions to America began later in the same year.

The 1870s saw further expansion, including a round-the-world tour and trips to Palestine and the Nile. The Egyptian enterprise was very different from that in Europe: it was grander and more luxurious – tourism for aristocrats rather than for the masses. For the British, Egypt was both a dependent state and a convenient stopping-off place on the most direct route to India; Thomas Cook, always keenly aware of the needs of his clientele, became a representative of British imperialism. The Egyptian government gave him exclusive control of all passenger steamers, and by 1890 the company had fifteen steamers which operated as floating hotels. It also had a hotel in Luxor – the first Cook's hotel.

India was the logical next step, and offices were opened in Bombay and Calcutta. Cook arranged ostentatious travelling parties for Indian princes as well as visiting Englishmen: they included such items as two hundred servants, ten elephants and thirty-three tame tigers. But mass travel was not forgotten: the company was also charged with the task of organizing the pilgrim traffic from India to Mecca.

Mark Twain, who enjoyed travel, paid a tribute to the innovative genius of Thomas Cook which the company still treasures. Cook, he said, 'has made travel easy and a pleasure. He will sell you a ticket to any place on the globe, or all the places, and give you all the time you need and much more besides. It provides hotels for you everywhere . . . and you cannot be overcharged for the coupons show just how much you must pay. . . .'

But not everyone approved. As Cook himself acknowledged, there were people who 'affect to treat with disdain those who occupy a lower social sphere than themselves and think that places of rare interest should be excluded from the gaze of common people'. It was, he said, 'too late in the day to talk such exclusive nonsense . . . railways and steamboats are the results of the common light of science and are for the people . . . the best of men, and the noblest of minds, rejoice to see the people follow in their foretrod routes of pleasure'.

An alert and vigorous man to the end, Cook lived to the age of eighty-four, and attributed his longevity in equal proportions to 'globe-trotting and temperance'. The business he founded is now a subsidiary of the Midland Bank and remains one of the largest travel organizations in the world. It arranges nearly two hundred thousand package holidays a year, has 15 per cent of the worldwide travellers' cheque market, and is the world's largest business travel agency.

Bernard Cornfeld

b. 1926

The mutual funds wizard

Bernie Cornfeld is chiefly remembered as the super-salesman who devised an enticing slogan ('Do you sincerely want to be rich?') and whose spectacular success in the 1960s was followed by an equally spectacular collapse.

His basic idea was almost childishly simple. Mutual funds (or unit trusts, as they are called in Britain) had been popular for some time, as a way of allowing people with modest means to invest in industry. The concept can be traced back to Britain in the late 1860s; an early exponent was a Scottish textile executive named Robert Fleming, grandfather of the man who invented James Bond. Its most consistent attraction has always been the claim that, by putting up a relatively small sum, an investor can participate in the advantages of a large, diversified and professionally managed block of investments. It is a sensible approach, and a great many people have benefited from it. But there is no guarantee of success, of course, and the investor has to pay for the privilege of having his money looked after by someone else.

Cornfeld not only managed to recruit and train a team of excellent salesmen, who called themselves 'financial counsellors', but also took the whole process a stage further. He turned his company, Investors Overseas Services, into the biggest and best known of the 'offshore' funds, which meant that its funds, and the companies that managed them, were carefully registered and domiciled wherever in the world they would best avoid taxation and regulation. He also created a 'Fund of Funds', which invested in other mutual funds. The scheme worked so well for a while that at one time the IOS empire had total funds of $2500 million under its control. Cornfeld's personal fortune was estimated at well over $100 million.

Bernie Cornfeld was born in Turkey and as a boy emigrated with his parents to America; he grew up in Brooklyn and graduated in 1950 with a BA in psychology. He spent a year as a social worker but decided that he wanted to make money and, armed with a useful understanding of human behaviour, joined a mutual fund business as a salesman. But competition in New York was tough and he decided to try his luck in Europe. Arriving in Paris in 1955 with a few hundred dollars in his wallet, he soon saw the possibilities of a large expatriate market – especially American servicemen. He decided to become an independent dealer and persuaded other Americans living in Paris at the time to help him. In 1958 he moved the base of his growing sales force to Geneva and later launched his own mutual funds.

The 'Fund of Funds', Cornfeld's most successful idea, was a gimmick which turned out to have tremendous popular appeal. Investment decisions were not just left to professionals; the ordinary man now had professionals choosing the professionals who made them. It meant paying two management fees, but most of Cornfeld's customers did not seem to mind. He then had another stroke of inspiration: why not reorganize things so that IOS could collect both management fees? All it required was that IOS itself should control the funds into which the money went.

The IOS sales force was soon busy combing the whole world for people's savings and putting them into the funds which the company ran. But the products had one basic flaw: in the long run one's sales talk has to be matched by performance, and Cornfeld failed to do so. The whole edifice eventually collapsed because the money was badly managed. When the world's stock markets went into a sharp decline, the value of his dizzy speculations plummeted and many investments were wiped out altogether. No one wanted to buy his fund shares any more; hordes of investors, painfully aware that his promises could not be kept, deserted him.

IOS was, first and last, a sales organization run by salesmen for salesmen. It was they who profited most from the vast flow of money which IOS handled. Cornfeld was an opportunist who understood greed and exploited it. His techniques should be studied by everyone who is seriously interested in the art of manipulating people.

His famous slogan, 'Do you sincerely want to be rich?', was addressed primarily to his recruits. He made them believe that, if they followed him, they could all become millionaires. His salesmen were always called 'associates' and they could qualify for the IOS Stock Option Plan, which arranged the distribution of shares in IOS itself, as distinct from shares in the

Cornfeld was an opportunist who understood greed and exploited it. . . . His famous slogan, 'Do you sincerely want to be rich?', was addressed primarily to his recruits. He made them believe that, if they followed him, they could all become millionaires.

mutual funds which IOS was selling. The price was determined by a formula based on the growth of IOS, and of its sales force and its sales. The shares could not be sold on the open market, but Cornfeld promised that the company would eventually be reorganized so that such a sale could become a possibility. He also gave gold watches to every 'associate' who did $1 million worth of business, and set up sales conferences which had an almost religious atmosphere. Cornfeld would talk with messianic fervour about the merits of 'people's capitalism'; he was invariably given a standing ovation.

His 'financial counsellors' did not have to be investment experts; he told them that after one week's training in salesmanship they would be able to get out and sell mutual funds to complete strangers anywhere in the world. He gave them a text cast in the form of a dialogue between salesman and prospect, which they were supposed to learn by heart.

'Mr Geldt,' it began, 'let's presume that you had $1 million. You don't mind presuming you have $1 million, do you?' (He didn't.)

It was then explained to Mr Geldt that if he really did happen to be a millionaire he certainly wouldn't be keeping his money in the bank. He would hire professional investment managers who would, through the advice of economists and statisticians, select numerous investment positions and spread the money out amongst them.

'Now then, Mr Geldt,' the salesman would say, 'unless you have been keeping something from me, you don't have $1 million.' However, some of the benefits of millionairehood could be available to even the smallest of investors. You too can have the advantages, Mr Geldt would be told, of 'a millionaire's method of investing'. This was 'a mutual fund'.

Computations were then produced, suggesting that a mutual fund investor could expect to see $10,000 turn into $54,000 within ten years. 'If this had happened to you, Mr Geldt, would you have been pleased?' the salesman would ask. And it was not even necessary to have $10,000 to put up at once. Just putting up $100 a month for ten years would result in a pay-out of $34,000.

One beneficial result of the rise and fall of Bernie Cornfeld is that the mutual fund business is now more tightly controlled than it was in the 1960s. There are many respectable funds, on both sides of the Atlantic, which have performed very well for investors. But there is still no guarantee of success: even the best professional adviser can sometimes be wrong.

Trammell Crow

b. 1914

Creator of the Dallas skyline

Trammell Crow has had a remarkable career in a business which has always attracted bold entrepreneurs – real estate. His vision, drive, willingness to take risks and ability to persuade others to back his ventures have made him the biggest private property developer in the United States.

As a young man he studied accountancy and worked for a time as a bank teller. His first real estate project, in 1948, was a humble warehouse in his home town of Dallas, built with the help of his wife's parental inheritance. The next step was the result of a lucky accident. He and his wife attended a flower show in Dallas and met a man called John Stemmons, who told him that his father was having difficulty finding developers to build on an embankment system he had constructed along the Trinity River. Crow decided to have a go. Today the name of the man he met at the flower show is commemorated in one of the city's most important highways, the Stemmons Freeway. Strung along its twelve lanes is a series of market halls that form the world's largest merchandising complex, plus two major hotels to accommodate the half-million retail buyers who spend billions in the complex each year. All of them were built by Trammell Crow.

One of his strengths has always been a talent for spotting trends and exploiting them before his competitors. He built thousands of warehouses to accommodate the post-war prosperity of the United States, and foresaw that the baby boom of the 1950s pointed to a strong need for apartments in the following decade. The Dallas market halls were a venture which at the time seemed so risky that many people doubted his business sense. But the gamble paid off. Since then Trammell Crow has continued to play a major role in fashioning the city's razzle-dazzle skyline. His most recent ventures include a replica of London's famed Crystal Palace – the InfoMart, with 900,000 square feet of space dedicated to wholesalers of computer hardware and software. He has also been the driving force behind numerous projects in other American cities, while the Brussels International Trade Mart, with its 1.6 million square feet, was his first market abroad.

The Trammell Crow Company is not just a build-and-sell operation. It owns, leases or manages a great deal of real estate. Crow has more than a hundred partners in fifty-seven national and international offices, all with a stake in the business. Industrial buildings make up just over half of the assets; offices and shopping centres account for most of the rest. The Dallas markets, though, have remained separate family concerns.

Like many developers in the USA, Crow hit a bad patch in the mid-1970s. He was said to be personally liable for $150 million, with contingent liabilities of $400 million. He survived, while others went under, because his creditors had faith in him. His attitude at the time was characteristically

'Work', he told me when I interviewed him in 1986, 'is more fun than fun.'

pugnacious: don't sell. Tough it out, tough it out. In the boom that followed, he gained more than he had lost. *Forbes* magazine has put his personal wealth at more than $500 million.

Crow says he is an optimist who likes to make things happen. In many ways he symbolizes what some people have called the 'Dallas spirit' – a strong determination to succeed, despite all odds. He has always worked hard. 'Work', he told me when I interviewed him in 1986, 'is more fun than fun.' He sits at an employee's desk surrounded by colleagues, because he likes to be 'where the action is'. He does, however, try to find as much time as possible for family life, which he says is very important to him. One of his sons works in the same office; his daughter Lucy runs the Apparel and Trade Mart.

Crow says that Dallas remains his favourite city. 'It may go through tough times now and then, but it still has great potential.' Partly due to his efforts, Dallas has become one of the five major distribution areas in the United States; it dominates the South-west. New York is the leading centre for the North-east; Atlanta for the South-east; Chicago for the Mid-west; and San Francisco and Los Angeles share the Western portion. Crow has interests in all of them.

Michael Cullen

1864–1936

'The world's most daring price-wrecker'

There has always been some dispute about the origins of one of the greatest innovations in food retailing – the supermarket. The idea caught on so quickly, and was adopted by so many companies, that quite a lot of people believed that they had invented the concept. The man with the best claim was Michael Cullen, who opened what is generally reckoned to have been the first supermarket in an abandoned garage in Jamaica, Queens, New York, on 30 August 1930.

Cullen was working for an Illinois food chain in the 1920s when he worked out a plan to develop self-service stores on a cash-and-carry basis, 5000 or 6000 square feet in area, with an equal amount of surrounding parking space and located outside the high-rent district. Loss leader and low mark-up merchandise would be flanked by high-profit items, mass displays of groceries would be featured in aisles that contained few fixtures, and heavy newspaper advertising would secure volume. Today, of course, all this is commonplace, but at the time his employers felt that it wouldn't work and rejected the proposal. Cullen gave up his job, raised some money and set out to prove them wrong. He succeeded: the supermarket was an immediate success. Within two years he was operating eight large units; by the time of his death he had fifteen.

With the advantage of hindsight, one can't help being surprised that it didn't happen much earlier. It was, after all, a logical development of ideas which had been around for some time. The Piggly Wiggly store chain, launched in 1916 by Clarence Saunders of Memphis, Tennessee, was already using self-selection, turnstiles and check-out counters as principal features. Drive-in markets for quick service had begun to appear in southern California in the 1920s. A & P chain had introduced cash-and-carry in 1912, and pioneered the 'combination store'. What Cullen did was to take these ideas, add his own concepts of grocery selling, and fuse them into a large, integrated market. He also had a flair for publicity: he called himself 'The world's most daring price wrecker'.

A & P was not the first food chain to take up the supermarket concept, but it eventually became the leading proponent of this type of selling. It played a key role in changing the food-buying habits of millions of Americans – and, later, of many more millions of shoppers around the world. It therefore deserves at least some of the credit for turning the supermarket into a popular institution. It also pioneered a system for pre-packaging meat cuts and, later, took on other merchandising ideas, such as the use of increased supermarket space to sell non-food items.

The A & P story is very much part of American business folklore. It began with a little New York tea store that was opened in 1859 by George Huntington Hartford and a partner. Hartford cut the price of tea from a dollar a pound to thirty cents by eliminating all middlemen. He was also a showman: he painted his store bright red and gold, hung Japanese lanterns, put his cashiers into pagodas, and hired a band to play on Saturdays. He sent a big red wagon drawn by eight horses through the streets of New York to advertise the business. A prize of $20,000 was offered to anyone who could guess the combined weight of the team and wagon, and all kinds of premiums were given away – dishpans, china, crockery and coloured pictures of babies.

Hartford gradually extended his range of staples, adding spices, coffee, soap, condensed milk, baking powder and so on. He also opened more stores: there were five by 1865 and eleven by 1869 when he adopted the more grandiose name of the Great Atlantic & Pacific Tea Company. By 1876 there were sixty-seven A & P stores, all with the familiar red-and-gold façade, all conventional grocery stores with charge accounts and delivery service.

His two sons, George and John, were chiefly responsible for later innovations. 'Mr George', as the eldest became known, organized a huge fleet of travelling 'stores' to service vast segments of the population which were cut off from the towns and cities by bad roads. 'Mr John', eight years younger than

'We went so fast', John Hartford later reminisced, 'that hobos hopping off freight trains got hired as managers.'

his brother, came up with the concept of 'economy stores' which would sell food only over the counter and for cash: the profit on each item would be kept low in order to produce a large volume. Neither his father nor his brother agreed with him, and it was only after many weeks of heated debate that 'Mr John' persuaded them to give him a chance to try out the idea. They invested $3000 and he opened his 'experimental store' in just about the toughest spot imaginable – round the corner from the company's main outlet in Jersey City. Within six months it had become the biggest moneymaker in the chain and the regular A & P was out of business. All the company's stores were converted to the new formula and new ones were opened at the rate of one every three days. 'We went so fast', John Hartford later reminisced, 'that hobos hopping off freight trains got hired as managers.' It led directly to the birth of the 'combination store', which was the forerunner of the supermarket.

Edward de Bono

b. 1933

Inventor of lateral thinking

Dr de Bono has made a considerable impact on the business world with his ideas on 'lateral thinking' – defined in the Oxford English Dictionary as 'a way of thinking which seeks the solution of intractable problems through unorthodox methods, or elements which would normally be ignored by logical thinking. . . . Lateral thinking leads to those simple ideas that are obvious only after they have been thought of.'

Born in Malta in 1933, Dr de Bono is a former Rhodes scholar who has taught at Oxford, Cambridge and Harvard. His books have been translated into many languages and have made him a millionaire.

Most people assume that intelligence and thinking ability are one and the same. Not so, says de Bono. To explain, he compares innate intelligence to the raw horsepower of a car and thinking ability to the skill with which the car is driven. In the same way that powerful cars can be driven poorly, so can many intelligent people be poor thinkers.

When do Bono teaches thinking to children, he tries to move them away from 'I am smart' or 'I'm pretty dumb' to a new concept: 'I am a thinker.' *Metacognition*, a word coined by him to mean 'thinking about thinking', cannot take place unless an individual is able to distance himself from his thinking abilities enough to admit, for example, 'My thinking was pretty awful yesterday.'

Rightness is what matters in vertical thinking, de Bono says. *Richness* is what matters in lateral thinking. The lateral thinker plays games with data, thinks outrageously and often erroneously, considers improbable options to shake his mind out of pre-set thinking patterns. Right/wrong judgment is suspended; ideas are seen as stepping stones to other ideas.

In *vertical* thinking, step follows step in an unbroken sequence; reasoning must be correct at every step; only relevant information is considered. In *lateral* thinking, non-sequential thought paths are explored; irrelevant information is considered; errors in reasoning are made, as it may be necessary to pass through a 'wrong' idea to reach a solution.

The intelligent, he says, should beware of common thinking snares. For example, at a business meeting John Smith listens to a new idea put forward by one of his associates and immediately begins attacking it. De Bono refers to this familiar phenomenon as the 'intelligence trap'. A person encounters a problem, makes a snap judgment based on his current mood or his past experience, and uses intelligence to defend his judgment instead of exploring the situation. Smith is trapped by his own intelligence and misses the chance to look into what might have been a valuable idea.

There are several de Bonian methods of escaping the intelligence trap. The first is the PMI: evaluating a problem, idea or situation by first listing the *pluses*, then the *minuses*, and finally those points that just seem *interesting*. The objective is broad-mindedness – avoiding the intelligence trap by delaying judgment. Although emotion plays a part in every decision we make, the decision may change if the emotional component is added *after* doing a PMI.

A group of toronto businessmen were presented with this proposition: 'A law should be passed decreeing that women be paid 10 per cent more than men for the same jobs.' At first the women unanimously endorsed this idea. They were then asked to do a PMI on the proposition. The PMI revealed that a crucial minus point had not been considered: as companies would have to pay women more than men, they would tend to hire men. The women rejected the proposal.

Some people seem to come up with ingenious solutions to problems all the time. Are there ways of making the rest of us more receptive to the spark of inspiration? According to de Bono, there are. He suggests several methods of generating imaginative alternatives to problem solving. One is *reversal*, turning a problem or situation upside down or inside out to see what new ideas are suggested. If a factory is polluting a river, a reversal solution would be to pass a law requiring factories to put their effluent pipes upstream instead of downstream. This

'The purpose of provocation in lateral thinking is to move you outside the normal,' de Bono says. 'You can't guarantee that you will get an answer, but there are so many possible tracks that you almost always get an idea.'

solution is not as far-fetched as it seems. Upsteam effluent pipes would mean that the factories would have to ingest the waters they had polluted. Another de Bonian thinking method is called *po*, for *provocative operation*, putting two seemingly unrelated or even contradictory ideas together to see where they lead. Here, de Bono is after what he calls the 'movement value' of an idea, using one idea as a stepping stone to another: 'All *po* cars should have square wheels', for example, or '*Po* planes should land upside down.' The *po* statements are not meant to be taken literally but as provocations to force the mind into new, potentially rich avenues of thought. Someone might say: 'Well, if planes landed upside down, the pilots would certainly have a better view of the runway.' This might lead to a discussion of where the pilot should be situated on an aircraft. 'The purpose of provocation in lateral thinking is to move you outside the normal', de Bono says. 'You can't guarantee that you will get an answer, but there are so many possible tracks that you almost always get an idea.'

Lateral thinking alone will usually not be sufficient to solve the problem. A second step, logic, is needed, whereby the ideas that have been generated are evaluated for feasibility or practicality. In lateral thinking it is extremely important to be aware of the assumptions you bring to a problem, those dominant ideas that smother the possibility of innovation. You cannot escape pre-set thinking patterns until you first become aware of them.

Many schools now incorporate de Bono's techniques in their curriculums, and he has been hired by numerous corporations to teach lateral thinking to their executives. De Bono himself says his best ideas come to him while shaving; it's just as well, perhaps, that he has never worn a beard.

Everette Lee de Golyer

1886–1956

Father of the oil industry

De Golyer is widely credited with bringing applied geophysics to the United States. A scientist and scholar who became a multi-millionaire by putting his knowledge to good use, he introduced highly successful techniques for finding underground oil.

His father was a Kansas mineral prospector and, as a boy, he developed a keen interest in the search for hidden wealth. But he soon grew tired of rule-of-thumb methods and enrolled at the University of Oklahoma, where he graduated in 1911 at the age of twenty-five. While still a student he worked during the summers as a field geologist for the Mexican Eagle Oil Company, then owned by British interests and later sold to Royal Dutch Shell.

On his first assignment he relocated the search in accordance with what he had learned about structural trends and brought in a spectacular gusher. Mexican Eagle promoted him to chief geologist and, later, head of the land department. In 1914 he opened his own offices as a consulting engineer to the petroleum industry.

On a trip to England in 1918, to participate in the sale of Mexican Eagle to Royal Dutch Shell, he was invited to form the Amerada Petroleum Company, of which he was made vice-president and general manager, then president and finally chairman. The enterprise prospered. De Golyer retired from the company in 1932, but continued with the Geophysical

Research Corporation, which discovered oilfields by scientific methods for the big oil companies. He also formed Core Laboratories, Inc., and the Atlatl Royalty Corporation to carry on oil discovery and ownership.

In the early days, most prospectors based their efforts largely on guesswork. De Golyer applied the knowledge of a trained, scientific mind nourished widely on the theoretical literature, much of it European, about the casual process of earth formations. He implemented his insights by introducing the use of the seismograph, gravimeter, torsion balance, electromagnetic surveys and explosives to send shock waves through the varieties of underground formations, thereby determining their structure. All this later became standard practice, but at the time it represented a significant departure from established methods.

De Golyer's efforts made him very rich, but he could have made a lot more if he had devoted himself solely to accumulating wealth. Looking on his fellow oil men with considerable reserve, he often remarked that 'A talent for making money can imply a lack of talent for leading a useful life.' De Golyer certainly did not suffer from that deficiency. He published a

Looking on his fellow oil men with considerable reserve, he often remarked that 'A talent for making money can imply a lack of talent for leading a useful life.'

long, impressive list of original scientific papers and wrote about the history and personalities of the South-west. He collected priceless rare books – on the South-west, on geology and geophysics, and on scientific methods and the history of science – and left them to the University of Oklahoma, the University of Texas and other institutions. The de Golyer Foundation was established to add to these valuable collections of books. He also served on scores of national and local cultural and scientific bodies, lectured to serious audiences at MIT and Princeton, and served in 1940 as Professor of Geology at the University of Texas. He held honorary degrees from many American and foreign universities.

Sadly, this brilliant man came to an unhappy end. After an illness of six years he shot himself at the age of seventy.

Richard Dennis

b. 1949

The successful contrarian

Many financial operators have made fortunes by doing exactly the opposite of what everyone advised them to do. One such man is Richard Dennis, one of the most remarkable traders in that most dangerous of markets, commodity futures. He is what is known as a 'contrarian' – someone who holds that public opinion is always wrong, that contrapuntal forces which run powerfully against the conventional wisdom of a given moment can make the disciplined contrarian rich. Richard Dennis has not only applied this approach to his own trading but has also founded a Washington think tank, the Roosevelt Center for American Policy Studies, with the aim of challenging orthodox thinking on a wide range of issues.

The buying and selling of commodities to be delivered in the future – which is what commodity trading is all about – goes back a long way. Assyrian wheat-growers are said to have sold the receipts for unharvested crops more than three thousand years ago. Today the world's major financial centres – New York, London, Chicago, Tokyo – all have markets in which producers and would-be buyers can make deals to buy and sell raw materials well ahead of their needs. In essence, this is a form of insurance. The producer sells his output forward if he feels the price is right rather than risk a future drop. In this way he gets a guaranteed price and therefore a guaranteed profit based on the current cost of production. The manufacturer or merchant is similarly assured of a supply of raw materials at a fixed price.

The speculator takes the risks the others don't want to bear. The glossy brochures from the exchanges call him a 'speculative investor' and insist that he plays a valuable – indeed essential – role. He provides an active market for all this hedging. But don't be misled: his sole interest is profit and the word 'investor' is inappropriate. He is a gambler who is drawn to commodities because they provide *action* – the sort of mercurial price movements that can mean big profits in a relatively short period of time. He rarely takes delivery, and in ninety-five deals out of a hundred the whole affair is strictly a paperchase.

If his judgment is wrong, the losses can be enormous. Putting money into commodities is, as someone once put it, 'like climbing aboard a big dipper which has no brakes and no seat-belts'. Nelson Bunker Hunt would certainly agree: he is the Texas billionaire, you will recall, whose punt on silver came so badly unstuck that he was presented with a sudden demand for $500 million.

Richard Dennis started trading in Chicago, in a modest way, while still a teenager. His father, a blue-collar worker, provided the $1400 needed to purchase a trading badge at the small mid-American Commodity Exchange, and his brother gave him a few hundred dollars out of his savings. But because Richard was under twenty-one he wasn't allowed to trade on the floor. He persuaded his father to stand in for him, while he directed from a seat on the sidelines. As soon as he reached his majority, he took his father's place.

From the beginning, Richard decided to reject certain fundamental trading precepts. Every new trader, for example, was advised never to 'sleep on a position' – never to hold a speculative position overnight – because you couldn't tell what might happen next. It was better, old hands said, to do what everyone else did, which was to 'sell down to the sleeping point' at the end of each day. Richard ignored them; he made it his rule *always* to hold positions overnight. As he saw it, the fact that so many traders were desperate to sell down to sleeping point presented an extra opportunity to make a profit.

By the end of 1972 he had accumulated more than $100,000

Putting money into commodities is, as someone once put it, 'like climbing aboard a big dipper which has no brakes and no seat-belts'.

---

in trading profits. He managed to hit the great run-up in the price of soybeans the following year and increased his capital to $500,000. It was enough to convince him that he should move down the street to the bigger playground at the Board of Trade. He became a millionaire in 1974. He was still only twenty-five and determined to stay on the Big Dipper, even though he knew that he could easily lose it all.

In 1977 he withdrew from the hurly-burly of the trading floor. There was no longer any need to be there, because everything he wanted to do could be done sitting in front of computer screens in a quiet, comfortable office. He had never cared for the hysteria which so often developed on the floor: in the office, one could make swift decisions in a more rational atmosphere, and others couldn't see what one was up to. Besides, a floor trader could, at the most, participate in only three markets at a time. In the late 1970s a lot of new commodities and financial instruments were being traded as futures and Richard Dennis wanted to be in them all. Computers were the key.

Financial futures are an extension of the commodities game. They were born among the soybeans and pork bellies on the

Chicago exchanges, and Dennis was not slow to recognize the potential for speculative gain. The two basic forms are interest rates and foreign currency. An interest rate future consists of a contract to buy (or sell) a given amount of a particular type of fixed income security (bonds, bills, even mortgages) for an agreed price at some future date. The value of the securities covered by the contract is susceptible to changes in interest rates between the time the contract is struck and the time delivery is made, which is usually between one and six months. If rates go up, the value goes down, and vice versa. The full price of the contract is not paid until it matures, though the buyer must put up a small percentage of the value of the contract. Thus, for a relatively modest outlay, a speculator or hedger can gamble on a large number of securities.

A currency future is, quite simply, a contract to buy or sell a given amount of a specific currency, such as the dollar or

Dennis is an outstanding example of a new breed of speculator: people who not only understand how complex markets work but who know how to make the most of sophisticated modern technology. They make Las Vegas high-rollers look like small-town poker players.

sterling, for an agreed price at some future date. In other words, the principle is exactly the same. With currencies so much more volatile than they used to be, it is hardly surprising that currency futures have become very popular.

Dennis complemented his early contrariarism with his own list of technical rules, based on his study of market behaviour and personal experience. He fed them into computers, together with historical facts about different markets. This helped him to assess the value of a strategy before making a new commitment. Computers also enabled him to trade around the clock: from screens fitted into the bedroom of his Lake Shore Drive apartment he could keep in constant touch with developments in financial centres around the world.

A few years ago, he inserted a notice in the *Wall Street Journal* offering to train some young traders from scratch. He had a thousand replies and selected a class from the most intelligent and naturally contrarian of the applicants. They were all people who had taken risks in the past and tried to do something different in their lives. He shared his ideas with them, and it seems that they did well afterwards.

But even Dennis is by no means infallible. He has sometimes made millions in a day, but he has also suffered heavy losses. In one week during 1986 he was reported to have lost as much as $25 million. 'It happens sometimes,' he said philosophically. He added: 'There are fifty trading weeks in a year.' By then, he was well able to afford such setbacks: his fortune was estimated at $200 million.

Dennis is an outstanding example of a new breed of speculator: people who not only understand how complex markets work but who know how to make the most of sophisticated modern technology. They make Las Vegas high-rollers look like small-town poker players. It takes strong nerves to ride without brakes and seat-belts, and it obviously helps if one is not unduly concerned with money as such. One has to risk the possibility that, as the jargon has it, you will go 'belly up' at some stage in the game. It may happen to him: who knows? Meanwhile, he has begun to give away 10 per cent of his net worth every year to charitable and political causes. He is particularly interested in politics – supporting the Democrats – and clearly hopes that his think tank will be able to influence social and economic trends.

Walt Disney

1901–66

America's 'happy accident'

Walt Disney not only understood children but always remained, at heart, a child himself. He saw the potential in fantasy and exploited it, but also enjoyed it as much as the millions who went to see his films and, later, visited Disneyland. It was typical of him that, when he bought his first electric train set at the age of forty-six, he set it up in a room next to his office so that he could play with it in his spare moments.

Disney showed that it pays to give one's imagination a free rein. He had the courage and vision to try bold new ideas, often against the advice of his colleagues and financial backers (he frequently staked everything on his next project) and he knew how to bring out the best in other creative people. His first business venture ended in bankruptcy, but he persisted. He went to Hollywood with $40 in his pocket and talked his elder brother, Roy, into joining him. It was a smart move: Roy was a capable businessman who time and time again managed to raise the money for his dreams. Walt's contribution, at meetings with sceptical bankers, was to act out all the parts of a Mickey Mouse or Donald Duck scenario. It must have been a splendid sight.

Mickey Mouse, of course, was the character which laid the foundation for their company's success. Walt thought it up on a train journey; it became a national craze and brought in badly needed income. Disney recognized that in the world of the fairytale, especially the cartoon fairytale, anything is possible. Animals can talk and behave like human beings; witches can fly; little boys can use a beanstalk to climb up into a world of giants. He took many of his plots from old fairytales – Cinderella, Snow White, Sleeping Beauty – but always added his own imaginative touches to them. His brother's help was invaluable, but it was Walt's talent and sunny optimism which made the company successful. He said in his later years:

> I've always been bored with just making money. I've wanted to *do* things, I wanted to build things. Get something *going*. People look at me in different ways. Some say 'The guy has no regard for money.' That is not true. I *have* had regard for money. But I'm not like some people who worship money as something you've got to have piled up in a big pile somewhere. I've only thought of money in one way, and that is to do something with it. I don't think there is anything I own that I will ever get the benefit of, except through doing things with it.

Disneyland was – and is – all of his fantasies cast as reality, built on a vast film set, neatly dovetailed into a fairytale world of robust adventure and pixie-dust dreams. It was such a huge success that the Disney Organization later built a similar Walt Disney World in Florida. When he started to buy land near Orlando, in great secrecy, few people had ever heard of this part of America. He was able to acquire 27,400 acres, twice the area of Manhattan. Disney did not live to see the opening

---

'. . . he probably did more to heal or at least to sooth troubled human spirits than all the psychiatrists in the world'.

---

of his new 'Magic Kingdom' in 1971, but his successors finished what he had begun. They also went to work on another idea he had come up with before his death: Epcot. The name stands for Experimental Prototype City of tomorrow. Walt envisaged a city of the future, a model community where the latest technology could be tested and used by scientists who lived there. The company eventually decided that the idea wasn't commercial enough and, instead, created a vast amusement gallery filled with innovations in science and technology. They also added another attraction: World Showcase, a group of national pavilions which reflect the past rather than the future. The clever trick has been to get others to pay heavily for the privilege of being part of this extravaganza. They managed to persuade major US corporations that it would lead to a better understanding of big business and that the publicity value would outweigh the cost. AT & T sponsored Spaceship Earth, a striking geosphere which houses an exhibition of the various stages of communication; Exxon paid for the Universe of Energy; General Motors contributed the World of Motion; General Electric financed a futuristic show called Horizons; Kodak footed a bill for a fantasy known as Journey into Imagination; Kraft chipped in with The Land; and United Technologies spent $60 million on a splendid exhibit called The Living Seas. Goodness knows how they all justified it to their stockholders, but the result is highly entertaining – Walt would have enjoyed it – and it makes a lot of money for the Disney Organization. The pavilions in World Showcase, the other part of Epcot, were sponsored by various Governments, including China and Japan.

Today the Florida venture is the biggest single tourist attraction in the United States, drawing more than 22 million visitors a year. It is a remarkable monument to a truly creative man. When Walt died, at the age of sixty-five, Eric Servareid paid him a moving tribute on the CBS Evening News. Disney, he said:

> . . . was an original, not just an American original, but an original, period. He was a happy accident; one of the happiest this century has experienced; and judging by the way it's been behaving in spite of all Disney tried to tell it about laughter, love, children, puppies, and sunrises, the century hardly deserved him . . . he probably did more to heal or at least to sooth troubled human spirits than all the psychiatrists in the world.

Charles Dow

1854–1920

Creator of the Dow-Jones index

Charles Dow was the first editor of the *Wall Street Journal*, and the creator of the oldest and most famous stock market index in America, the Dow Jones industrial average.

He and a fellow journalist, Edward Jones, were publishers of a financial newsletter (the forerunner of the *Wall Street Journal*) when the index made its first appearance in 1884. Dow had evolved what is now known as the Dow theory, which is based on the view that an index of stocks and shares reflects all that is generally known about the outlook for business in general, and expresses all the hopes and fears about the prospects for the individual companies whose stocks make up the index.

The first list was composed mainly of railroad stocks. None is in the Dow today; in fact, the only surviving name in that original group is General Electric, which continues to be one of the nation's leading blue chip corporations. The list grew to twenty companies in 1916. Then, in 1928, Dow Jones & Co. moulded the modern Dow Jones industrial average, listing thirty companies.

The index quickly became a business tool, because it was the only one which could be easily calculated hour by hour. Until the late 1940s it was used mainly by analysts, but during the 1950s and 1960s it became the popular measure of the market. In those decades, the number of shareholders in the USA rose from 5 million to more than 30 million and movements in the Dow were widely publicized. Lyndon Johnson saw it as a measure of his popularity, and brokers found it the simplest way to relate market activity to all those investment newcomers.

The Dow is not calculated as a pure average, that is, by dividing the sum of the prices of its thirty component stocks by thirty. In order to maintain statistical continuity the average is calculated by using a 'divisor' that is periodically adjusted to reflect changes in the prices and the numbers of shares as the result of stock splits by the companies. When Charles Dow started, the divisor was thirty. Now it's 0.889. The Dow is refigured every time one of its stocks is traded in. The daily high is an average of the high of all the thirty stocks.

. . . the venerable Dow . . . is part of the language of American finance.

Changes in the components of the index are entirely the province of the editors of the *Wall Street Journal*. The companies added or removed are not consulted about the decisions, nor is the stock exchange. The editors say that their aim is to reflect changing influences in corporate America. They included American Express among the big thirty in 1982, in recognition of the large role that financial services nowadays play in the US economy, and later selected McDonald's to represent the fast food revolution.

The Dow has been accused of many things – misleading the public, distorting the market, creating near-panic with large point fluctuations, causing an unfavourable attitude toward the financial community, and containing too few stocks to represent the market fairly. It is certainly far from perfect. Analysts who examined its performance over a ten-year period found that, although the index had risen by only 17.9 per cent, the average of all the stocks listed on the Big Board had climbed by as much as 60 per cent. Other indexes are more comprehensive and probably more reflective of the true state of the overall market: Standard & Poor's index, for example, is based on five hundred stocks.

Wall Street professionals say that using the Dow to gauge

the performance of the entire market is like predicting the weather by holding a wetted finger to the wind. The 'market' in the USA could mean half a dozen stock exchanges and more than thirty thousand stocks. It is a valid point. An index based on averages (which includes Standard & Poor's) is just that – averages. It provides a fix on what stocks in general are doing, but it is not a foolproof guide and it has little to tell the individual investor, who must buy stocks in particular. But the venerable Dow *is* important, because of its psychological impact. Its ups and downs are believed to measure the mood of the market, and therefore have considerable influence on investment decisions. It is part of the language of American finance.

In Britain, the *Financial Times* index has much the same function. It was started in 1935 and, like the Dow, is based on thirty leading stocks.

Peter Drucker

b. 1909

Pioneer of 'management by objectives'

Peter Drucker, who was born in Vienna, is sometimes credited with 'inventing' the modern manager. It is the kind of extravagant statement which he would be the first to deny, but there is no doubt that he has played a major role in the shaping of management thinking. He has taught new ways of thinking and looking at the organization, and has given the field new phrases and concepts. His main achievement has been to make the concept of management a matter of everyday thought for the people who conduct the affairs of organizations.

The achievement is all the more remarkable when one considers that Drucker himself has never been part of an organization. He has never run a business, never met a payroll, never worried as a manager. He freely admits that he wouldn't be any good at it. He sees himself as a man who is primarily concerned not with the practice but with the philosophy of management.

Drucker was a pioneer of the now well-known concept of 'management by objectives'. He didn't invent the term, but put it in a central position. Management by objectives shifts the focus from processes to goals, to the purpose of the activity rather than the activity itself. Instead of asking 'What do I do?' the manager is led to ask 'What is the objective towards which we are working?' Under this concept, the manager is held responsible for results rather than for activities. It is no longer a matter of how well he understands the machinery, or how many meetings he holds, or what volume of correspondence he is able to turn out, but rather how his activities pay off in terms of the objectives of the organization.

As Drucker sees it, there is no one single objective for any organization. However, at the same time there should not be a profusion of objectives, big and small, hoarded in every nook and cranny of the enterprise. Objectives must be set up in every area where performance and results directly affect the prosperity and survival of the business.

'We can't start talking objectives', he says, 'until we know what they are. The things we desire are not objectives. Corporations and institutions alike mistake good intentions for objectives. Health care is a good intention, not an objective. Nothing operational follows from it. When you do not figure out the real objectives, you substitute procedure for thinking.'

Many businessmen would probably say that they have one objective: profit. Drucker does not accept profit as an objective at all in the sense in which he talks about objectives. Profit is a necessity for survival. It is the wherewithal to pay the cost of today and tomorrow. Since objectives are conducive to survival, profit is involved in objectives. But profit is not primarily what management by objectives is all about.

Organizational objectives must grow out of a thorough knowledge of what the business is and what it should be. Specific targets, not abstractions, render it possible to make specific assignments. Objectives, says Drucker, should enable us to do five things: organize and explain the whole range of business phenomena in a few general statements; test these statements; predict behaviour; gauge the soundness of decisions before they are made; and enable businessmen to analyze

'Corporations and institutions alike mistake good intentions for objectives. . . . When you do not figure out the real objectives, you substitute procedure for thinking.'

and improve performance. There are eight areas in which objectives should be set: market standing, innovation, productivity, physical and financial resources, profitability, manager performance and development, worker performance and attitude, and public responsibility.

Drucker believes that the task of setting objectives should be pushed as far down the organizational chart as possible. Take the goals that are to be set for subordinate managers. The objectives of the individual, he points out, are a function of the objectives of the larger unit of which he is a part. For example, the objectives set for the district sales manager are defined by the contribution that he and his salesmen should make to the sales force as a whole. Higher management has the authority to approve or disapprove the goals. But the development of the objectives is part of the manager's responsibility. He should participate fully in setting them. Indeed, says Drucker, it is his first responsibility. He must understand the purpose of management by objectives, know the goal of the unit of which he is a part, and have the judgment and integrity to generate goals for himself that fit the concept.

Having set his own goals, the manager judges his performance against these goals. Obviously he needs sufficient information and coherent enough controls to do this. The measurements don't have to be highly quantitative: it is folly to try to reduce a management function to a series of tiny components, each of which can be reduced to numbers. However, the controls must be 'clear, simple and rational'.

Management by objectives has become standard practice in many companies – it is the dominant concept in management today – but there has been less widespread acceptance of the suggestion that the individual manager should be given the means of controlling himself. Drucker insists that it is essential to do so. What the business enterprise needs, he says, 'is a principle of management that will give full scope to individual strength and responsibility, as well as common direction to vision and effort, establish teamwork, and harmonise the goals of the individual with the commonweal'.

As a management philosopher, Drucker has always been an advocate of participation. One of his other ideas, first put forward in his book *The New Society* (1950), was the concept of the 'plant community'. Business, he said, would be dominant in the new order. But this would not be 'capitalism' in the sense in which we have long considered it. Rank-and-file relationships with top management would no longer be adversary relationships. The plant community would offer genuine 'industrial citizenship'; in the new multi-level corporate institution each member would be involved in the management of those parts of the operation appropriate to his involvement, and each would derive 'status and function' (a favourite Drucker phrase) from this involvement.

In the new order, the 'managerial attitude' would be part of the intellectual equipment of even the lowliest worker. This would enable everyone in the organization to see his job, his work and his product the way the manager sees them, that is, in relation to the work of the group and the product as a whole. Profit-sharing plans would be devised in a way that would give the worker a meaningful share in the success of the enterprise.

The idea has since been taken up by politicians in search of policies which might appeal to the electorate, and some companies have moved towards the kind of participation envisaged, but the 'New Society' has not come about. The plant community is not a reality. Drucker's critics say that his enthusiasm for the concept showed how little he really knew about the way that business works; his admirers maintain that, as usual, he was simply ahead of his time.

Richard Duke

1929–77

The man who invented 'lawn care'

Dick Duke had a simple idea in the 1960s: he reckoned there was scope for a business that knew how to take care of people's lawns. It led to the creation of a company which, by 1985, had annual sales of more than $300 million.

Duke and his father were at the time running a garden centre in Troy, Ohio. They were selling, among other things, premixed lawn fertilizer, and customers kept asking them for advice on how to use it. How often should they put it down, and how could they ensure that it was evenly distributed? How much did the average lawn need? Duke thought that many of them would probably be willing to pay someone to do the job for them. He was right.

Two basic factors helped to ensure the success of the enterprise. One was a liquid blend of fertilizer, weed killer and bug killer which quickly made a lawn uniformly green and healthy. The other was clever marketing, based on the belief that people would respond to personal, friendly service. Duke invented a new title for the men hired to do the job: they became 'lawn care specialists'. He sold the garden centre, bought two trucks, and designed tanks, spray nozzles and chemical-resistant hoses. The trucks would go out each day and spray the liquid on to people's lawns, usually while they were at work. All *they* had to do was to sign a piece of paper which assured them that their gardens would get this efficacious treatment four times a year, at an annual cost of between $50 and $100, depending on the size of the lawn.

Duke was good at finding and training people who were not only capable of doing the job but who also had a pleasant personality. They managed to make customers feel that they really did *care about their lawns.*

The ChemLawn Corporation began operations in the summer of 1968, serving Troy and nearby towns. Its first five hundred customers all lived within a ten-mile radius of the base. Duke's father became the company salesman, but the 'lawn care specialists' also picked up a lot of new business. Neighbours would see them at work and ask for the same service. Duke was good at finding and training people who were not only capable of doing the job but who also had a pleasant personality. They managed to make customers feel that they really *did* care about their lawns. He gave them a great deal of independence and they responded by doing their best for him: they worked hard and they were loyal.

ChemLawn soon started to expand beyond Ohio. During the next few years it set up operations in a large number of cities. Duke moved his own family to Georgia. Then, in 1977, he died suddenly of a heart attack. He was only forty-eight, and it was a tragic blow for everyone, as well as the business, which by then had annual sales of $49 million. Many companies, faced with similar circumstances, would have plunged into a crisis. But Duke had already appointed a president and a competent financial officer, and the employees rallied around them. His long-standing policy of giving people a real sense of personal responsibility paid off; ChemLawn not only survived, but continued to grow rapidly.

The ChemLawn story shows what can be achieved if one listens to the marketplace, develops a concept for which there is a genuine need, hires the right people and acts boldly. Dick Duke and his father only had $40,000 of capital when they began. But Dick had given a lot of thought to the venture and he was confident that, at the very least, it would make more money than the garden centre had done. He invested their modest sum in trucks and spraying equipment, took on workers who shared his faith in the idea, and then expanded as the contracts – and cash – started to come in. It was a well thought out, low-risk effort to meet one of the needs of suburban America, and it worked even better than anyone had dared to hope.

George Eastman

1854–1932

'You press the button, we do the rest'

It was George Eastman, more than anyone else, who first turned photography from a profession into a hobby when, in 1888, he introduced a simple camera that anyone could use. He had had a tough childhood. His father died when he was eight, and his schooling ended at fourteen when he went out into the world to earn his own living and help his widowed mother and two sisters, one of whom was crippled by polio. In the classic HORATIO ALGER tradition, he worked as an office boy in an insurance company. But he was intelligent and a hard worker, and by the time he was twenty he had advanced himself to the position of junior clerk in a bank in Rochester, New York.

Photography came into his life by chance in 1877. He wanted to go on vacation to Santo Domingo and a friend suggested that he should make a photographic record of his trip. Eastman gamely bought everything he would need, and took lessons in how to use all his equipment. He found that it amounted to what he later called a 'packhorse load'. The camera was as big as a soap box and required a heavy tripod; the dark tent had to be large enough to get into while spreading emulsion on the glass plates before exposure, and later for developing the plates. In addition there were chemicals, glass tanks, a water jug, scales and boxes for storing the plates. The trip to Santo Domingo fell through, but Eastman became completely absorbed in photography.

At that time photographs were made by the wet-plate method: the photographer dipped a clear glass plate into light-sensitive chemicals, put it in the camera, took his picture, and developed the plate in his dark-room before the chemicals dried. Eastman felt that there had to be a better way and set out to make a dry plate which could be prepared well ahead of time, used when needed and then developed at leisure. He worked in his kitchen laboratory at night, and in the morning returned to his job at the bank. By 1880 he had created a dry plate with the sensitized surface protected by a coating of gelatine.

At first his efforts to simplify the complex process of picture-taking were for his own use and personal enjoyment. Before long, however, he saw the great potential in making dry plates for sale to commercial photographers. He gave up his job at the bank and, with $3000 of capital and a partner, Henry Strong, he set up in business as the Eastman Dry Plate Company on the third floor of a factory building in Rochester. Eastman managed every phase of the operation, from finding customers and publicizing the firm to keeping an eye on production and improving the plates. There were many problems and obstacles, but before the end of 1881 the company was able to move into a four-storey building.

Eastman now concentrated his efforts on replacing the heavy glass plates he was making with a lighter and more flexible material, and finally succeeded in adapting paper to carry the emulsion. He and his associates also devised a roll holder so that any camera could use the new film. But to create a mass market for the film a simple camera was needed.

The one he came up with, in 1888, was a rectangular box, small and light, loaded with a roll of paper long enough for a hundred exposures. It did not require any juggling with focusing or exposure time: the user simply aimed the camera and clicked the shutter, then advanced the film with a key and cocked the shutter for the next picture by pulling a cord. When the film was used up the camera was sent to the Eastman plant, where the exposed strip was removed, developed and printed, and a new one inserted for a charge of $10. The pictures were round and only two-and-a-half inches across, but it was the first time a novice had been able to take any kind of photographs.

Eastman named his camera the Kodak. 'I chose that name', he explained,

> because I knew a trade name must be short, vigorous, incapable of being mis-spelled to an extent that will destroy its identity, and, in order to satisfy trademark laws, it must mean nothing. The letter K had been a favourite with me – it seemed a strong, incisive sort of letter. Therefore the word I wanted had to start with K. Then it became a question of trying out a great number of combinations of letters that made words and ending with K. The word Kodak is the result.

He also came up with an appealing slogan for his advertisement: 'You press the button, we do the rest.'

Even before the first Kodak appeared, Eastman was working towards a film that would not need paper or other backing. In 1889 Henry Reichenbach, a chemist working for him, discovered a celluloid material that was everything they needed. The camera no longer had to be sent to Rochester to be filled; amateur photographers could take the exposed film to local developing centres or even develop it themselves. The market quickly expanded, and Eastman made the most of it. His company became a multi-million dollar business. At the same time, thousands of small establishments sprang up to develop films and make prints for photographers.

Paradoxically, few photographs were ever taken of Eastman himself. He was a shy, reticent man who shunned personal publicity. After he had become enormously wealthy, many of his gifts to institutions were made anonymously. One such gift was the $20 million he gave to the Massachusetts Institute of Technology as 'Mr Smith'. The true identity of the donor did not become known until many years later.

He took a keen interest in music and painting, and loved the outdoor life. 'What we do during our working hours determines what we have; what we do in our leisure hours determines what we are,' he often said. He strongly believed that the 'progress of the world depends almost entirely upon

'What we do during our working hours determines what we have; what we do in our leisure hours determines what we are.'

education', and gave away most of his money during his lifetime – $100 million – to art, education, and to scientific and medical institutions. When he died the *New York Times* said of him: 'Eastman was a stupendous factor in the education of the modern world – fostering music, endowing learning, supporting science in its researches and teaching, helping the lowliest in their struggles towards the light, making his own city a center of the arts, and glorifying his own country in the eyes of the world.' No man could wish for a better epitaph.

Thomas A. Edison

1847–1931

The inventor-entrepreneur

Everyone knows that Thomas Edison was a great inventor. Less well known, perhaps, is the fact that he was also a shrewd entrepreneur. For him it wasn't enough to solve scientific problems. Most of his efforts were concerned with developing usable products and services which he felt would meet a need in the marketplace.

No doubt his childhood experiences helped to nurture this pragmatic approach to his work. Astonishingly, Edison left school at the age of twelve. his father got him a job hawking newspapers and sundries on the train that ran between Port Huron and Detroit. He did it for three years, which taught him something about the art of salesmanship. When he had to choose a trade, he decided to become a telegrapher. He doesn't seem to have been a particularly good one (once, it is said, his inattention caused a train crash), but it got him interested in the practical applications of electrical technology.

The outstanding feature of Edison's personality was his unflagging curiosity about everything, which led him to conduct countless experiments throughout his long life and which produced more than a thousand patented inventions. A trained scientist might have been content with a major breakthrough in one special field. Edison had a much wider range of interests and he possessed at least two other important qualities: he was adventurous and he was persistent.

His first patented invention, filed in 1868, was (of all things) an electrical vote recorder. It was an idea which was way ahead of its time and he failed to find a buyer. He didn't make the same mistake with his next project – a stock ticker for exchange and brokerage houses, which was better than the one they were using at the time. He sold it for $40,000. Then followed a carbon telephone transmitter and a non-magnetic telephone sounder, bought by Western Union for $100,000 each, and a telephone receiver, sold to the English Bell Company for £30,000. (Edison conceded that Alexander Graham Bell had invented the telephone, but he had managed to make improvements.) These transactions gave him the funds to create one of America's first research and development laboratories, at Menlo Park, New Jersey. He was twenty-nine at the time and he had the good sense to hire people who possessed the skills and knowledge that he lacked.

The most famous invention to emanate from Menlo Park was, of course, modern electric lighting. We take it so much for granted these days that it's hard to understand the widespread resistance it met with at the time. But people were used to lighting their homes and offices with gas, which was reliable and relatively inexpensive, and the gas companies had a vested interest in maintaining the system.

Edison knew that he couldn't just produce a light bulb: he had to come up with an entire system to replace gas and sell it not only to financial backers but also to the public. So his laboratory produced dynamos, generators, distribution mains, feeder wires, meters and controls, as well as the bulb. And Edison, the inventor-entrepreneur, did his best to make his concept acceptable by describing his 'lamps' in terms of 'candlepower', setting them at the same intensity as gas light, and charging his customers for 'burners' on bills which were modelled after those sent out by the gas companies. He also recognized that property owners would be worried about the safety aspect, and worked out an arrangement with the Board of Fire Underwriters, whereby people who installed electric lighting were assured that their rates would not rise if their wiring was checked before it was hooked up.

It was an expensive enterprise, and in order to raise capital he had to sell a sizeable chunk of his stock in the Edison Electric

Light Company, which was set up in 1878 'to own, manufacture, operate, and license the use of various apparatus used in producing light, heat, and power by electricity'. A group of investors, including the Vanderbilts and J. P. Morgan, bought one-sixth of the company for $5000. Morgan, the great financier, was quick to see the potential and not only installed one of Edison's generators in his New York home but also played a significant role in subsequent fund-raising efforts. Edison's

A group of investors, including the Vanderbilts and J. P. Morgan, bought one-sixth of the company for $5000. Morgan . . . was quick to see the potential and not only installed one of Edison's generators in his New York home but also played a significant role in subsequent fund-raising efforts.

vision was that electricity would be produced in huge central stations, just as gas was produced from coal in gas houses. It would then be conveyed through underground conduits to nearby customers, who would pay a fee to receive service from the network.

Together with some of his backers, in 1880 he established the Edison Electric Illuminating Company of New York and applied to the city fathers for the right to electrify some of its street lighting. He demonstrated his invention at Menlo Park, gave lavish dinners at one of New York's best restaurants, and worked hard to get the press on his side. He eventually won the franchise, and Edison's Pearl Street station went into operation in September 1882. Initially, electricity was sent to fifty-eight locations. By December there were 203 customers, all near the station.

The project did not start to make money until 1885; by then, however, Edison and his associates were already pushing ahead with the next phase of their plan. The idea was simple: the rights to Edison's electrical patents would be exchanged for stock in various Edison 'illuminating companies' set up throughout the world and financed by local investors. These companies would also be obliged to buy equipment from the various Edison facilities which manufactured them.

Boston became the second largest city to have an 'illuminating company', and others followed. But Edison was no longer the only one in the field: by now he had a number of rivals and some of them thought they had found a better way. Edison's system operated on direct current (DC), in which electricity flows in one direction, from source to user. Because DC's maximum voltage was relatively low, it could be used economically only in small areas with high consumer demand. Other inventors, notably George Westinghouse, had come up with alternating current (AC) distribution systems, which could supply power cheaply to less densely populated areas.

Edison reacted in much the same way as the gas companies had done when *his* invention first appeared on the scene: he defended his interests by dismissing the whole idea of alternating current and, when that didn't have any effect, challenging the system on economic and technical grounds. He even tried to exploit the issue of public safety. It was a surprisingly petty thing to do, but there was a lot at stake and, like so many inventors, he no doubt resented the notion that someone else could do better. It didn't work: by the turn of the century even the Edison companies were producing AC systems.

Thomas Edison was responsible for many other important inventions over the years – concepts which laid the foundation for major industries. They included the phonograph, electric traction motors and storage batteries, the mimeo machine and motion pictures.

Brian Epstein

1934–67

The man who made the Beatles

Every manager in the rock music business dreams of finding a goldmine, as Brian Epstein did when he walked into a Liverpool cellar club in 1961 and discovered four scruffy young men who called themselves the Beatles. To most people they were just another local group, dressed in leather trousers and jackets and playing good time rock and roll. No one, not even Epstein, could have predicted that they would become a worldwide entertainment phenomenon, earning hundreds of millions of dollars. But he thought they were marvellous and decided that they needed his help.

Epstein's parents owned the city's largest record store, which he ran. He knew nothing about managing a beat group, and his parents were appalled when they heard of his intentions (they wanted him to concentrate on the store). But he had a flair for showmanship and his fascination for the Beatles quickly became an obsession. It was partly sexual: Epstein was gay and he was deeply attracted to the young men, especially John Lennon.

They signed an agreement, and he embarked on what his parents and friends regarded as a hopeless task. His first step was to refashion the group's image. He insisted that they forsake their leather and cowboy boots and wear identical suits. Although this was a brilliant stroke on Epstein's part, developing the striking visual image that was to become a trademark, John Lennon hated the idea and tried to convince the group that it was selling out. But Epstein got his way. He next tried to get them a recording contract, making hundreds of phone calls, writing volumes of correspondence and making dozens of personal visits. He was turned down by one company after another, but persisted. Finally, an executive from the Parlophone label agreed to give the Beatles an audition. He wasn't impressed by their performance, but thought they had potential and eventually offered them a contract. The terms were poor, but after so many rejections Epstein felt that he was lucky to get anything at all.

Their first record . . . would have got nowhere but for Epstein's fierce determination. . . . His mother was enlisted to walk all over Liverpool from shop to shop, asking if they had 'Love Me Do'.

Parlophone didn't think much of the drummer, Pete Best, so Epstein took on the task of firing him. In the next twenty-four months the Beatles would earn a massive fortune, making Best the most luckless of all might-have-beens: he became a baker. The new drummer was Ringo Starr, who readily obeyed Epstein's order to cut his hair and wear a suit, like the rest of the group.

Their first record was called 'Love Me Do', and would have got nowhere but for Epstein's fierce determination. He ordered ten thousand copies for his own store, and started a letter-writing campaign to Radio Luxembourg and the BBC, requesting the Beatles' song. His mother was enlisted to walk all over Liverpool from shop to shop, asking if they had 'Love Me Do'. Epstein began to organize and promote his own concerts, all of which headlined the Beatles. More records followed and finally, in March 1963, they had their first number one hit. Epstein kept them touring and managed to persuade Lew Grade, then head of ATV, to put them on Britain's most popular television variety show, *Sunday Night at the London Palladium*. He also got them an invitation to take part in the most prestigious of all shows, the *Royal Command Performance*. The following day the *Daily Mirror* summed up the reaction in a word the whole world would soon hear: 'Beatlemania!'

Epstein carefully packed all the cuttings into his suitcase and boarded a plane for New York. America was the biggest market, and he desperately wanted to claim it for the Beatles. Again, though, he was turned down by the major companies. Capitol Records said: 'They won't do anything in this market.' Epstein finally managed to sign the 'Love Me Do' single to a small record label in Chicago called Vee Jay. It sold only a few hundred copies.

The big break came when Epstein succeeded in booking them on the *Ed Sullivan Show*, the top-rated TV entertainment show in 1963. Sullivan knew how well they were doing in Britain and saw them as a novelty item; he said they could headline two shows, on successive Sundays. Epstein went back to Capitol Records and played their latest single, 'I Want to Hold Your Hand'. Capitol reluctantly agreed to release it on a limited basis, and it was an enormous hit. A companion album, *Meet the Beatles*, was rushed into American record stores and overnight it became the fastest-selling LP in American recording history.

Epstein later decided that the Beatles should make a movie, and they did. He also sent them on lucrative American tours: they filled vast stadiums. His one major mistake was to sign away the merchandising rights for a modest percentage. He simply under-rated the potential.

It is possible that the boys from the Liverpool cellar would have been successful even without the hard work of their mentor. Two of them – John and Paul – were not only good performers but also brilliant song-writers. But it is questionable whether they would have made quite the same impact. Epstein was the driving force. He was innovative, persistent and loyal. He provided much-needed discipline as well as flair. It is interesting to recall what happened after he died in 1967, apparently from an accidental overdose of carbitol (the public believed that it was suicide). The Beatles embarked on several unhappy ventures, including an awful film called *The Magical Mystery Tour* and a business they named Apple.

Their Apple store in London lost money from the day it opened its doors and eventually they gave away all the stock. People came to the Beatles with all kinds of absurd ideas. There was a man with a formula for a pill that could make you into whoever you wanted to be. There was a plan to save whales and another to build a commune in India. There was a woman who made tactile art from patent leather covered in oil. The group put money into fruitless projects like the design of a new 'demobilization suit' and a puppet show in Brighton. Audition tapes for Apple Records arrived by the thousands and many new singers were signed up. Most of them were flops. They got themselves another manager, Allen Klein, but the relationship turned sour and contributed to the eventual break-up of the group. John and Paul went on to do their own thing and made more money. But the showbiz phenomenon called the Beatles ended a few years after the death of the man who had started it all.

Carl Fisher

1874–1939

The Magic City of the Sunshine State

Many people have made millions out of real estate development in Florida and will, no doubt, continue to do so. The credit for opening up the Sunshine State, and paving the way for the boom that was to follow, belongs to oil and railroad magnate HENRY FLAGLER. But other entrepreneurs played a significant role in later years. Fisher was one of the first. He was a car dealer, not a real estate man, but he recognized the scope for development when he went to Miami for a vacation in 1910 and decided to do something about it.

After building a winter home there he set his sights on Miami Beach, then mostly sand and mangrove swamp. With a partner, John S. Collins, he built a bridge to connect the peninsula to the city. Dredges were brought in to bring up much of the bottom of Biscayne Bay, and this was used to fill the mangrove swamps. Sand from the Atlantic was sucked up and deposited on the beaches to make them more attractive. Several man-made beaches were created at the mouth of Biscayne Bay, as the forerunner for lagoons which Fisher thought would please prospective buyers. He then advertised Miami Beach in northern newspapers as a 'place to escape from winter'. The promotion was only a limited success, but Fisher and his partner went ahead and formed the town of Miami Beach in 1915.

His aim was to sell the land at a large profit, so that he could finance his real dream: a coast-to-coast highway. Flagler had been a railroad man; Fisher was more interested in automobiles. He presented the idea to a group of friends in Indianapolis, his home town, and got their support. Long before it was completed he came up with another project, which he called the Dixie Highway. It was to run from Indianapolis to Miami, his two favourite places. It was eventually built in the 1920s, in time for the great land boom of that extraordinary decade. Motorists arrived in large numbers, to be greeted by slick salesmen. Fisher, who had kept a lot of land, made a fortune.

So did others. Many of the early buyers found that they could resell for up to fifty times what they had paid. In Miami Beach dealers were doing business in hotel lobbies, warehouses, tents and makeshift shanties, or milling about in a kind of open-air market on the sidewalks. Every evening charabancs rolled through the streets, loaded with realtors shouting their offers over the sound of trombones and saxophones. The city of Miami had trouble maintaining a police force because so many patrolmen turned to real estate.

The promotion of particular areas went to ludicrous extremes, with carnivals and show business acts staged to attract investors. Gangsters moved in and the gullible, impressed by the genuine profits made at the start of the boom, were sold land which comprised swamps of palm groves; others, when they got round to inspecting their property, found that the advertised 'outside Miami Beach' in fact meant seventy miles outside.

Every evening charabancs rolled through the streets, loaded with realtors shouting their offers over the sound of trombones and saxophones.

One of the most grandiose projects was Coral Gables, the brainchild of GEORGE E. MERRICK, who announced that it would be 'the Venice of America', complete with arched bridges and gondolas. Merrick invented many of the lures and gimmicks that have served developers ever since. He hired three thousand salesmen and brought prospects in buses from New York, Boston and Chicago. Coral Gables promised not only home sites but golf courses, a clubhouse and a marina, all on canals dredged out of the sand.

Two other imaginative promoters were ADDISON AND WILSON MIZNER. Addison, who had taken part in the Alaska Gold Rush, was a self-taught, unlicensed architect who had built palaces for the Palm Beach millionaires in what his biographer, Alva Johnston, described as the 'Bastard-Spanish-Moorish - Romanesque - Gothic - Renaissance - Bull Market-Damn-the-Expense Style'. His brother Wilson was a famous wit, raconteur and bon vivant. Together they launched Boca Raton, billed as 'the Bride of the Gulf Stream', the 'Anteroom of Heaven'. Boca Raton (actually Spanish for Rat's Mouth) was approached by the 'World's Widest Highway', twenty lanes abreast with a Grand Canal in the centre. It was also the shortest highway, running less than half a mile before it ended in the pinewoods.

The Mizners said that their resort was intended for 'the best people . . . smart society'. Lots were ready for sale in May 1925, and the initial response was good. But many people were already wondering whether the Florida boom could last, and they were right to do so. It ran out of steam in 1926, and that same year a hurricane struck the coast, completely inundating Miami Beach and blowing the roofs off many houses. Suddenly there was no bottom to the market. The slump in land values crippled not only small investors but also some very big developers.

Carl Fisher and others ran advertisements telling tourists that Florida was healthier than ever, in every way. But Fisher himself had already left. He was busy with a new project in New York. With the help of friends, many of whom had done well out of investing in Miami Beach, he raised $2.5 million

Boca Raton . . . was approached by the 'World's Widest Highway', twenty lanes abreast with a Grand Canal in the centre. It was also the shortest highway, running less than half a mile before it ended in the pinewoods.

and bought 10,000 acres at Montauk, at the eastern end of Long Island. Here, he thought, was the site for another Newport, if not Palm Beach. It was close to New York City, had a decent natural harbour and a reasonable summer climate. But the venture turned out to be a disaster for him. In 1935 the Carl G. Fisher Company was taken over by the creditors and Fisher himself, no longer wealthy, died in 1939.

The Florida resorts did not recover for quite some time.

There was another hurricane in 1928, followed by the stock market crash of 1929. But Miami Beach, Coral Gables and Boca Raton have all enriched their subsequent owners. Today's prices are multiples of the highest levels reached in the 1920s.

Jet travel has made it easy to get there, and the much-publicized climate continues to lure refugees from the chilly northern winter weather. As in Fisher's day, many new homes are bought by retired people. The state has the nation's highest concentration of elderly residents, and they are still arriving in large numbers, with New York and Ohio providing the biggest share. The successors of Fisher, Merrick and the Mizners have been very good at selling the idea that retirement can and should be fun. They offer the enticing prospect of a new life in a 'careful adult condominium community' or a 'planned activities community'. These are usually new resorts built around a golf course, with a choice of villas or apartments, tennis courts, a swimming pool and other leisure facilities. Many overlook the ocean, or a river, or a lake, and also have a marina. There has also been a rapid growth in old and new services, including medical care. South Florida alone now has forty-three hospitals, many of which sell their services through glossy advertisements.

Miami, Fisher's 'Magic City', has become a bi-lingual, bi-cultural metropolis. Half of its year-round inhabitants speak Spanish as their first language, and many jobs require both Spanish and English. It is widely considered to be the place to be if you have business in South America and the Caribbean, or if you come from there and have business with the rest of the world. Nearly two hundred multi-national corporations have established their Latin American headquarters here, and the banks have also arrived in force. One highly visible result of all this activity has been massive commercial development: new office blocks, hotels and high-rise condominiums have transformed the skyline.

But Miami also has its seamier side: racial tension, drug-related crime and some of America's worst poverty within hailing distance of some of the world's most conspicuous consumption. Many of the elderly have moved away, to the new resorts and condominium communities along Florida's Gold Coast, and to other parts of the state. Palm Beach remains the favourite haven of the rich, but there are plenty of other places to choose from. The delightful Pinella Sun Coast, for example, now bristles with fashionable resorts such as Clearwater, Sarasota and Dunedin. The coastal areas also offer a wide choice of industrial and office parks – landscaped gardens and smart new buildings have replaced scrubland to accommodate the influx of hi-tech companies. Like the retirement communities, the 'silicon seaside' has the twin merits of an attractive setting and useful amenities.

Between 1980 and 1985 Florida's population grew by 16 per cent to nearly 11.2 million. By 1990 it is expected to reach 12.5 million, and it should pass the 13.6 million mark by 1995. Many forecasters reckon that early in the next century the number will be close to 20 million. This is bound to produce all kinds of problems: the University of Florida estimates, for example, that by the year 2000 the state will need to spend at least $33 billion on new and improved roads, sewers and water-treatment facilities. But, clearly, it also presents considerable opportunities for businessmen who can afford to look ahead.

Henry M. Flagler

1830–1913

The man who made Florida

Henry Morrison Flagler made a fortune from oil: he was a partner of John D. Rockefeller and one of the founders of Standard Oil. But he is best remembered as the man who made Florida a playground for the rich.

He actually did much more than that. He opened it up to the rest of the country by constructing the Florida East Coast Railroad, built hospitals and schools as well as luxury hotels, encouraged utility companies to expand in the area, helped banks, and in general provided the Sunshine State with the economic infrastructure it previously had lacked. Flagler gave Florida the reputation of being 'the state of the future'.

None of this appears to have been in his mind when he first went there on a visit in the winter of 1878. His wife Mary was ill and the family doctor had suggested that the sun would do her good. Flagler was charmed with the scenery and the climate but appalled by the poor hotels and the worse transportation. Three-quarters of the state was isolated at this time. St Augustine alone drew tourists to the Atlantic coast, while Tampa was not much of a draw on the Gulf. The fastest-growing vacation spot of the day was Palatka, on the St John's River, because the nearby sulphur springs were said to cure all sorts of ailments.

The Flaglers made further visits in 1879 and 1880. Mary died in 1881, but by then Henry had become quite enthusiastic about Florida's potential. He married again in 1883, and took his second wife to St Augustine for their honeymoon. Combining business with pleasure, he looked the area over for investment possibilities. He was an energetic man and, at fifty-three, already somewhat bored with the petroleum business. He would remain high in the Standard Oil hierarchy, but from that time on the development of Florida land and transportation would consume most of his spare time.

He build a smart new hotel in St Augustine, with 540 rooms and a large casino, designed to appeal to his wealthy friends. There was a large sulphur pool in the grounds for those who came to Florida for health reasons, and many recreation facilities including golf and tennis. He also arranged for the purchase of the local railroad, which he improved and extended. He bought two more railroads in the years that followed, and arranged for special through trains to leave New York for St Augustine during the season. The Florida Specials were first-class in every respect. They were lavishly decorated, with plush club cars and luxurious Pullmans, and made the trip in thirty hours, an amazing time in the 1880s.

Flagler scarcely stopped to enjoy his first success in tourism before he entered a new phase of the business. He bought a hotel in Ormond, just north of Daytona, and modernized it. He also set about acquiring land in Palm Beach, then known as Palm City. (Flagler renamed it at his wife's suggestion.) Although the area was settled, and several large estates and citrus fruit interests were established, it was isolated, with the Atlantic to the east and tropical forests on the other three sides. It would hardly pay to construct a railway line merely for the benefit of tourists. The 'season' lasted only about two months; what would the line do for the rest of the year? The answer was to transport Florida citrus fruits to Jacksonville and further north, expanding the market for these products, which in the 1890s was still small.

Flagler was not interested in land speculation, though he might easily have made another fortune at it. Instead, he concentrated on construction and promotion. As soon as he owned sufficient land for his purpose, he announced his plans to build a new hotel, the Royal Poinciana, which would rival those of the Riviera. 'I shall build upon this spot a magnificent playground for the people of the nation,' was the way he put it. But, of course, he was well aware that only the rich would be able to play there. He also acquired land in what is now West Palm Beach, which he said would be used for light industry, the loading of citrus fruit and the storage of supplies, as well as rows of small houses. 'That is the city I am building for my help,' he said.

Construction work on the railroad and the hotel began in

It would hardly pay to construct a railway line merely for the benefit of tourists. The 'season' lasted only about two months. . . . The answer was to transport Florida citrus fruits to Jacksonville and further north, expanding the market for these products. . . .

May 1893, and both were finished in February of the following year. The Royal Poinciana could accommodate 1750 guests. There were tennis courts, auto racing tracks and a fine golf course, as well as pools, archery ranges and a gambling casino that soon became the most famous in the nation. It was so successful that in 1895 Flagler opened a second hotel, the Breakers.

The rich came down regularly each winter – some, like the Vanderbilts, the Morgans, the Whitneys and the Mellons, in their own elegantly fitted railroad cars. Many built plush homes of their own; even today, Palm Beach is second home to some of the wealthiest people in the world.

Flagler next turned his attention to the area south of Palm Beach. He extended the railroad to Miami, which until then had been linked to the rest of the world only by sea, and built another hotel there. He also embarked on a project which many of his friends regarded as unthinkable: building a railroad 156 miles out to sea, along a series of bridges. It spanned twenty-nine islands of the Florida Keys and connected Key

West (and Havana by ferry) to the rest of Florida. Flagler hoped to construct a modern port in Key West – one that would attract Cuban tobacco and sugar imports, and provide facilities for the export of American manufactured goods to the island.

He was seventy-five when construction began, and saw the project as the grand climax to all his other developments. The task took seven years to complete. It was not a sound economic venture, and after a hurricane washed out much of the roadbed in 1935 the island line was never rebuilt, though its trestles now carry the Key West Highway. But Flagler never knew that it had failed. He died in 1913, at the age of eighty-three. He had invested a total of $50 million in Florida, and still managed to leave an estate of more than $100 million to his widow. (See also CARL FISHER.)

Henry Ford

1863–1947

'Any colour they like . . . as long as it's black'

Henry Ford had nothing to do with inventing the internal combustion engine, or even with the assembly-line method of manufacture, which was already old when he was born. What he did was to take both the invention and the method and tinker them into near perfection. He also had ideas about wages and profits which other employers found hard to accept: in his day he was considered a radical, even a revolutionary.

When he launched his Model T automobile in 1909, motor cars were generally considered to be the ostentatious toys of the wealthy. The Model T was a stark, almost grim, affair. But it had two undeniable merits: it was efficient and it was cheap. Ford's innovative concept was a reliable car that would sell for no more than the price of a horse and buggy. Its initial cost and its upkeep were intended to be within the means of 'the little people'.

The concept was later copied in Hitler's Germany and elsewhere, but at the time it was so novel that five of Henry Ford's original partners decided to get out. Ford bought their stock, which gave him majority control of the company. His remaining associates were solidly opposed to mass production: they were 'inexpressibly shocked' and even contemplated stock action to stop the madness. But Ford went ahead and the Model T soon became the sensational gadget of the United States. It was the only automobile that went into folklore. Selling for a little under $1000 in 1909, its price dropped spasmodically over the years to as low as $295. By World War I 250,000 Model T cars had been made and sold: those manufactured in 1914 accounted for 45 per cent of all automobiles made in the USA that year.

Then, also in 1914, Ford rocked American industry with another move characterized as 'crazy': he announced that his company was instituting a wage scale based on a minimum of $5 a day – twice as much as the highest common labour wage in the country. Moreover, the Ford working day was henceforth to be eight, not nine, hours a day. 'Industry must manage to keep wages high and prices low,' he said, 'One's own employees should be one's own best customers.' There it was in capsule form, the new theory – namely that the wage earner is more important as a consumer than as a producer. Yet he had to be up and doing; he had to *produce*. Ford's assembly line saw to that. It had no place for men who needed to go to the toilets during shifts; such weaklings were weeded out as soon as discovered, and other men were paid to discover them. He was implacably against the labour unions, which would interfere with his manufacturing methods. But when he eventually surrendered he gave them everything they asked for and a lot they had not demanded.

Ford was a great believer in putting most of his profits into expansion. This led to a celebrated legal case when his five stockholders took him to court to force him to distribute the company's earnings. Ford told the court that the profits of the Ford Motor Company were neither his nor the stockholders'. 'After they [the employees] have had their wages,' he said, 'and a share of the profits, it is my duty to take what remains and put it back into the industry to create more work for more men

'Industry must manage to keep wages high and prices low. One's own employees should be one's own best customers.'

at higher wages.' He denied that either generosity or his conscience had anything to do with it: it was simply good business. He lost the case. 'It is not', said the court, 'within the lawful powers of a corporation to shape and conduct its affairs for the merely incidental benefit of stockholders and for the purpose of benefiting others.'

Ford promptly resigned, though retaining his seat on the board of directors, and hinted that he might start a new company, a concern with no stockholders to harass him. The directors panicked and sold out to him. The Ford Motor Company became a family property.

The Model T lasted almost two decades. In 1928 Ford came out with a new car – the Model A, which lasted only five years. His competitors made it obsolete, not in performance but in appearance. They recognized what Henry Ford had stubbornly refused to acknowledge: that most Americans wanted a new-style car not every twenty years, or every five years, but annually. The Ford plant shut down again, this time to come out with the V-8. It was as good a car as any other at its price, but then all makes of cars were good.

Henry Ford was a farmer's son who hated banks and

bankers, abhorred idle people and denounced the profit motive. He was the champion of the man with the hoe or the hammer. He died a billionaire, and his company is still one of the big names in the industry, but after correctly identifying a need he made the classic mistake of the production man: he failed to keep pace with the changing demands of the market. He contemptuously dismissed fashion or style; one of his much-quoted comments was that 'They can have any colour they like, as long as it's black.' It allowed his competitors to exploit what he had begun.

Milton Friedman

b. 1912

The guru of monetarism

Milton Friedman, who won a Nobel Prize in 1976, is widely regarded as the most influential economist since JOHN MAYNARD KEYNES. He has made many valuable contributions to economic science, but is best known for his work on what is popularly called 'monetarism'.

Friedman was born in Brooklyn, New York, the son of a shopkeeper. At college he showed a particular aptitude for mathematics and at one time considered becoming an insurance actuary. But having experienced the Depression, during which his father was perpetually on the brink of bankruptcy, he felt that the most serious problems in the world were those of economics. He received his graduate training at the University of Chicago, and later became the most famous advocate of the 'Chicago school' of economic thought.

Friedman first made a reputation as an innovator of statistics. He had the original idea of sequential analysis, which is the foundation for all quality control. But he soon broadened his range. His subsequent contributions to economic theory and policy have been based on his strong belief in doctrines relating to a 'free man', which are diametrically opposed to the concept which stresses 'welfare' and 'equality' over freedom.

In one of his books, *Free Choice*, he traces the success of western economic and social advancement to the ideas embodied in two works which appeared in 1776, Adam Smith's *The Wealth of Nations* and Thomas Jefferson's *Declaration of Independence. The Wealth of Nations* identified market forces, powered by the desire of individuals to enter mutually advantageous trade, as a superior co-ordinator of human action for the general benefit of society. Friedman feels that coercion is the greatest threat to mankind and, as Jefferson did, reckons that government produces the most debilitating coercion of all. He insists that

> Economic freedom is an essential requisite for political freedom. By enabling people to co-operate with one another without coercion or central direction, it reduces the area over which political power is exercised. In addition, by dispersing power, the free market provides an offset to whatever concentration of political power may arise. The combination of economic and political power in the same hands is a sure recipe for tyranny.

The government's role, he argues, is to 'serve as an umpire to prevent individuals from coercing one another', rather than 'to serve as a parent charged with the duty of coercing some to aid others'.

Friedman's free market alternatives include limits on government's power to tax and spend, removal of tariffs and quotas in foreign trade, abolition of price and wage controls, and the removal of other impediments to free choice. All this, of course, accords with the views of many right-wing politicians. Friedman's influence stems largely from the fact that he has been able to give intellectual weight to their case, while at the same time managing to explain complex issues in language they can understand. Other academics, please note.

When he first achieved prominence, the Keynesian approach was more fashionable. But many people, especially in Britain, had begun to question the belief, so dear to socialists, that government solutions are necessarily superior solutions. The election of a Conservative government in Britain in 1979 provided Friedman with his most fervent

'The combination of economic and political power in the same hands is a sure recipe for tyranny.'

supporter – Margaret Thatcher, whose father had also been a small shopkeeper. She not only agreed with most of his arguments, but also resolved to take appropriate action.

A key element of the strategy she introduced after becoming Prime Minister was monetary policy. Friedman has since said that monetarism was simply a new name for an old doctrine, but there is no doubt that his pioneering work to restore and extend monetarist theory played a big part in its acceptance by the British government – and, later, by the governments of other countries.

The modern version of monetarism, or the quantity theory of money, states that:

1. There is a stable relationship between the amount of money supplied to an economy and the amount of spending generated.

2. The money/spending relationship will vary in a predictable manner in response to a few variables such as interest rates and inflationary expectations.

3. Changes in spending generated by changes in money supply will induce temporary changes in economic output.

4. Changes in money supply ultimately affect only the price level.

5. Interest rates, after adjustment for inflationary expectations, are determined by time preference, productivity and the physical return on capital.

6. The money supply is an independently targetable policy objective of government.

According to Friedman, 'There is no other empirical relation in economics that has been observed to recur so uniformly under so wide a variety of circumstances as the relationship between substantial changes over short periods in the stock of money and prices.'

In *A Monetary History of the United States*, which is probably his single most important work, he and Schwartz make a persuasive case that the Great Depression was caused not by a failure of free markets, but by a sharp and sustained decline in the money supply for which the government was largely responsible. The historical evidence confirmed his earlier belief that 'The central problem is not to construct a highly sensitive instrument that can continuously offset instability introduced by other factors, but rather to prevent monetary arrangements from themselves becoming a primary source of instability.' He advocated a policy that would maintain a constant, predictable, non-inflationary money growth rate so that destabilizing changes from monetary policy would be eliminated.

The principal objective of Mrs Thatcher's government, when it first took office, was to reduce the rate of inflation, would had reached alarming levels under the previous Labour administration. Mrs Thatcher was vigorously opposed to ideas like wage and price controls, which not only ran counter to her own belief in the merits of a free market but had also been tried before without lasting success. Friedman's answer had much more appeal. Within a matter of months, variations in money supply were attracting as much attention in the business pages of the newspapers as other indicators, like the balance of payments statistics, had done in earlier years. Friedman became the guru everyone wanted to interview.

In a speech to the Institute of Economic Affairs in London, he complained that monetarism had been 'misinterpreted and misrepresented' by the press. According to the British papers, it meant 'anything that Margaret Thatcher at any time had expressed as a desirable object of policy'. But monetarism had 'nothing whatever to do with the question of what the appropriate size of government ought to be, with what taxes should be, with whether you ought to have nationalized or denationalized industries. To make my point most clearly, let me inform you that among my fellow monetarists are Karl Marx and the leaders of Communist China . . . but while we agree on monetarism, I assure you there's not much else we agree on.'

Friedman's irritation was understandable; there certainly had been a tendency to simplify. But he had every reason to be pleased with the general direction of Mrs Thatcher's economic strategy, though he would clearly have liked to see her go much further. He also had the satisfaction of seeing Britain's inflation rate fall to the lowest level for many years.

Inevitably, many economists strongly disagree not only with his (and Mrs Thatcher's) enthusiasm for 'economic freedom' but also with his case for monetarism. It is certainly not the cure-all some people would like it to be – but then Friedman has never said it was. He has also been criticized for being 'populist'. He has frequently appeared on television, written a

'. . . among my fellow monetarists are Karl Marx and the leaders of Communist China. . . .'

column for *Newsweek*, published books with simple titles, talked to audiences of businessmen and politicians in plain English, and even told jokes against his own profession. Many academics find this hard to accept. But economics is the servant of the people, not its master. It should have practical as well as theoretical value, and it helps if those who have to implement the theories, and take responsibility for the result, know what economists are talking about.

George Gallup

1902–84

The forecaster who got it right

George Gallup developed public opinion polling and did much to make it a key tool of politics, advertising and many other activities. The idea was not new in American life: it had been known under the name of 'straw ballots' for more than a century. As an election came along a newspaper would canvass a number of representative people to secure an indication of how the voting would go. This had been practised on an extensive scale by a weekly journal, the *Literary Digest*, whose results proved fairly accurate until the election of 1936 when a hopelessly wrong prophecy ended the career of the publication. Gallup was the man who got it right, and it brought him instant fame.

Gallup had a PhD in psychology from the University of Iowa, but he was more a practical-minded thinker than a scholar. His solid six-foot presence and his staid dark suits gave him the appearance of a prosperous businessman – which he also was. He was for years the largest stockholder and chairman of the Gallup Organization, the corporation that carried out much of his attitude sampling.

After graduating, Gallup lectured at the state university for six years, and was then successively head of a new Department of Journalism and Professor of Journalism at North-Western University in Chicago. But he came to opinion polls from a research post at the advertising agency of Young & Rubicam, where he carried out editorial and advertising surveys for numerous newspapers and weekly magazines. In 1935 he founded the Gallup Poll, with its headquarters in Princeton,

New Jersey, and an editorial office in New York. The organization was rather grandly christened the American Institute of Public Opinion, and a similar British Institute was established in 1936.

The aim was to test and measure public opinion by methods which he had found to be both practical and accurate in advertising. Gallup trained his assistants to go round a number of houses asking questions. He did not deal with large numbers, but made it his aim to take a representative cross-section of the community.

In the 1936 election, the *Literary Digest*'s prediction was based on 10 million mock ballot cards mailed to people who figured in telephone directories or on the list of car owners. The poll showed Alf Landon winning with 57 per cent of the vote, and Roosevelt trailing with 43 per cent. In fact Roosevelt won with 62.5 per cent. The *Digest*, it turned out, had made two crude mistakes. First, its sample excluded anybody who did not own a car or telephone – at that time, anyone with below-average income. Secondly, only 2.4 million people returned their poll cards; and the *Digest* could not have known which party's supporters were more inclined to respond.

Gallup's prediction was based on a scientifically constructed

Gallup used to say that every person had a 'fundamental right to give expression to the worth that is in him'.

'stratified random sample' of the electorate, totalling only a few thousand. Yet it turned out to be correct. The resulting publicity brought him many commissions, and he introduced the concept of a 'continuous audit' of public opinion. Yet even Gallup was not infallible. His reputation only just survived an incorrect forecast in 1948 that Thomas Dewey would defeat Harry Truman, an error which he said was caused partly by ending the polling too early.

Today the system of testing cross-sections of the public, not only repeatedly during election campaigns but also on almost every controversial issue which arises, is widely used around the world. Opinion polling has become an industry, with numerous organizations competing for attention. Presidents and Prime Ministers anxiously wait for the latest verdicts on their popularity. But the polls are not confined to politics: they have tended to become moral, as well as political, social and cultural, arbiters. In Britain, for example, they have played their part in such profound moral issues as the reform of the laws on homosexual conduct, on abortion and on capital punishment. In the USA, they helped to end the country's involvement in Vietnam.

Many people object to what they see as 'trial by opinion poll'. Politicians say that the repeated polls themselves can have an undue influence on voters. When Gallup was asked about this some years ago, he replied: 'One might as well insist that a thermometer makes the weather.' But there is little doubt that the polls do have *some* influence. Many voters are swayed by the alleged opinions of a majority, and polls which show a strong lead for a particular candidate can create a 'bandwagon' effect. And there is ample evidence that much-publicized opinion polls have helped to persuade lawmakers to press ahead with reforms, sometimes against their own judgment.

Gallup used to say that every person had a 'fundamental right to give expression to the worth that is in him'. He emphasized the 'grave danger to democracy which arises when the ordinary citizen begins to say: "It doesn't matter what I think – they'll run things their own way anyhow."' It was a valid point, but it is nevertheless questionable whether opinion polls, in which the individual rates as little more than a code mark, provide a proper basis for making policy decisions. Half a dozen poll organizations may provide widely differing answers; who is to say which one accurately reflects the public's view? Polls on complex issues commissioned by pressure groups are sometimes dubious – not in the sample but in the use of loaded questions. In a democracy, the ordinary citizen has other ways of expressing his or her approval or disapproval, notably by using his vote at the ballot box. Gallup himself once said that he never voted, 'because I've always felt I shouldn't get involved in politics'. It was the kind of remark one feels inclined to take with a large pinch of salt: surely he recognized that his polls had become *part* of politics?

Bill Gates

b. 1955

Software's whizz-kid

According to *Fortune* magazine, no one ever made more money at an earlier age than William H. Gates III, known to everyone as Bill. He is certainly an astonishing young man, even by the high-flying standards of the computer industry. In the spring of 1987, his stake in the company he co-founded at the age of nineteen was estimated to be worth £1 billion; he was still only thirty-one.

Gates, who looks like a university student, has helped to change the way American business works by creating some of the most widely used personal computer software. Aside from the microprocessor, software is the most important part of a computer and he talks zealously about his 'vision' of bringing computing power 'to the masses'. His Seattle-based company, Microsoft, has become one of the biggest in the business.

He comes from a prominent Seattle family. His father is a partner in a leading law firm, his mother a member of the University of Washington Board of Regents and a director of First Interstate Bank. He says he grew up in a 'rich environment in which to learn'. Like so many young people these days, he got hooked on computers while still at school. He was fascinated not only by the technology but also by its practical uses. He and some friends developed a computerized payroll system for the school, and also used a computer to count the holes punched in cards by machines that monitor highway traffic. In 1973 he enrolled at Harvard, but he and one of his friends, Paul G. Allen, still spent a lot of time trying to think up new businesses involving computers.

Gates avidly read all the magazines devoted to the subject, and in January 1975 he came across a cover story in *Popular Electronics* which seemed to offer an interesting opportunity. It was about a company which had developed a personal computer and needed a computer language that hobbyists could use to program the machine. Gates and Allen thought they could write a condensed version of the language BASIC, used on large computers, that would fit the new machine's limited memory. They did so, and soon had a number of other customers. Gates decided to drop out of Harvard and to set up a partnership with Allen. They called their new business Microsoft.

Their lucky break came in 1980 when IBM, which had

. . . he talks zealously about his 'vision' of bringing computing power 'to the masses'.

begun to recognize the mass-market potential of commercial computers, asked them to write an operating system. The IBM contract allowed them to expand rapidly: by the end of the following year they had a staff of 125 and an annual turnover of $16 million. The link with the giant corporation is still of great importance; most IBM personal computers use Microsoft's product.

Gates has shown great skill at keeping one step ahead. When

IBM began to develop a new generation of computers, it decided at first to design its own program. But he persuaded them that his most recent software package, Windows, had a two-year head-start over IBM's product. He said he would work with the company's engineers to modify it to their liking. IBM changed its mind and Windows, which presents information in an eye-catching format, is now a key part of the new machines. Gates expects it to become an industry standard. He also sells software to other companies and reckons that his business will soon be the top company in the field.

Though he lacks a degree in computer science, Gates is widely regarded as a technical genius. Unlike so many other whizz-kids he also appears to be a shrewd businessman. He has become a self-taught expert on legal matters, marketing, distribution and accounting. But he has had the good sense to hire professional managers and he tends to leave most of the management to them, which allows him to concentrate on technology.

He can be tough – several managers have been fired over the years, and in 1986 he cut a long-time relationship with his Japanese distributor because he felt that he wasn't pushing hard enough. But he clearly knows how to inspire enthusiasm. Microsoft now has more than 1500 employees, mostly young people (the average age is thirty-one). They work long hours, with Gates setting the pace. A bachelor, he rarely gets home before midnight on weekdays and usually works at weekends. He says his ambition is to put a personal computer on every desk and in every home, by developing nifty new software programs.

Gates is the company's chief strategist. He describes himself as a hands-on manager with a passion for excellence. When he starts work on a project, he picks a team of about ten people from engineering and marketing. It sets goals, divides up the work, and then meets every two weeks to discuss problems. There are frequent arguments, but his methods get results. Microsoft makes impressive profits. The company went public in 1986, and stockholders have since had good reason to be pleased with its performance.

Gates held on to 45 per cent of the shares. He has given his old high school more than a million dollars for a science building, but he seems to spend little on himself. He likes to go to parties, but he rarely takes a holiday and shuns most of the toys of the rich. His main indulgence is a Jaguar XJ6 Vanden Plas.

With IBM's business firmly in hand, Microsoft's prospects looks bright. Inevitably, though, there are people who think that his luck won't last. Competition is stiff and even a genius can make mistakes. It has, after all, happened to others. If IBM *had* decided to go ahead with its own design, Gates would have been in trouble. But it *didn't*. His great strength is that he has a remarkable talent for adapting himself to the needs of an ever-changing industry. He is young, energetic and intelligent, and he has demonstrated that he has staying power. He says that there are still great opportunities ahead, and there is no doubt about his determination to make the most of them.

Harold Sydney Geneen

b. 1910

The Michelangelo of management

A French magazine once described Harold Geneen as the Michelangelo of management, and others hailed him as 'the best professional we've had in this generation'. These fulsome tributes were based partly on the intricate and rigorous system of controls he introduced at ITT, which later became the subject of study in business schools and management courses all over America, and partly on his bold and often controversial policy of rapid growth by acquisition. According to Anthony Sampson, he 'helped to create a new kind of industrial animal, a conglomerate which was also a multinational; a company that could make anything anywhere'. Audacious and autocratic, hard-working and imaginative, Geneen came to rule over a thousand companies scattered throughout the world.

Geneen was born in Bournemouth, the conservative seaside resort on the south coast of England, where his father was a concert manager, but the family moved to the United States when he was only one year old and he became a naturalized American. His parents separated soon afterwards; young Harold remained with his mother, who sent him to a boarding school at Suffield, Connecticut, which he left at sixteen. He found a job as a page boy at the New York Stock Exchange, and took night classes in accountancy at New York University.

In 1935 he joined the accountancy firm of Lybrand, Ross Brothers & Co. During the next seven years his work consisted mostly of servicing clients' accounts, and in the process Geneen became an expert problem-solver. He not only learned how business functions but also saw what his clients were doing wrong and came up with practical solutions. Not surprisingly, American Can eventually offered him a top accounting position, which he accepted. He soon came to play a key role in management, but found that the board did not agree with his view that growth, not stability, should be the prime goal of any vital enterprise. He left American Can in 1946 to take the job of controller at Bell & Howell, and then controller at Jones & Laughlin. In 1956 he moved again – this time to Rayteon, the giant electronics company, which made him executive vice-president. The job gave him a lot of power, and he created a new structure for the company, basing it on the one established at General Motors by ALFRED SLOAN, one of his few heroes. But he still had not achieved his own goal: to become the head of a major organization. The president of Raytheon had no intention of stepping aside, so when ITT asked Geneen to become its president in 1959 he accepted with alacrity.

Founded in 1920 as a communications service company operating outside the United States, ITT in 1959 was still essentially that, its business overwhelmingly overseas, its assets just under the $1 million mark. The board of directors hired Geneen primarily to straighten out the jumble of companies and finance left by his predecessors, and he embarked on a major effort at streamlining and restructuring operations. As part of this, he introduced his system of tight controls. 'I want no surprises,' he told executives – a warning he repeated often in the years that followed.

But Geneen was also determined to expand his new empire: his aim, he declared, was to double revenue and earnings within five years. It was a formidable undertaking, but he succeeded with the help of some significant acquisitions, paid for mostly with ITT shares. They included two important insurance companies, a new field for ITT. Geneen, however, was far from satisfied. The pace of buying accelerated; in one year he acquired companies at the rate of one a month.

The scope of ITT's activities, Geneen proudly declared, extended 'from the Arctic to the Antarctic and quite literally from the bottom of the sea to the moon. . . .'

By 1969 he had completed more than a hundred mergers, and in the process had transformed ITT from a loosely knit group of telephone companies, operating abroad, into a highly centralized organization controlling an unprecedented range of industries. It owned, among other things, well-known companies like Avis, Sheraton and Continental Banking, and operated in sixty-seven countries. The scope of ITT's activities, Geneen proudly declared, extended 'from the Arctic to the

Antarctic and quite literally from the bottom of the sea to the moon.' It was the ninth largest corporation in America and the biggest conglomerate.

Geneen did not like the word 'conglomerate'; he preferred to talk about 'diversification'. He rejected the charge that he had built his empire in a haphazard fashion. It was all part of his master plan, he said. When asked to explain the plan, he wrote that the corporation's purpose were:

1. To diversify into industries and markets which have good prospects for above-average long-term growth and profitability.

2. To achieve a sound balance between foreign earnings and domestic earnings.

3. To achieve a sound balance between high-risk capital-intensive manufacturing operations and less risky service operations.

4. To achieve a sound balance between high-risk engineering labour-intensive electronics manufacturing and less risky commercial and industrial manufacturing.

5. To achieve a sound ratio between commercial/industrial products and services, and consumer products and services.

6. To achieve a sound ratio between government/defence/space operations and commercial/industrial/consumer products and services in both foreign and domestic markets.

7. To achieve a sound balance between cyclical products and services.

Not all his bids were successful. The most serious setback came when he tried to acquire the third TV network, the American Broadcasting Corporation, for $400 million. The merger was approved by stockholders, but the Justice Department intervened and in 1968 Geneen called off the deal. Meantime, ITT had also run into trouble with anti-trust legislation and was forced to divest itself of part of the business of a subsidiary, Avis. Further controversy followed in 1970, when ITT was accused of manoeuvres to block the election of the socialist Salvador Allende as President of Chile.

Undeterred, Geneen continued on the takeover trail. In 1972 he acquired twenty-two companies. But by then ITT was under increasing attack in the press and by government. Geneen's enemies said he was running a heartless, amoral business, a grasping giant out to dominate large sectors of the economy and a malevolent force overseas. Anthony Sampson's highly critical book, *The Sovereign State of ITT*, appeared at a time when many people had begun to feel that multi-nationals like ITT had grown too powerful, and it was an instant best-seller. Geneen, however, remained president until 1977 and he continued as chairman until 1980.

Even now the mention of his name tends to evoke a strong response, inside ITT and in the business world generally. Some people think he was a genius; others say he was a prime example of the Ugly American. My view is that he was a bit of both. He was not an attractive personality, and he did not spend much time discussing moral values. He was ruthless and autocratic. But he was certainly a man with exceptional abilities, a manager who combined great administrative skill with considerable entrepreneurial flair.

Geneen's strength lay in his talent for building on the foundations laid by others. ITT had been created by someone else; he took over at the age of fifty and turned it into one of America's most formidable business empires. His much-admired system

Some people think he was a genius; others say he was a prime example of the Ugly American.

of controls was heavily influenced by the earlier work of Alfred Sloan, but it was highly effective and later copied by many others. He did not start companies, but he made them more efficient. He was difficult to work for, but he trained a new race of managers, many of whom later left to join, or to run, other companies, so that ITT was dubbed 'Geneen University'. He made mistakes, but when he finally retired in 1980 he was able to look back on an impressive list of achievements.

King C. Gillette

1855–1932

Inventor of the safety razor

Successful entrepreneurs often claim that their best ideas have come to them while shaving. This is certainly true of the man who revolutionized shaving habits by inventing the first safety razor – King C. Gillette.

Gillette was born in Font du Lac, Wisconsin, and from the time he was seventeen years old, when his father lost everything in the great Chicago fire, he was on his own. At twenty-one he was earning his living as a travelling salesman, but his real interest lay in inventions. He was awarded several patents but had neither the time nor the money to make commercial use of them. In 1891 he was persuaded by a friend, William Painter, to join his sales force at the Baltimore Seal Company, which made rubber bottle stoppers for beer and soft drinks. Later, Painter invented the Crown Cork – the tiny cap with the cork lining which is still extensively used – and the name of the company was changed to the Crown Cork and Seal Company. Painter and Gillette often talked about their mutual interest in inventions, and in the course of one of these discussions Painter urged his friend to 'concentrate on just one thing – something like the Crown Cork – that people use once and throw away'.

Gillette agreed that the suggestion had a lot of merit and listed every material need he could think of – to no avail. Then, in the summer of 1895, it happened. In Gillette's own words:

> It was born as naturally as though its embryonic form had matured in thought and only waited its appropriate time for birth. One morning when I started to shave, I found my razor dull, and it

was not only dull but it was beyond the point of successful stropping. It needed honing which meant it would have to be taken to a barber or cutler. 'A razor is only a sharp edge', I said to myself, 'and all back of it is just support. Why do they go to all the expense and trouble of fashioning a backing that has nothing to do with shaving? And why do they forge a great piece of steel and then spend so much labor in hollow grinding it when they could get the same result by putting an edge on a piece of steel only thick enough to hold an edge?

As I stood there with the razor in my hand, my eyes resting on it as lightly as a bird settling down on its nest, the Gillette razor was born – more with the rapidity of a dream than by a process of reasoning. In a moment I saw it all: the way the blade could be held in a holder; the idea of sharpening the two opposite edges on the thin piece of steel; the clamping plates for the blade, with a handle half-way between the two edges of the blade.

All this came more in pictures than in conscious thought as though the razor were already a finished thing and held before my eyes. I stood there before that mirror in a trance of joy. My wife was visiting Ohio and I hurriedly wrote to her: 'I've got it! Our fortune is made!' Fool that I was, I knew little about razors and nothing about steel, and I could not foresee the trials and tribulations I was to pass through before the razor was a success. But I believed in it with my whole heart.

After his sudden inspiration, Gillette rushed off to a hardware store and bought some pieces of brass steel ribbon used for clock springs, a small band vise, and some files. With these materials, he made the first razor. He also made endless sketches. But the 'trance of joy' turned out to have been premature. He could not get any financial backing for his invention. For six years he tried in vain to raise the money; during this time he continued his experiments with steel blades. The 'experts' whom he consulted advised him to forget it; they insisted that he would never succeed in putting an edge on sheet steel that would shave.

Gillette recalled later:

'But I didn't know enough to quit. If I had been technically trained, I would have given up, or probably would never have begun. I was a dreamer, and in search of the gold at the foot of the rainbow. I dared where wise ones feared to tread.

I tried every cutler and machine shop in Boston and some in New York and Newark in an effort to find someone who knew something about hardening and tempering thin steel so it would keep its flatness and not be warped by strains. Even the Massachusetts Institute of Technology experimented and failed absolutely in securing satisfactory results.

Finally, in 1901, Gillette persuaded some friends to raise $5000 and form a company. He started manufacturing in a room above a Boston fish store. There a young graduate from MIT, William E. Nickerson, refined Gillette's original safety razor and developed processes for hardening and sharpening sheet steel. The $5000 was soon gone and the company ran into debt. It was rescued by a Boston investor, John Joyce, who recognized the possibilities of the razor and put up the funds needed to launch it. In the first year, 1903, a total of 51 razors and 168 blades were sold. The following year saw a dramatic increase in business: sales rose to 90,844 razors and 123,648 blades. The company prospered, and so did Gillette. His persistence had paid off at last.

'But I didn't know enough to quit. . . . I was a dreamer, and in search of the gold at the foot of the rainbow. I dared where wise ones feared to tread.'

Another innovator, GERALD B. LAMBERT (1886–1967), later became president of the Gillette Safety Razor Company and invented a one-piece razor. He also introduced the famous Blue Blade. When Lambert took over, in 1931, the patents on Gillette's razor and blades had expired and there were many competitors. The business was in trouble. Lambert decided that the answer was to improve the product.

Research had shown that the public no longer believed the

company's claim that its blade was better than all the others. Lambert put in new machinery and when he knew that he had a better blade he asked one of his engineers if he could colour it blue. The engineer said yes, it could certainly be done. He would just put on a blue lacquer. Lambert then got an advertising agency to produce full-page ads with the eye-catching headline: 'A frank confession of the Gillette Safety Razor Co.' The ads went on to say, in effect, that the old blades had been

---

After he had restored the company's fortunes, he resigned. . . . Many innovators . . . are only really happy if they can make a creative contribution to a business.

---

bad and that the company admitted it. But now there was a new blade and it was the sharpest blade ever made. There was no fear that the reader would get the old stock. This new blade could be identified at once by its blue carton and the Blue Blade inside.

As Lambert later recalled in his autobiography,

> The results were what we expected. Millions of shavers who had hated our old blade but couldn't do anything about it had tiraded against us. Now, to their joy, they found they had been right all along. Their hearts began to warm to us. After you have confessed, people are very tolerant. Jimmy says 'Mama, I was a bad boy'. She pats him on the head and forgives him. And they were sure that there was no confusing the new blade with the old.
>
> Sometime after these ads broke, I heard a yarn that tickled me. It seems that six brokers in Wall Street who were interested in Gillette stock came uptown after the ads broke and had dinner together. One fellow started to scold about me personally. This man Lambert, he ranted, is crazy. He will ruin the company. Just imagine admitting that a company had been all wrong! Then he asked each one at the table if he had by any chance seen the ad. It seems they had all seen it, but that was natural, they explained. They were interested in the stock, weren't they? Someone asked if

anyone there had bought any blades. With various excuses and apologies they all admitted that they had bought the new blades. The facts suddenly dawned on one of them and he spoke of it. The ad had 100 per cent attention value and had made a 100 per cent sale. Not a bad record. After a drink they decided not to tell their customers to sell their Gillette stock after all.

Lambert was already a rich man when he accepted the presidency of Gillette, and he worked there without a salary. It was the challenge which appealed to him. After he had restored the company's fortunes, he resigned and went back to his sailing yachts and estates. The thrill had gone. Many innovators know the feeling; like Lambert, they are only really happy if they can make a creative contribution to a business.

Yoram Globus

b. 1942

The 'Go-Glo' boys

Yoram Globus is one of two Israelis who, in 1979, decided to try their luck in Hollywood and who startled the movie industry with their audacious and innovative ideas. The other partner is his cousin, MENAHEM GOLAN (b. 1929), who changed his name from Globus to commemorate his country's military victory on the Golan Heights.

The entrepreneurial cousins, dubbed the 'Go-Glo' boys by Wall Street brokers, have always loved the cinema. As children in Israel, they spent hundreds of hours watching movies in a theatre owned by Yoram's father. Yoram later became a projectionist, while Menahem went off to study theatre direction at the Old Vic in London and eventually became one of Israel's foremost theatre directors. But Menahem decided that he would rather make films, and the two of them teamed up to produce *Sallah*, a comedy featuring Topol in his first movie. They had to sell their houses to raise the money. *Sallah* was a critical success, and received an Oscar nomination for best foreign film. Their company hit its commercial stride with another movie called *Lemon Popsicle* and, in the years that followed, they became the most successful studio in Israel.

Their dream, though, was to make 'American movies' with stars for a worldwide audience. They reckoned that they could do it at an average cost of $5–6 million – much less than the major studios were spending. So they went to Los Angeles and shopped around for an American company to buy. They found a small, ailing business called Cannon, which had been responsible for exploitation films with titles like *The Happy Hooker*. The only hitch was that they didn't have the money. They solved the problem in an ingenious way: they persuaded the company to let them take its films to Cannes and sell them to an international market, and then used the commission to acquire the business.

But Hollywood wasn't prepared to welcome the brash newcomers with open arms. 'The first two years were very difficult,' Globus later recalled. 'Nobody returned my phone calls. No agent, no actor. Believe me, we had some nights when we were really down and said, "Let's forget it and go back home." '

They didn't. Instead, they continued to produce movies in the old Cannon tradition – low-budget trash like *The Apple*, directed by Golan and described in a Cannon catalogue as 'a futuristic musical fantasy about the over-sexed, over-drugged, glamorized decadence of the music world in 1994'. It was certainly not art, but the films *were* cheap and, through aggressive international marketing, the cousins turned profits.

What made Cannon different as an American film-maker was the concept of pre-selling every film to foreign markets and ancillary markets (videotapes, videodiscs, TV and satellite transmissions) as soon as they had a script and a title. Globus told an interviewer in 1985 that by the time they started production they usually had guarantees of worldwide revenues exceeding the picture's budget, even if it flopped at the box office. That year, they produced more films than any other studio.

As production expanded, the cousins added another unconventional element to their formula for financial success. They made a concerted effort to acquire movie theatres. 'Theatrical exhibition is very important for the ancillary rights,' Globus said. 'When a picture has had exposure in the theatrical market, the value of the videocassette or cable or television is much higher.' It also put Cannon in an excellent position to ensure that its movies got released.

After making a good deal of money with action-packed quickies, dismissed by critics as 'Cannon fodder', they were in a position to sign up some of the big stars – Katharine Hepburn, Anthony Quinn, Charles Bronson, Julie Andrews, Sylvester Stallone. They also started to include better-quality movies in their output, like Franco Zeffirelli's *Otello*, starring Placido Domingo, and the much-acclaimed *Runaway Train*, which was nominated for two Academy Awards.

Norman Mailer, who was hired for Jean-Luc Godard's

Norman Mailer . . . praised them warmly. 'They're positive entrepreneurs,' he said. 'They're nineteenth-century spirits.'

version of *King Lear*, praised them warmly. 'They're positive entrepreneurs,' he said. 'They're nineteenth-century spirits.' According to Mailer, most people who had power in Hollywood got it by saying 'No'. The cousins were different: they preferred to say 'Yes' to interesting projects and then make them as cheaply as possible. Of course, he went on, it might get them into terrible trouble.

It did. The cousins became involved in box office fiascos like

John Derek's *Bolero* and Roman Polanski's *Pirates*, which cost $34 million to make and was hammered by the critics. Asked how it happened, Golan simply said: 'We all make mistakes.' There were others. By the end of 1986 the main problem appeared to be that, in their enthusiasm for new projects and acquisitions, they had over-stretched themselves financially. Despite their system of pre-selling, they had accumulated debts estimated at $600 million. To reduce it, they signed a deal with Warner Bros which cost them half their European cinemas; they also agreed to sell their Screen Entertainment library to Weintraub Entertainment. Meanwhile, the Securities and Exchange Commission had begun to scrutinize the company's accounting methods.

The movie business has always been what veteran actor Charlton Heston calls a 'crap game'. Public tastes are notoriously fickle and even the most experienced film-makers have had their share of disasters. It was perhaps inevitable, given the scale of their operations in the 1980s, that the 'Go-Glo' boys should discover that they, too, were not infallible – or invulnerable.

But no one would deny that they have made a formidable impact on the industry. They have helped to change the way Hollywood works. The practice of pre-selling has become widespread, and studios have become much more aware of the potential in overseas markets. They have also become more determined to eliminate waste and change attitudes. There is general agreement, nowadays, that costs got out of hand in the 1970s. Globus and Golan, the upstarts from Israel, showed that there was a better way.

Hetty Green

1834–1916

The Witch of Wall Street

Hetty Green was the first woman who made it big on Wall Street. When she started to play the New York Stock Exchange in the 1870s it was considered to be a place for males only. She soon demonstrated what nonsense that was. Her extraordinary skill (and eccentric parsimoniousness) made her the richest woman in the world; when she died she left $100 million, considerably more than the famous financier J. Pierpont Morgan.

She was born Henrietta Howland Robinson in New Bedford, Massachusetts. Her forebears were shipowners, and she had got her first taste of finance as a girl of eight by reading stock market news to her grandfather. She inherited several million dollars and in 1867 married Edward H. Green, who had made about a million of his own in the China trade. On their wedding day, the couple signed an agreement that each should remain independent of the other in all financial affairs. Eighteen years later, as if making good his wife's premonition, Green went broke, listing as his assets 'seven dollars and a gold watch'.

Hetty made her first killing on Wall Street by buying depreciated US government bonds right after the Civil War, when many investors feared that they would never be redeemed at full value. After that she specialized in railroad bonds and stocks, and engineered several spectacular coups by driving stocks up and down by heavy purchases or sales, sometimes bringing off a 'corner' in which traders who 'sold short' were trapped until she sold them shares at her own price.

Her secret of success, she always said, was to buy cheap and sell dear. This, of course, is not as easy as it sounds. One can lose money even on the best stocks if one gets the timing wrong. There are usually good reasons why some are cheap and others dear. The trick is to recognize the potential of a stock before anyone else does, or to spot a likely general trend. But you also have to know when to get out, because a paper profit is just that until you have the money in the bank: it may evaporate if you hang on too long. Many people have had the unnerving experience of watching a stock rise to dizzy levels and then plummet like a stone.

This is what happened to a lot of speculators in the panic of 1907. Hetty Green survived because, by some reason or instinct, she usually seemed to know when it was time to buy and to sell. The story has often been told how, one day in the spring of that year, she came home, her dress bulging with securities. She explained to a friend that she had just taken all her holdings out of the Knickerbocker Trust Company. 'If you have any money in that place,' she advised, 'get it out first thing tomorrow.' The friend asked why. 'The men in that bank are too good-looking,' Hetty replied. 'You mark my words.' A few months later, on 21 October, a run began on the Knickerbocker Bank and by noon it had closed its doors. That was the beginning of the panic of 1907.

Hetty had, by then, become well known for her incredible frugality. Despite her wealth, she lived in obscure and shabby boarding houses and invariably wore the same voluminous dress, originally black but turning slightly brown and green with age. Sewn inside her petticoat were many pockets, each large enough to hold the contents of a safe-deposit box. Every day she would travel by public bus or ferry to her Wall Street 'office', which was the vault of the Chemical National Bank. Here she would sit on the floor, clipping coupons, reading the financial news and receiving callers, among them some of Wall Street's most eminent figures.

She ate the cheapest foods in the cheapest restaurants, leaving no tip, or did her own cooking on a gas ring in her room.

She had an investment income of thousands of dollars a day, but haggled over the price of shoes. The manager of a Manhattan store once recalled the time when he commented to Hetty that her veil was torn. If she would come to his store, he said, he would give her one of the best veils in stock. 'Will you?' she said. 'That is nice of you.' He had forgotten about the incident when one morning an agitated assistant came to him, saying that Hetty Green was downstairs at the counter demanding a

'If you have any money in that place,' she advised, 'get it out first thing tomorrow. . . . The men in that bank are too good-looking.'

veil for nothing. He went down and had a salesgirl drape the best veil in stock over Hetty's battered hat. She was delighted. 'I wonder', she asked, 'if you have any skirts you could let me have at a reduced price?' The manager let her have one for fifty cents. She paid for it, and ever after told her friends that it was the best store in town to buy things at reasonable prices.

Her son Ned was the saddest victim of her parsimony. When he hurt his knee she dressed the boy in rags and took him to a New York doctor, begging treatment as a charity patient. When the doctor learned who she was and demanded payment, she took Ned away and never came back. Some years later the leg had to be amputated. But Hetty was not deliberately unkind – she just hated to spend money. She trained Ned carefully in business and when he was twenty-four gave him a small railroad in Texas, which he ran well. She had no further use of her husband after he went broke, but gave him enough to live in a genteel hotel.

In 1916 the old lady suffered a stroke brought on by a fierce argument with the cook in the home of a friend with whom Hetty was living. She was taken to the modern brownstone of her son where, while beridden for some weeks, she was looked after by nurses engaged and paid for by Ned. The nurses were instructed never to appear in their white uniforms, but to dress as servants, which were relatively inexpensive. Ned remarked that the appearance at her bedside of a white-uniformed nurse would have been sufficient to kill his mother on sight.

Hetty Green – the 'Witch of Wall Street', as the press dubbed her -- never took any interest in art, books, houses or any of the toys of the rich. She did not support any causes. The huge fortune she left to her son and daughter consisted entirely of what are called liquid assets.

One can only guess at the reasons for her unusual behaviour. Was it some deep-rooted feeling of insecurity which she couldn't shake off? Or was it simply love of money for its own sake? Her stock market expertise made her more than a match for the bulls and bears of Wall Street, but her main purpose in life seems to have been to make more and more millions. It was a sorry aspect of a truly fascinating character.

Andrew S. Hallidie

1836–1900

The folly that became a national monument

Andrew Hallidie is the Scotsman who gave San Francisco what today must surely rate as the most useful of any national monuments anywhere – the cable car. Until he came along, horses and wagons had to labour up the city's steep hills. But it was not humanitarian pity for horses that led to his development of the world's first cable car. He owned a San Francisco company that manufactured wire rope (cable), which had been invented by his father in 1835. Andrew thought it would be good business to have a device that would grip an underground cable and pull street cars up the hills.

On 1 August 1873 he and his backers gathered atop Nob Hill for the maiden run. The driver who had been hired for this historic occasion looked at the shiny new tracks disappearing into the summer fog, thought of the steep, steep hill below him,

'They turn corners almost at right angles, cross other lines and, for all I know, may run up the side of houses,' wrote Rudyard Kipling in 1889.

shook his head at the new-fangled contraption, and said 'No!' He wasn't the only one to express doubts: the cable car was known as 'Hallidie's folly'. So Hallidie himself got into the driver's seat. He navigated the car half a mile down a grade of 307 feet on Clay Street between Jones and Geary. He then turned it round on the Kearny Street turntable, and returned to the top of Nob Hill. That afternoon, on its first official, public trip, the tiny car was mobbed by eager riders.

The success of that first run led to the construction of 112 miles of track by 1880, conquering and linking all the major ups and downs of San Francisco. They sustained major damage in the 1906 earthquake, but the system was rebuilt. At one time, several dozen routes were operated by as many as eight private companies. Only three lines remain; they are now part of the City's Municipal Railway System. From time to time there have been attempts to scuttle them. In the late 1940s, cold-hearted city accountants decided they were no longer needed, but a Citizens' Committee to Save the Cable Cars rode to the rescue – and won. The importance of their victory was recognized in 1964, when the National Parks Service named Hallidie's folly a National Historic Landmark.

They did disappear for a while in the early 1980s so that the system could be overhauled, at a cost of $60 million. San Francisco's citizens and corporations raised $10 million, and assorted government agencies kicked in the rest.

Tourists, of course, love the funny little cars, which begin to run each day at 6 a.m. As the Hallidie Grip grabs the cable and the car lurches forward, you hear the sharp, distinctive sounds of this curious mechanism at work: the metallic clunk of wheel on rail, the whirl of the cable, the crisp tinkle of the bell. 'They turn corners almost at right angles, cross other lines and, for all I know, may run up the side of houses,' wrote Rudyard Kipling in 1889. Millions of other visitors have been equally amazed by their dexterity. There is now a Cable Car Museum, which is popular with tourists, at Washington and Mason Streets. Reopened in 1984 after extensive renovation, it has informative exhibits, cable car memorabilia, and an underground viewing room from which one can observe the huge sheaves – grooved wheels that guide the cables under the street. In the jet age, riding a San Francisco cable car is a delightful old-fashioned experience which one hopes will continue to be available for a long time to come.

Armand Hammer

b. 1898

Wheeler-dealer of East and West

Dr Armand Hammer made the first of several fortunes in an unusual way. Though an American, and a great believer in the merits of capitalism, he originally became rich in the Russia of Lenin and Stalin. Nikita Khrushchev, who was also intrigued by his ideas, once told the following story in a speech reported in *Pravda*:

> Hammer went to V. I. Lenin and said he had decided to seek a concession for the manufacture of pencils. V. I. Lenin looked at him with surprise and said: 'Why do you want a concession for the manufacture of pencils?
>
> 'Mr Lenin,' said Hammer, 'you have set a goal that everybody should learn to read and write and you haven't any pencils. Therefore, I will manufacture the pencils!'

He did just that. It was the Soviet Union's first pencil factory and he stayed in the business for nine years. But he used his Kremlin contacts to engineer numerous other deals – and later, back in America, he embarked on other successful ventures, notably in the oil business.

Hammer's father was a physician born in tsarist Russia, who emigrated to America and opened a drugstore. He struggled with mounting debts until his son took over the store and turned it into a money-maker. Armand had studied to be a doctor at Columbia University's College of Physicians. But business intrigued him and, looking for ways to expand the firm, he hit on a bold idea. Why not go back to his father's old country and see what he could sell? The market was huge, and there clearly was a need for everything. The Soviets, struggling to cope in the aftermath of the Revolution, appeared willing to hand out concessions to Westerners who offered to help. So he travelled to Moscow and managed to get an appointment with Lenin.

But pencils were only the start: he also had a go at operating an asbestos mine and at importing farm tractors. His principal problem was that the Soviet government – and everyone else – seemed to be short of cash. Very well, Hammer decided; there was always barter. He started to wheel and deal: in one celebrated coup he brought in a million tons of wheat from the United States, accepting payment in furs and caviar.

But Hammer was shrewd enough to get out while his luck held. He realized that in time the Russians would insist on making their own pencils, and that under Stalin life was completely unpredictable. Roubles were of no use in the West, so he put his money into one thing that he knew would have lasting value – tsarist treasures. He sold his factory to the government, which allowed him to take his collection home. Soon after returning to New York he opened an art gallery in Manhattan and wrote a book describing his quest for the Romanov heirlooms. It attracted a lot of publicity, and

His principal problem was that the Soviet government . . . seemed to be short of cash. Very well, Hammer decided; there was always barter. . . . In one celebrated coup he brought in a million tons of wheat from the United States, accepting payment in furs and caviar.

Hammer went on a tour around the country, selling pieces to wealthy Americans. Barter has since become a widely accepted method of trading with the Soviets, but the Kremlin nowadays guards its treasures more carefully – even if they did belong to the tsars.

With a substantial amount of money in the bank, Hammer turned his talents to other fields. He went into the whisky barrel business, using his Moscow contacts to buy staves for the barrels, and then bought an obscure brand of bourbon which he built into a top-seller. Schenley eventually bought him out for $6½ million. He also started to raise Aberdeen Angus cattle, and in 1954 sold his breeding herd for $1 million.

His next move took him into an altogether different game. He went to Los Angeles and invested in a struggling little oil company, Occidental Petroleum, which was drilling two wildcat wells. Within a year he had become the biggest stockholder and was made president. Over the next decade he built Occidental into a mammoth complex of oil, agricultural chemicals and other products, with an annual turnover of more than $660 million.

One of his biggest coups during this period was once again abroad – in Libya. When news of a major oil strike in that country reached the United States, Hammer went to see the government of King Idris and, beating more than a dozen rivals, won two valuable oil concessions. A key factor was his offer to put 5 per cent of Occidental's Libyan pre-tax profits into an agricultural project to turn the oasis of Kufra, the king's birthplace, into fertile, crop-producing land.

The Libyan deal made a lot of money for Occidental – until, suddenly, the king was toppled by a group of young army officers, who threatened to cancel foreign oil concessions and sharply raised the government's taxes. By then, however, Hammer had taken Occidental into other lucrative ventures, beyond oil. He became a prominent player on the merger scene, making skilful use of leverage and buying up other major enterprises. Even his unsuccessful bids yielded a substantial profit: he walked away with $18 million, for example, after a company he was trying to buy, Kern County Land, rushed into the arms of the Tenneco Corporation. As Kern's largest single stockholder he was in a position to thwart the merger, so Tenneco agreed to buy his shares for considerably more than he had paid.

Hammer went back to the USSR, on a visit, in 1961. The US government had made him an adviser on foreign trade, and this time he secured an appointment with first deputy premier Mikoyan. They chatted about the past, and Hammer told him what he had done since leaving Moscow. He showed Mikoyan a brochure which contained descriptions of his breeding bulls, and left it with him. The next day he had a telephone call from Khrushchev's office: the Soviet leader would like to see him. Khrushchev said he had seen the brochure and had been impressed; he now understood why American steaks were so good – US cattle were three times the size of Soviet livestock. He questioned Hammer about the American way of breeding prize bulls and vowed to bring his country's cattle up to US standards. At the end of their conversation, Khrushchev gave him a gift – a pencil engraved with a picture of the Kremlin.

Hugh Hefner

b. 1926

Playboy of the western world

Hugh Hefner was the first magazine publisher to exploit the male chauvinist's vision of the Good Life. When he launched *Playboy* in 1953, Hollywood still seemed to take the view that man wanted to identify with generals like Patton, gunfighters like Wyatt Earp, and swashbuckling adventurers who leaped from chandelier to chandelier in a never-ending quest to rescue damsels in distress. Movie moguls made vigorous use of the casting couch but insisted that their heroes and heroines should be above reproach; stories of their raunchy private lives were skilfully suppressed. Errol Flynn was allowed to kiss the heroine, but that was all. Hefner decided to rebel against this hypocrisy – and, as everyone knows, made a fortune in the process.

Hefner's father was an accountant who worked for a large corporation. He spent long hours at the office and had little time for his children. Hef, the older of two sons, produced his first 'newspaper' at the age of eight; it consisted of news and cartoons, all written and drawn by himself. Each issue was painstakingly typed out on an old Royal typewriter and sold by the young publisher, who knocked on doors in his neighbourhood offering copies at a penny apiece. He followed this with a school journal called *The Pepper*, and at fifteen he launched *Shudder Magazine* – a periodical with a circulation of one copy (the original). It was passed around by hand for his 'subscribers' to read. Hefner then spent two years in the army, and afterwards enrolled at the University of Illinois, where he promptly started another publication, a campus humour magazine called *The Shaft*.

But these were all amateur efforts, and Hefner was determined to have a proper magazine of his own. 'The only thing wrong with that dream', he said later, 'was money – I didn't have any.' He nevertheless conceived the idea of a picture magazine for and about the people of Chicago, and placed an advertisement in the *Chicago Tribune* offering printers the opportunity to go into partnership with him. Only one responded, and he wanted Hefner to pay for the paper and ink. Hef couldn't afford to do so, so he reluctantly decided that the project would have to be temporarily shelved. He also decided that the only way to get any money at all was to look for a steady job. But editorial jobs in publishing were few and far between, and he eventually became a copywriter for a men's fashion store, at night drawing cartoons which he sent out to newspapers and magazines. He was later hired by *Esquire* to

'The only reason I tried it was that I had no conception of the almost insurmountable difficulties and the odds against my success.'

write direct mail subscription copy, but when the head of his department refused to give him a $5 raise he quit.

Hefner had $600 of borrowed money when he decided to have a go at the men's magazine market (he pledged his furniture as collateral) and he spent most of that on the rights to reproduce colour photographs of Marilyn Monroe in the nude. He wrote a letter to the twenty-five largest news-stand wholesalers throughout the United States, outlining the contents of the magazine he had in mind, and the response encouraged him to press on. He formed a company, sold shares in it to relatives and friends, persuaded a printer to give him credit, bought second rights to articles, and put the first issue together on his kitchen table, naming it after a make of sports car then struggling to get into production.

Hefner was lucky: *Playboy* caught on at once. If it hadn't, he would almost certainly have been forced to give up. Recalling

Playboy *worked, he thought, 'because it was the right idea in the right place at the right time'. . . .* Playboy *offered recognizable signposts to the freedoms and fantasies of the new morality.*

those days, he later said: 'The only reason I tried it was that I had no conception of the almost insurmountable difficulties and the odds against my success. If I had known what I know now, I doubt if I would have even tried.' *Playboy* worked, he thought, 'because it was the right idea in the right place at the right time'.

It was the era of the post-war boom: young men had more cash than ever before, and they were demanding better lives with more access to fun and freedom. *Playboy* offered recognizable signposts to the freedoms and fantasies of the new morality. Hefner himself had, in the words of his long-time associate Victor Lownes, 'broken free of the trappings of bourgeois domesticity' and he set out to show, through his own highly publicized lifestyle, that dreams need not remain dreams. As soon as he could afford it he bought his own pleasure palace, where he held court surrounded by fawning acolytes and nubile creatures eager to make his every wish come true.

With the magazine a runaway success, Lownes suggested to him that a Playboy Club would 'fit in perfectly with the image we're trying to create'. Hef agreed, and the first club was opened in Chicago on 29 February 1960. The magazine was already using the Bunny symbol, but it was strictly male, with black bow-tie. It was one of Hef's girlfriends who suggested that the club waitresses should be 'dressed as rabbits'. He thought it a 'sexy notion' and a costume was devised, with collar, cuffs, a black bow-tie and bunny ears. Other clubs followed, and Hefner also moved into films, gambling and hotels.

The London gambling operation, run by Lownes, was phenomenally successful for some years. It helped Hefner to get a good price when he decided on a public flotation of Playboy Enterprises in 1971. During the next decade, gambling made a staggering fortune for the company. In 1980, it also applied for a casino licence in Atlantic City. But then disaster struck. The British police, prodded by some of Playboy's rivals, announced that it intended to object to the renewal of the London licence. The action was based on technicalities, but Hefner promptly fired Victor Lownes, who had done so much for him, and appointed a new chief executive, Admiral Sir John Treacher. Just what bearings the admiral had in a gaming casino was a mystery to everyone, but presumably Hef thought the court would be impressed by his title. They might have been, but Playboy lost the licence anyway. A bitter Lownes noted afterwards that no actions were ever taken against him or anyone in the company.

The loss of all those gambling millions was a severe blow to Hefner (and to his shareholders), especially as some of his other business activities were also doing far from well. Hotels and clubs were closed down, and in 1985 the 'rabbits' disappeared from the scene. The magazine itself continued to attract a substantial readership, but it faced strong competition from many imitators. Some went a good deal further than *Playboy*, leaving little to the imagination, and Hefner also had to compete with the proliferation of porn videos. There was not a lot he could do about it, because an equally raunchy approach would have got the magazine banned in many states and advertisers would have deserted him in large numbers.

In the 1950s *Playboy* had indeed been 'the right idea in the right place at the right time'. Hefner had seen the potential before anyone else, and had made a great deal of money out of it. Some of his magazine innovations, like the famous centre-fold of a busty girl coyly clad in a G-string, were a big hit when they were first revealed to a startled public. Another clever move was to add respectability to the magazine by publishing the work of serious novelists. But times change, and there are always people with new ideas. By the mid-1980s the whole concept of the 'Playboy' was looking curiously old-fashioned. Hefner himself was still ensconced in his own 'Magic Kingdom', a plush Californian mansion well protected by security guards. There, he continued to lead the kind of life promoted by his magazine: watching movies, playing poker and pinball machines, giving parties, and – well, you know what. One good idea had provided him with three decades of pleasure, which isn't a bad reward for an innovator.

Conrad Hilton

1887–1979

A chain of hotels around the world

Conrad Hilton, founder of the hotel chain that bears his name, originally wanted to be a banker. 'That', he told his mother as a young man, 'is the real ambition of my life. Some day, you wait and see. I'll have three or four banks all up and down the Rio Grande. You'll be proud of me.'

It nearly happened. He went to Cisco, a Texas cow town in the middle of an oil boom, and went straight from the railway station to the first bank he saw. It was for sale. The absentee owner wanted $75,000 for it. Hilton only had $5000, but he called a banker friend in El Paso, who said it sounded like a good deal and promised to put up the rest. But when he sent off a telegram – 'WILL BUY BANK' – the owner wired: 'PRICE RAISED. WILL NOT ACCEPT LESS THAN $80,000.' Hilton was furious. That night he stayed at a small hotel in town, and got talking to the man who ran it. He said he was doing good business, but felt he could make more money in the oil-fields. Hilton resolved, there and then, to buy the hotel instead. It was the start of a remarkable career which was to make him world-famous.

The two-storey Mobley Hotel wasn't much to look at – it was a convenient place to sleep, nothing more. When a friend came to inspect it, he was dismayed. '*That*', he said, 'is a hotel?' Hilton told him it was a cross between a flop-house and a goldmine. 'Just be glad the people around town have so much oil in their eyes they can't see it.' The friend was eventually persuaded to become the manager. But Hilton still had to complete the deal. He and the owner agreed on a price – $40,000 – and he began to put together his first buying group. An oil man and a rancher friend agreed to contribute $5000 each, and his mother mailed him a cheque for another $5000. He borrowed the rest from a local bank.

In his autobiography, *Be My Guest*, Hilton later said that 'I hadn't been in the hotel business five minutes before I knew this was *it*.' The Mobley was so busy that he and the manager had to sleep in the office – where, he said, he dreamed of 'Texas wearing a chain of Hilton hotels'.

During the next few months, he hit upon some basic principles for operating hotels. One was that you have to find out what is the best use of space; the manner in which waste space is unearthed and utilized can mean the difference between a plus and a minus in an operation. Another was that you have to build *esprit de corps*. He got all the employees together and told them that it was largely they who were responsible for whether the hotel guests were pleased and would ever come back. Hilton continued to do both for the rest of his life.

His second hotel was another unimpressive place, in Fort Worth. It was in bad shape, but it had sixty-eight rooms and he found that he could lease it for $25,000. He managed to raise the money (his mother was again among those who helped out) and brought in painters, carpenters and cleaners. He hired a manager, and the hotel was soon making useful profits.

The third hotel was in downtown Dallas. It was called the Waldorf, but the name was the only thing it had in common

When a friend came to inspect it, he was dismayed. 'That', *he said,* '*is a hotel?*' *Hilton told him it was a cross between a flop-house and a goldmine.*

with the famous establishment in New York which he was to buy many years later. It was a six-storey building with 150 rooms and a few baths; there was also a fifty-room annexe, without any baths at all. He bought the lease, and moved in as acting manager.

But his real ambition was to build a tall hotel, the newest of the new, with the name of Hilton on it. 'This time', he told his mother, 'I am really going big. And the first thing I'll need is to raise a million dollars.' A million was a lot of money in those days – for most people it still is. The way Hilton went about the task of fulfilling his ambition is a fascinating example of skilful wheeler-dealing.

He found the site he wanted, in the Dallas business district, and optioned it from the owner, a real estate man named George W. Loudermilk. He worked out that he could probably realize $100,000 on his own, one-tenth of what he needed, and get two-tenths more from his regular backers. But what was three-tenths of a million? And there was nothing to invest in at this point but a wild dream. If he raised the money and gave it to Loudermilk, he would have nothing left with which to erect the building.

His solution was to suggest that, instead of buying the land, he should lease it for ninety-nine years. 'I'm not Methuselah,' Loudermilk shouted. 'I won't *live* ninety-nine years.' But Hilton told him: 'If I don't pay, you get not only the land but the building.' When he had agreed to that, Hilton added: 'And I'd also like the lease to have a clause authorizing me to float a loan on the real estate.'

He got the deal, but he still needed the million. He put up $100,000 of his own, and a bank in St Louis agreed to lend him $500,000, to be paid in instalments as each storey of the building was finished, but with the understanding that at all times he must have enough cash on hand to finish the job or they would stop advancing money. He borrowed another $150,000 from the contractor, and wrote or talked to people whom he knew were interested in investing, telling them what he had to offer. The venture capital he needed came in very quickly, and in July 1924 the contractor started work on the first Hilton hotel.

But, as so often happens, everything cost more than he had expected. He began to run out of money when the hotel was only half finished, and the bank put on the pressure. So he went back to Loudermilk and said: 'Look, would you take over and finish the building and then lease the whole thing back to me?' This way, he stressed, Loudermilk would own both the land and the building. Loudermilk indignantly rejected the idea, but later gave in. In August 1925 the Dallas Hilton opened with great ceremony; it was an instant success.

Conrad Hilton went on to buy more hotels, not only in Texas but also in other parts of the United States. He organized Hilton Hotels Inc. to consolidate all the properties in one group. But when the stock market crashed in 1929 he once again found himself in deep trouble. Hotel occupancy dropped sharply, and so did his revenues. It became increasingly difficult to meet all the operating expenses *and* to pay interests on the loans. He bought some time by borrowing $300,000 from the American Life Insurance Company in Galveston, putting up the Hilton Hotels stock as security. But the worst was yet to come. When the $300,000 was gone, and he could not meet the payments, the insurance company took over the hotels.

It was a bleak moment, but what happened next restored some of his faith in himself. The family which controlled American Life offered him back the management of the hotels together with a flock of very sick ones of their own. They suggested merging the lot into the National Hotel Company, in which he would be one-third owner and general manager. He secured a contract which stipulated that, if they should fall out, they would partition the hotels on the same basis, two-thirds and one-third. They did fall out, eventually, and he managed to regain some of his hotels. When the Depression ended, he embarked on a new period of expansion; as before, he formed buying groups to acquire properties like the Sir Francis Drake in San Francisco.

Hilton always said that 'To accomplish big things, you must first dream big dreams . . . without this master plan, you have nothing.' His dream, still, was to have a great Hilton hotels chain. In the years that followed he bought a number of

He got all the employees together and told them that it was largely they who were responsible for whether the hotel guests were pleased and would ever come back.

properties, including the Roosevelt in New York and, in 1943, the Plaza, one of the world's leading society hangouts. He also married the tempestuous Zsa Zsa Gabor. Finally, he got a chance to get his hands on the greatest of them all – the Waldorf in New York. His board of directors was firmly opposed to the idea, and as president of the Hilton Hotels Corporation he couldn't buy without their approval. But he *could* do what he had done thirty years earlier in Cisco – he could put up his personal money and form a buying group to raise the rest. He did just that, and when the chips were down the board agreed to participate in the syndicate. They told him: 'Now you have gone this far, this hotel is going to belong to the Hilton Hotels Corporation.'

Around the same time, he also embarked on what he later called 'the fourth and, in many ways, most satisfying phase of my inn-keeping'. This was the creation of Hilton hotels *outside* the USA. The government urged him on, taking the view that it would help to promote international goodwill and bring American dollars into the economies of countries that needed help. But Hilton did not need much prompting: he recognized that travel was growing rapidly, and he liked the notion of having his name on hotels all around the world.

The Puerto Rico Industrial Company, a government agency, had written to half a dozen American hoteliers asking if they were interested in operating a hotel in San Juan. Hilton replied in Spanish, expressing enthusiasm and outlining a formula which set the pattern for what was to become a big international chain. The company would not only have to build the hotel, but also furnish and equip it. Hilton would provide consultants to help with all this, and would then come in with operating capital, managerial controls and techniques, and extensive worldwide sales promotion. His group would run the hotel under a long-term percentage rental agreement with renewal options, two-thirds of the gross operating profits to go to the owners and one-third to Hilton Hotels. He would also hire Puerto Ricans to form a large percentage of the staff and provide on-the-job training in the USA, so that their own people could learn the techniques of modern hotel management.

They wrote back at once accepting the terms. But, again, Hilton's directors were reluctant to go along with him. They felt the overseas market was too risky. When he persisted, they suggested that he should set up his own corporation, with its own board of directors. They would provide limited amounts of money. Thus Hilton International Inc. was born. Its slogan was 'World Peace through International Trade and Travel'. The San Juan project went ahead, and Hilton hotels subsequently opened in many other cities.

Hilton made one other big American deal before his death at an advanced age. He bought the Statler hotels group for $110 million, which at the time was reckoned to be the biggest single real estate transaction in US history.

Robert Holmes a'Court

b. 1938

The successful loser

Like the United States, Australia is a country which likes to make heroes out of its winners. Robert Holmes a'Court was one of the first Australian entrepreneurs who showed that you can also make money by losing. When, in 1979, he failed to win control of Ansett, one of the country's two internal airlines, he sold his share stake to RUPERT MURDOCH and cleared a profit of A$10 million. He repeated the feat in 1981, making A$15 million from an unsuccessful bid for Elder's, the Adelaide finance group.

Holmes a'Court was born in Johannesburg, South Africa, and inherited his chivalric name from a line of nineteenth-century British landowners. His father, the younger son of a younger son, was a farmer in Rhodesia. In the 1950s the family moved to New Zealand. Robert was sent to law school in Perth, and has remained in Australia ever since.

Not long after he qualified, he started his own law practice, employing his wife and mother as office staff. He gained clients by offering cut rates and a speedier service. The going rate for incorporating a company was A$200 and it took two weeks. Holmes a'Court did it in a day for A$75. When the Law Society wrote to him, complaining about his charges, he replied: 'I am only in my first year of practice. I am earning more than the Chief Justice, and you tell me that I am under-charging!'

In 1970 he found himself acting as legal adviser in the affairs of a textile firm, WA Worsted and Woollen Mills, which had run into serious financial problems. He brought control for A$75,000 (most of which he borrowed from his bank manager), and persuaded the state government to write off its loans rather than see the town's main source of employment close down. Perth was soon buzzing with rumours that he planned to use the company for something quite different from making blankets. The Australian stock exchanges were in the middle of a frenzy that had accompanied the nickel boom. Small, ailing companies were being taken over because they had a stock exchange listing and were then being used by the smart operators to sell the punters shares in mineral prospects. Without doing a thing, Holmes a'Court saw his WA Woollen Mills shares, worth only 10 cents two months earlier, move to A$1.75. No one was surprised, therefore, when Holmes a'Court announced that he was, indeed, going into mining. He bought some mineral rights and used the excitement generated by the deal to place one million WA Woollen Mills shares on the market at A$1.50 through a firm of Sydney stockbrokers.

Holmes a'Court had made his first million from business dealings, but he still didn't think of himself primarily as a businessman. 'I saw my venture into business with WA Woollen as a temporary thing,' he recalled later. 'I planned to return to law. Thinking back on it, what is extraordinary is the lack of purpose and intent I had. So much happened by accident.' The Perth business establishment took a different view: they regarded him as a charming but devious entrepreneur who had every intention of becoming very big. It was an accurate judgment.

Left Robert Maxwell, the Czech refugee who became a powerful British publisher and MP. *Below* Rupert Murdoch, the Australian press baron whose activities have spread to Britain. *Below left* Murdoch's fellow Australian, former lawyer Robert Holmes a'Court. *Bottom of page* Agent to the sports superstars, Mark MacCormack, with Gina Swainson (Miss World) and Carolyn Seaward (Miss UK) in London, 1980.

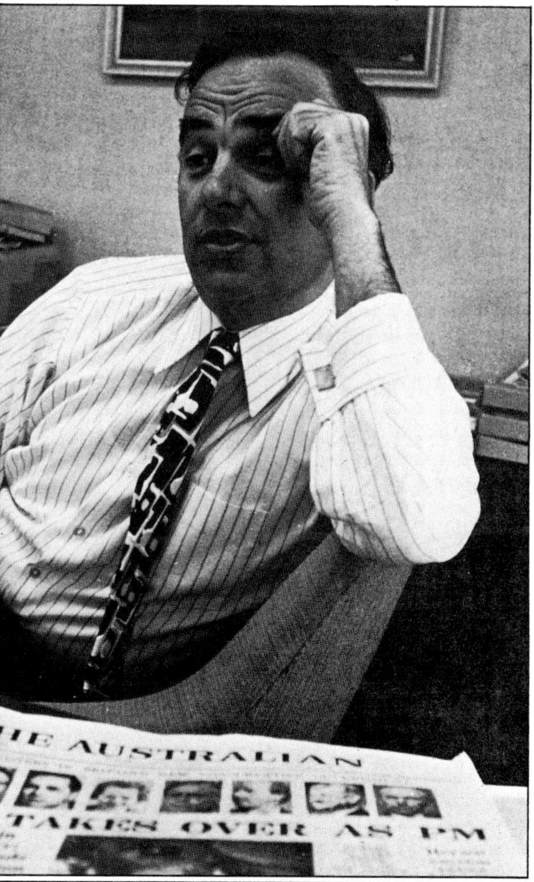

Top left Gilbert Trigano, the ex-actor who set up Club Med for sun-lovers. *Top right* Billy Butlin's holiday camps were intended to offer holidays with built-in entertainment for ordinary families. *Above* Walt Disney with his most famous creation *Left* King of today's musical theatre, Andrew Lloyd Webber , bottom of photograph, with his wife, Sara Brightman, and Michael Crawford – stars of *The Phantom of the Opera*.

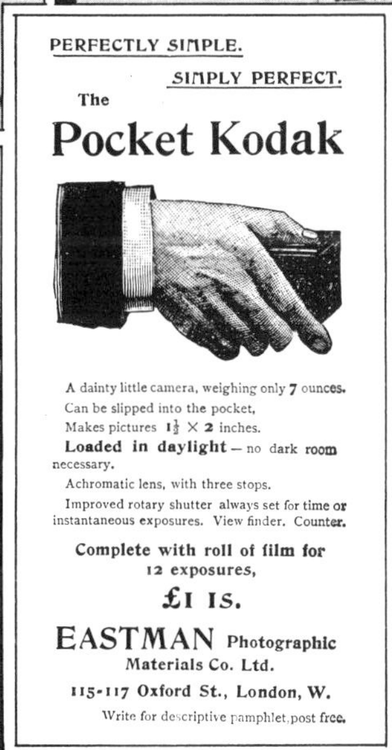
PERFECTLY SIMPLE.
SIMPLY PERFECT.
The
Pocket Kodak
A dainty little camera, weighing only 7 ounces.
Can be slipped into the pocket,
Makes pictures 1½ × 2 inches.
Loaded in daylight — no dark room necessary.
Achromatic lens, with three stops.
Improved rotary shutter always set for time or instantaneous exposures. View finder. Counter.
Complete with roll of film for 12 exposures,
£1 1s.
EASTMAN Photographic Materials Co. Ltd.
115-117 Oxford St., London, W.
Write for descriptive pamphlet, post free.

Top left An early Thomas Cook's office in Jerusalem. *Top right* What Cook did in the nineteenth century, Freddie Laker did for air travel in the twentieth. *Left* Another entrepreneur of the air and expert self-publicist, Richard Branson started his career in pop music. *Above* Charles Eastman's Kodak brought photography to the man in the street.

THIS PAGE *Top left* Lee Iacocca, supersalesman of the US auto industry. *Top right* Gianni Agnelli, head of Italy's Fiat. *Above* Andrew Hallidie's cable cars revolutionized San Francisco. *Right* George Mortimer Pullman brought luxury and comfort to the railroads.

OPPOSITE *Top left* Louis B. Mayer, creator of the Hollywood star system, with Gene Kelly. *Top right* Aristotle Onassis, whose courage to take risks made him a multimillionaire shipowner. *Below* Henry Ford with his son in a Model F in 1904.

Above left Terence Conran brought uncluttered simplicity to British homes in the sixties. *Above centre* Maurice (left) and Charles Saatchi have rapidly swept to the forefront of the UK advertising world. *Above right* Anita Roddick's return to natural ingredients in cosmetics exactly caught the spirit of the seventies. *Right* Andy Warhol, pop artist, entrepreneur, publicist and salesman *par excellence*.

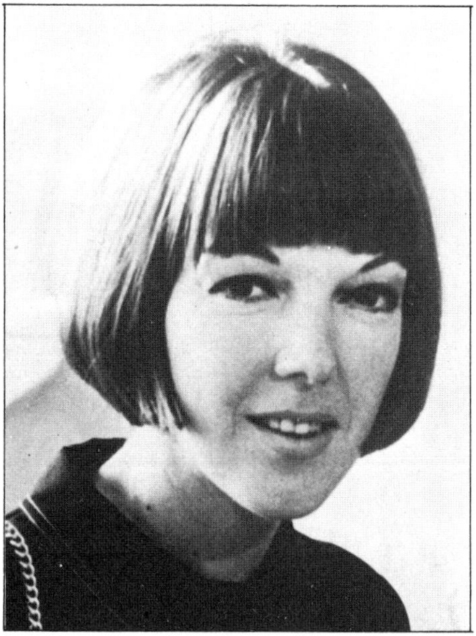

'op of page Mary Quant, with her Vidal
›assoon hairdo and mini-skirts, set a new
tyle for the young in the sixties. *Above* Laura
ıshley found her inspiration in the fashions
f the past. *Right* In the twenties Coco Chanel
ıtroduced women to revolutionary soft, fluid
nes and inexpensive costume jewellery.

Above Milton Friedman, guru of the economic doctrine of monetarism. *Right* Helena Rubinstein, founder of a great cosmetics empire at the beginning of the century. *Below left* Hugh Hefner enjoys his Playboy image. *Below right* Bernie Cornfeld, the mutual funds wizard, appreciates some of the pleasures of life.

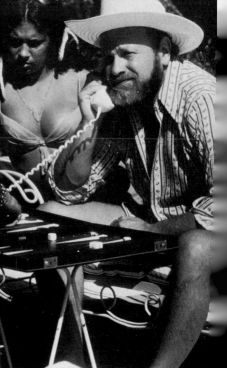

Holmes a'Court achieved his next exponential expansion by using techniques that were familiar to everyone who had bothered to study the ways of Wall Street, like the 'leveraged buy-out'. This was the way he bought Bell Brothers, a transport company which leased many of the giant earth-moving machines used in the enormous open-cast ore mines in Western Australia. Bell Brothers had once been a high-priced stock, but the business had fallen on hard times and the total value of the shares on the Perth stock exchange was less than the value of all the company's assets. Holmes a'Court saw it as something he could exploit. He didn't have the money to buy Bell's shares but went to his bankers and put to them what was, for that time, an extraordinary proposition. Would they lend him the money to buy Bell Brothers? He had no security himself to cover the loan, but, he said, would the bank accept Bell's assets as security for the loan? But, said the bankers, you don't own Bell's assets. Ah, said Holmes a'Court, but I will if you lend me the money to buy them. The bankers saw the merits of his argument and were impressed: here, obviously, was a young man who would go far.

His bid was successful, and Bell became the base for his future operations. In the years that followed he bid for a number of well-known Australian companies, including

---

'Business is Darwinism – only the fittest survive.'

Ansett, Elder's, EMU Wine and Griffin Coal. On each occasion he had to announce that his takeover plans had been frustrated and that he had been forced to sell out those shares he had acquired – at a handsome profit. But not all his activities ended in what, I suppose, should be called successful failure. Some of the bids were accepted, and by the early 1980s he had interests in many different fields – transport, engineering, oil and minerals, textiles, hotels, television and newspapers.

When I first met him in his Perth office towards the end of 1980, he had just decided to launch a new weekly paper, the *Perth Western Mail*. Knowing his track record, I had expected to find a strong, aggressive personality. The man who greeted me was a tall, languid intellectual who talked about his life and ambitions in a voice so soft that it was hard to catch some of the things he was saying. Behind his desk were the layouts of the paper, pasted up on boards, and he outlined the contents of the first issue. I thought he was just another millionaire with a new toy: I failed to recognize that the relaxed manner and soft voice concealed a sharp business brain and steely determination.

Others made the same mistake when he quietly built up a stake in Associated Communications Corporation, a British entertainment empire created by the flamboyant Lord Grade. ACC had run into financial difficulties, based chiefly on Grade's involvement in disastrous film projects like *Raise the Titanic*. Holmes a'Court pounced at the right moment and gained control. He has since made headlines with a series of other spectacular deals.

Holmes a'Court is a planner, a financial strategist (and keen chess player) who looks for openings, works out fallback positions for every contingency, and proceeds methodically from one stage to the next. He takes risks, but they are calculated risks. He thinks that the only kind of power worth having is economic power, and that the key to it is almost unlimited access to credit, made possible by an impressive track record and bold schemes. He insists that, if he were wiped out tomorrow, he could do it all over again. All he would need, he claims, would be a stake of $20,000 and he would turn it into half a million within six months. How? 'If you have to ask me that, there is no point in my telling you.' He is a firm believer in the theory of natural selection. 'Business', he says, 'is Darwinism – only the fittest survive.'

Soichiro Honda

b. 1906

'Supply creates its own demand'

Although he came from a very different culture, Soichiro Honda had much in common with HENRY FORD. He, too, was a small-town boy with an intuitive mechanical genius who created a business empire that still bears his name. He also shared Ford's disdain for formal education.

'I am not impressed by diplomas,' Honda told me when I interviewed him in Tokyo in 1968.

> They don't do the work. I went to a technical high school, but was dismissed. I was twenty-eight when I joined, and I had already held down a job. I attended only the classes I wanted to go to. Other students memorized the lessons, but I compared them with my practical experience. My marks were not as good as those of others, and I didn't take the final examination. The principal called me in and said I have to leave. I told him that I didn't want a diploma. They had less value than a cinema ticket. A ticket at least guaranteed that you would get in. A diploma guaranteed nothing.

The son of a blacksmith, Honda was fascinated by mechanical things almost as soon as he could walk. Impatient and ambitious, he left school at sixteen to become an apprentice in an auto repair shop. He later devoted much time and effort to the technique of casting, in an attempt to make a piston ring. He went to the technical high school primarily because he hoped he might learn something to help him in this endeavour.

Within a year of being asked to leave, he succeeded in manufacturing identifiably sound and functional devices. After a slow start, he gained Toyota's financial support. During

World War II he invented machinery for automatic piston ring manufacture and automatic planing for aircraft propellers, allowing relatively untrained women to produce these goods as the men went off to battle. He even managed to find uses for the aluminium wing tanks that American planes dropped while bombing his home town. 'Truman's gifts,' he called them. But he lost two factories to fire bombs, and after the surrender he decided to break away from Toyota. He sold what was left of his piston ring business for $125,000 and looked around for new challenges. His next step was eventually to lead to worldwide fame, though he did not know it at the time.

Honda's car had been immobilized by the fuel shortage, along with many others, which made it difficult to get around. He solved the problem by the novel device of attaching a motor to a bicycle. His neighbours were impressed enough to ask him to make more. Using a small gasoline engine which had been used for electrical generators during the war, he contrived a makeshift motorbike. When the surplus engines ran out, he decided to build motors himself. Faced with government controls on gasoline and restrictions on the manufacture of gasoline-using machines, he built a motor that ran on pine resin, which he recalled had been used as a substitute for aircraft fuel towards the end of the war. This innovation, based on a temporary problem, was the start of what later grew into the world's leading motorcycle company.

With the income from his contraptions, he set out to design and manufacture a real motorcycle, which he called the Dream. There was not yet a market for such a machine, but as he said later: 'We do not make something because the demand, the market, is there. With our technology we can create demand, we can create the market. Supply creates its own demand.'

The Dream was a sleek and powerful motorcycle with a four-cycle engine. Honda hired an experienced businessman, Takeo Fujisawa, to look after sales and the business side generally. Fujisawa wrote a letter to all the eighteen thousand bicycle shops in Japan. Five thousand dealers, who came to make up one of Japan's first and largest distribution networks, responded favourably. But Honda recognized that his Dream appealed only to a limited section of what was potentially a huge market: he would have to come up with something likely to command a more popular following. In 1952, a year after the launch of the Dream, he introduced a small, cheap, and efficient Cub engine that ran either on Honda's red-and-white frame or clipped conveniently on to a bicycle. It was a tremendous success.

He went on to produce the Super-Cub, which combined the power and excitement of big machines with the convenience and efficiency of scooters. It was built in his own modern factory, priced well below the competition, and advertised to a mass market. ('You meet the nicest people on a Honda'.) By the 1960s the company was exportig motorcycles all over the world, decimating the competition and dominating the industry.

It then began building cars. This did not suit the plans of MITI (the Ministry of International Trade and Industry, a sort of super-agency that plays a major role in Japan), which wanted to mould the auto industry into an international force and saw no room for Honda. He defied MITI and spent several years making a succession of cars that were, for the most part, forgettable and not very well received. But he kept on trying. 'Success', he later told a graduating class at Michigan Technology University, 'can be achieved only through repeated failure and introspection. In fact, success represents 1 per cent of your work which results only from the 99 per cent that is called failure.' In less than twenty years, the company's annual auto production went from twenty thousand cars to over a million.

From the beginning, Honda ran his business in his own special way. He hired young people and gave them responsibility immediately. He was contemptuous of the *gakkubatsu*, the old-boy network of university graduates, and scorned the *zaibatsu*, the industrial monoliths like Kawasaki and Mitsubishi. In the west Honda would have been considered a maverick; by Japanese standards, he was a radical.

He told me, in that interview, that he hated the Japanese seniority system, under which promotion is governed by length of service rather than merit. 'I promote by ability,' he said. 'Many people take pride in saying, at their retirement ceremony, that they got through their working lives without making mistakes. I prefer them to say that they made many errors, but always tried to advance. People who never made

'This company has grown to today's dimensions because it had no traditions.'

mistakes simply did what their boss told them to do. They are not the kind they want.'

What qualities did he look for? 'First,' he said, 'I try to find out what a man is good at, and whether he has ideas of his own. Then I assess whether he can get along with others. A man must have self-confidence, but he must be modest enough to learn from others.' And the secret of his own success? 'Imagination, resourcefulness, fresh ideas, sound theories, and economy of time. Life is based on seeing, listening, and experimenting. But experimenting is the most important. This company has grown to today's dimensions because it had no traditions.'

Japan, he went on, had done well out of losing the war.

> We'd never have the freedom we have now. I'd never have been allowed to get where I have got. With everything flattened, we could start from scratch, plan from the word go, and think big. You can see it in Tokyo to this day: the blitzed areas are booming, but those which escaped are backward. I love this new freedom. It allows me to go down to the shop floor. I couldn't bear sitting in the presidential suite, as I should have had to do in an old-fashioned firm, supposing I had risen to the top.

Honda rarely appeared at his own office. He much preferred working among the hundreds of technicians employed on basic research. The actual running of the business was left to bankers and accountants. 'Every man', Honda said, 'should concentrate on the things he can do best.'

When we met, at the company's research centre on the outskirts of Tokyo, he was wearing grease-stained overalls. He was a small man with rosy cheeks, a healthy tan and a mouthful of gold teeth. He laughed a lot, and generally seemed to be enjoying life. Wealth, he told me, had given him the freedom to do what he wanted to do – which, in his case, meant experimenting with new ideas. He didn't get much time for leisure, and he didn't have a yacht or anything like that. 'I have three cars – a Lotus Elite, a Fiat and a Honda sports car. But I drive them myself.' My house? 'Yes, it's large and luxurious. When I go abroad I get invited to a lot of big houses, and I have to have somewhere to entertain people who come to Tokyo.'

I asked him what advice he would give to his sons. 'Simply to do what they would like to do. One must be happy at work. That's the most important thing of all.'

On the wall of the small room where we talked was a large notice headed 'Management Policy'. It listed five points: proceed always with ambition and youthfulness; respect sound theory, develop fresh ideas and make the most effective use of time; enjoy your work and always brighten your working atmosphere; strive constantly for a harmonious flow of work;

'One must be happy at work. That's the most important thing of all.'

be ever mindful of the value of research and endeavour.

Soichiro Honda and Takeo Fujisawa retired on the company's twenty-fifth anniversary in 1973. Neither man was remotely approaching his dotage, and their departure was unusual in a nation accustomed to a gerontocracy. But Honda had been held back by his youth in the early days and he wasn't about to place the same obstacle before others. The company was left to the younger generation, men considered middle-management at other Japanese firms. Honda's successor, Kiyoshi Kawashima, was forty-three; when he retired, ten years later, another young man, Tadashi Kune, stepped in.

Howard Hughes

1905–74

The business hero turned eccentric

Howard Hughes is chiefly remembered for his eccentric behaviour in old age, but he was also an innovative businessman who turned his inheritance – estimated at $500,000 – into one of the greatest fortunes in America. His father was an oil wildcatter who developed a new kind of drilling bit, one which could cut through hard rock far beneath the earth's surface and thus open up huge reservoirs of oil which had so far been unattainable. He started a business to manufacture and lease it. When Hughes Senior died, he left three-quarters of the shares to his son, then only eighteen.

Howard had been a mediocre student at school, and his relatives thought that he should let his stock be handled by some kind of voting trust until he was twenty-one. But the young man, it soon appeared, was in a hurry. He went to court and argued that he was competent to vote his own shares. The judge found in his favour, but felt that he had to add a word of warning. 'I would like to suggest', he said, 'that you find older men to help you carry the burden of your new responsibility for a few years. Your education should not stop here. You should go back to college.' Hughes nodded politely, but he had no intention of going back into any classroom. He was impatient to try himself against the real world.

During the next few years he not only expanded his father's company and bought out his relatives' shares, but also went into the movie business. He invested in Hollywood companies of various kinds, including a production studio, a lab that was experimenting with colour film, and another that was trying to develop talkies. He made several movies, including a costly epic called *Hell's Angels*, which dealt with aerial combat in World War I. By the time he was twenty-five his net worth was conservatively estimated at $20 million.

Hughes next turned his attention to an entirely different field. While filming *Hell's Angels* he had become fascinated by aeroplanes. Without saying a word to any of his associates, he learned to fly and, using a false name, got himself a job as co-pilot with a small airline in Texas. On his return, he bought himself a private plane and established a small service and repair shop in California. He spent a lot of time tinkering with a succession of planes, and the service shop rapidly evolved into a rebuilding plant. Flying his own aircraft, Hughes began to win air races. A rebuilt Lockheed, with Hughes at the controls, went around the world and made headlines in 1938. Other owners asked him to do work on their planes, and the business eventually became the Hughes Aircraft Company.

He now began to look around the airline industry for a possible investment. The industry was young and not in good shape. But Hughes was convinced that somebody, some day, would make a lot of money from an international airline service. So for a sum reputed to be around $12 million he bought control of a small company called Transcontinental and Western Airline. He later changed its name to Trans World, but kept the initials – TWA.

His various ventures kept him very busy in the years that followed. He found good people to help him, but he made all the important decisions. More movies followed, including *The Outlaw*, a controversial but highly successful film starring Jane Russell, who had been a minor photographer's model until Hughes spotted her and turned the buxom young lady into a star. Hughes Tool, the original company, continued to grow, while the aircraft company gained useful defence contracts. TWA, however, had a hard time – but Hughes refused to give up. When he finally sold his stock in 1966 he received more than half a billion dollars.

Three major enterprises would have been enough for any other man, but they were not enough for Hughes. In the late 1940s he abruptly plunged into yet another new business – electronics. He founded a company which went after government contracts to

---

The industry was young and not in good shape. But Hughes was convinced that somebody, some day, would make a lot of money from an international airline service.

---

develop weapon-aiming devices, radar, missile-guidance systems and space gadgets of all kinds. By the middle of the 1950s its sales were running at the rate of $500 million a year.

By then Hughes had also taken a fancy to Las Vegas – that garish playground in the Nevada desert which nowadays calls itself 'the entertainment capital of the world'. Using his vast wealth he began buying hotels, gambling casinos and large tracts of real estate in and around the city. It turned out to be one of the shrewdest moves of all. With his help, Las Vegas grew to be an impressive money-making machine. At one time it had simply been a railway watering-stop. When Hughes got there, it had already become a magnet for gamblers from all over the United States. But its best years were yet to come – by the 1970s it was attracting 9 million visitors a year and earning more than any other 'resort' in the world. People came to try their luck, but most of them lost more money than they made: it was, and still is, an El Dorado for casino owners.

Sadly, Hughes's behaviour became increasingly bizarre. He had always been a maverick, with an open contempt for the formal structures of corporate life. From an early stage he had conducted his business from public telephones and hotel rooms – wherever he happened to be. His associates seldom knew where he was on a given day. Now he became a recluse: he shut himself away in hotel rooms, failed to keep appointments and often did not return telephone calls for weeks. His managers couldn't get him to make decisions, and many key people decided to leave. His empire started to fall apart.

The media was fascinated: here was one of the richest men in America, an enormously successful entrepreneur, who had apparently gone quite mad. Rumours circulated about his strange appearance. He looked, it was said, like a crone – painfully thin, with hair down to his waist, a withered face and immensely long fingernails. But so little was known about him at that stage that author Clifford Irving decided he could risk writing a fake 'official biography'. Hughes exposed him in a telephone call.

Howard Hughes was a complex man: intelligent, restless, bold, hard-working, iconoclastic. He had a huge range of interests – and he made them pay. Despite his sorry end, he was an authentic American business hero.

Lee Iacocca

b. 1924

'If you can find a better car, buy it'

Lee Iacocca is known to millions of people around the world through his autobiography, called simply *Iacocca*. It is the biggest-selling book ever written by a businessman (with the help of a professional author). In the United States it has made him an industrial folk hero, a corporate capitalist with populist appeal, a guy (one of his favourite words) who tells it like it is. Everyone knows about his famous feud with Henry Ford II, who fired him, and everyone knows how he became chairman of Chrysler and fought back.

The first HENRY FORD personified the engineer; ALFRED SLOAN of General Motors was the great manager; Lee Iacocca has always been the super-salesman. Long before the book was published, he became a celebrity by appealing in a series of nationwide television commercials extolling the merits of Chrysler products. 'I am not asking you to buy one of our cars on faith,' he said. 'I'm asking you to compare.' Or, more aggressively, 'You can go with Chrysler, or you can go with someone else – and take your chances.' Then came the quintessential Iacocca tag-line, the slightly belligerent ad that turned the promise of automotive quality into a dare. 'If you can find a better car,' he barked, 'buy it.' It was a novel approach to salesmanship, but it worked.

Iacocca was born and raised in Allentown, Pennsylvania. His father was an Italian immigrant who had arrived in the United States in 1902 at the age of twelve. Iacocca says he was 'a restless and inventive man who was always trying new things'; he taught his son that in America you could become anything you wanted to be, if you wanted it badly enough and were willing to work for it.

Lee took an engineering degree at Lehigh University and then spent a year at Princeton. His goal was to get a job at Ford, and he started in Detroit in 1946 as a management trainee. But he soon lost interest in engineering; he was eager to be where he felt the real action was – marketing or sales. During the next nine years he hustled up the regional sales ranks. Finally, weeks after his marriage in 1956, Iacocca was called back to headquarters as marketing manager under the chief 'whizz-kid', Ford vice-president Robert McNamara, who later became Defence Secretary in the Kennedy administration. One of Iacocca's innovations, in 1956, was a highly successful $56-a-month credit plan for Ford buyers, which he marketed under the slogan '56 for 56'.

In 1960, at the age of thirty-six, he took over as head of the Ford car division. In his book he says that the years he spent in this job were the happiest period of his life. He introduced various management techniques, including a quarterly review system for executives, but he is primarily remembered for the marketing skills he displayed at the time.

When he launched the Mustang in 1964 he promoted it up to the hilt. The newspapers and the television networks were

The first Henry Ford personified the engineer; Alfred Sloan of General Motors was the great manager; Lee Iacocca has always been the super-salesman.

blanketed with Mustang ads. A hundred members of the press were invited to take part in a giant seventy-car Mustang rally from New York to Dearborn. The car was displayed in fifteen of the country's busiest airports and in the lobbies of two hundred Holiday Inns from coast to coast. At the University of Michigan football games the company contracted for several acres of space in the parking lot and put up huge signs that said 'Mustang Coral'. And millions of mail-order shots were sent to small car-owners across the country. *Time* and *Newsweek* both featured the car and its corporate patron, Lee Iacocca, on their covers. Iacocca, *Time* declared, was 'the hottest young man in Detroit', brilliant, 'an ingenious automotive merchandising expert'.

The car had a special appeal to the youth market, and was a tremendous hit. Iacocca was promoted to vice-president of the corporate and truck group, which put him in charge of the planning, production and marketing of all cars and trucks in both the Ford and Lincoln-Mercury divisions. The Lincoln-Mercury products were regarded as unexciting, and Iacocca got to work on new models. In 1967 he launched a new luxury sports car, the Cougar, with typical showbiz flair. Dealers were invited to sail to the Caribbean island of St Thomas, where after a meal on a beach at sunset a World War II amphibious landing cract thrashed ashore and lowered its ramp. Out on to the sand popped a brand-new white Cougar driven by singer Vic Damone, who proceeded to croon. Like the Mustang, it was an immediate success. Other new cars also did well, and in 1970 Iacocca became president of Ford.

His first move as president did not exactly make him popular: he convened a meeting with top managers to discuss how to cut costs. He also instituted a programme which he called 'Shuck the losers'. Managers, he said, had three years either to make their departments profitable or to sell them off. He ended up closing nearly twenty major losers in the early 1970s. But he also launched new products, notably a small, fuel-efficient car for the European market, the Fiesta. He went to Japan and made a deal with SOICHIRO HONDA; the Japanese company agreed to supply a transmission and an engine in a box, ready to drop into any car Ford wanted to make. But when he returned to Detroit, Henry Ford vetoed the idea. Other arguments followed, and in 1978 Iacocca was demoted and then fired.

The company had just completed the two best years in its history, so it seemed an odd decision. According to Iacocca, the only reason Henry gave was that 'sometimes you just don't like somebody'. Ford later made it clear that there was more to it than that, but there obviously was a personality conflict: Iacocca was probably right in assuming that the grandson of the founder resented the prominence that his subordinate had achieved.

In the book Ford is depicted as paranoid, vulgar, personally extravagant at the company's expense, cruel and sexist. But Iacocca himself clearly is not without his faults: executives who worked for him at Ford, and later at Chrysler, have called him intimidating, unmerciful, arrogant, ruthless and opportunistic. Whatever the truth, there is no doubt that he made a triumphant comeback as head of Chrysler.

His settlement at Ford included $1.5 million in severance

pay, but there was a clause which stipulated that he would lose the money if he worked for another car company. The Chrysler board said they would pay him that amount if he agreed to join them. He soon learned why: the company was in deep trouble. The day he took over, in September 1979, it announced a third-quarter loss of $160 million, the worst deficit in its history. The management was in disarray, there was no overall system of financial control, stocks of unsold cars were alarmingly high and morale was understandably low.

Iacocca had to lay off thousands of workers, strip out several layers of management and sell some of the company's assets, including the tank division, which had lucrative defence contracts and was therefore attractive to buyers. He also hired some of his former executives at Ford and brought others out of retirement. But it was not enough. Chrysler badly needed a major infusion of cash to survive. Iacocca tried to tap Arab sources and talked to Volkswagen about a possible merger,

Dealers were invited to sail to the Caribbean island of St Thomas, where after a meal on a beach at sunset a World War II amphibious landing craft thrashed ashore and lowered its ramp. Out on to the sand popped a brand-new white Cougar driven by singer Vic Damone, who proceeded to croon.

but it all came to nothing. Finally he decided to ask the US government for a $1 billion loan guarantee.

The idea met with vigorous opposition, in and out of Congress. Many influential people felt that Chrysler should be allowed to go broke. Iacocca had to argue his case before numerous public hearings. He said that there were precedents, that Chrysler was under new management which would not repeat the mistakes of the past, that he was sure the company could be made profitable again, and that, if it were to go broke, it would cost the country a great deal more than a billion in unemployment, welfare and other expenses. The bill was eventually passed, but he still had a hard time getting the money out of the banks. And, while all this was going on, he had to continue with his efforts to stop the losses.

From 1979 to 1982 the cliff-hanger drama of corporate survival unfolded in the press almost like a weekly serial. At one point, Iacocca even proposed that the company should try to merge with Ford. Henry Ford had already announced his retirement, and Iacocca offered to do the same. But Philip Caldwell, who had taken over as chairman of Ford, said he had no intention of opening negotiations with Chrysler. Iacocca struggled on, slashing away at costs and introducing a new fuel-efficient, front-wheel drive car which, after a shaky start, proved to be a winner. In 1982 the company made a modest profit; in 1983 it made $925 million. Iacocca was actually in a position to make a new stock offering and, not long afterwards, paid back the entire government-guaranteed loan seven years before it was due. The super-salesman couldn't resist another bit of showmanship: at a ceremony in New York he presented his bankers with a cheque for $813,487,500.

Iacocca is an earthy, talkative, energetic, volatile character who can certainly be ruthless when he wants to be. But one certainly has to admire the resolute way he stood up for Chrysler in its time of crisis; without him, it might easily have been the biggest bankruptcy in American history.

Masaru Ibuka

b. 1908

'It is easier to earn a living by doing something others are not doing'

Many businessmen have achieved success through stumbling on to someone else's idea and recognizing the potential. In Masaru Ibuka's case it was transistor technology, which he used to make radios 'small enough so each individual will be able to carry them around for his own use, with power that will enable civilization to reach even those areas without electric power'. It made his company, Sony, a household word far beyond the shores of Japan.

Ibuka began his career as an obscure inventor after graduating in engineering at Waseda University in 1933. He failed the entry examination for lifetime employment at Toshiba, and decided to start his own small business. He was fortunate enough to find a partner, AKIO MORITA, who had a flair for finance and salesmanship. They had met during World War II on a Japanese navy research project and in 1946 set up operations in a small corner room on the third floor of a war-ravaged Tokyo department store building. They had little in the way of capital beyond a dilapidated Datsun truck, and struggled to produce automatic rice cookers. They also repaired radios and sold short-wave converters to Japanese radio owners hungry for foreign news. Raw materials were scarce and, Ibuka recalled later, 'We were forced to do everything just to live.' The experience taught him that 'It is easier to earn a living by doing something others are not doing.' It remained his guiding principle.

The company was incorporated in May 1946. Its prospectus,

written by Ibuka, expressed some of his visionary qualities. 'At this time of inception of the New Japan,' he wrote, 'we will try to create conditions where persons could come together in a spirit of teamwork, and exercise to their hearts' desire their technological capacity . . . such an organization could bring untold pleasure and untold benefits.'

He also committed himself to 'eliminate any untoward profit-seeking' and to eschew 'expansion of size for the sake of size'. Rather, he said, 'We shall emphasize activities that large enterprises because of their size cannot enter. . . . Utilizing to the utmost the unique features of our firm, welcoming technological difficulties . . . focusing on highly sophisticated technical products of great usefulness in our society, we shall open up through mutual co-operation channels of production and sales equal to those of large business organizations.'

Early products included voltmeters, an electrical gauge designed by Ibuka, and a tape recorder – then still a truly original consumer product in the Japanese market. But the big break came when Ibuka visited the United States to enquire into American uses of the tape recorder and instead found out about semiconductor technology. He made a down payment of $25,000 to license the technology from Bell and, on his return, persuaded Morita and other colleagues that there was a bright future for transistor radios. But the powerful Ministry for International Trade and Industry thought the idea was preposterous, and at first refused to give the required allocation of foreign exchange. In early 1954, however, the Ministry gave in and Sony was on its way.

Ibuka recognized that to exploit the full potential of the transistor – to make a pocket radio – required miniaturization of all the other radio parts. Most of the component manufacturers thought it was impossible to reduce the scale of their products, but Ibuka persisted and by the time Sony launched its pocket radio in international markets the company and its subcontractors had taken the world lead in electronic miniaturization. Sony went on to pioneer a long series of consumer products, including the first transistor TV in 1960, the Betamax VCR in 1975 and the Walkman.

Ibuka decided, early on, that his strength lay in finding and developing new ideas and that the business side ought to be left to others. 'In my field,' he said, 'research and development cannot be left to a department. This is one of the big mistakes so often made in Europe. I take the view that the president, or chairman, must be directly in charge of it. He must recognize its importance, and push it in the right direction.'

Akio Morita, a brilliant salesman, shared his view that 'It is easier to earn a living by doing something others are not doing.' Sony's philosophy was – and is – to develop a product when there is no market, and then create one. Morita liked to tell a favourite story. Two shoe salesmen find themselves in a rustic, backward part of Africa. The first salesman wires back to his head office: 'There is no prospect of sales. No one wears shoes here.' The other salesman wires: 'No one wears shoes here. We can dominate the market. Send all possible stock.'

Two shoe salesman find themselves in a rustic, backward part of Africa. The first salesman wires back to his head office: 'There is no prospect of sales. No one wears shoes here.' The other salesman wires: 'No one wears shoes here. We can dominate the market. Send all possible stock.'

Sony's approach paid off handsomely, especially in the United States, where American consumers were delighted with the new products. They were later imitated and even excelled by others, but Sony has continued to be an innovator – and, in the process, has kept its founder's promise to 'bring untold pleasures and untold benefits'.

Steven Jobs

b. 1955

Genius in a garage

Steven Jobs is one of the most remarkable young innovators in the computer business; as the founder of Apple, he became a genuine American business hero while still in his twenties. His career to date also shows how difficult it often is for truly creative people to adjust themselves to new disciplines when the business they have started grows big and successful.

Jobs grew up in California and, like so many teenagers of his day, found himself attracted to eastern philosophy. He dropped out of college, let his hair grow long, smoked dope and frequently went without shoes. He wanted to go to India but couldn't afford the passage. To earn money, he began doing bits of work for the Atari Corporation, helping to build video games. Jobs was no engineer, but he was quick and smart. In the summer of 1974, he finally made it to India. He had his head shaven by a guru, and attended religious festivals and visited monasteries. He contemplated going to Japan to join a monastery, but returned to California instead.

There he met Stephen Wozniak, who was five years older, and they became good friends. Wozniak was also a college drop-out, but he was fascinated by digital electronics and computers and managed to get himself hired by Hewlett-Packard. He was assigned to calculators, not computers, and found the job disappointing. After hours, Wozniak worked hard building a small, easy-to-use computer. The invention of the microprocessor had made such a machine theoretically possible, and Wozniak became obsessed with the idea of creating one. In 1976, he succeeded. The machine was smaller than a portable typewriter, but it could perform the feats of much larger computers. Hewlett-Packard turned him down when he asked if he could pursue his hobby for the company. The one person who recognized that these smaller machines might have some kind of broader appeal was his friend Steven Jobs. They talked about it endlessly and finally Jobs persuaded him that they should start a little company of their own.

Jobs, then twenty-one, opened a makeshift production line in the garage of his parents' home. He raised $1300 by selling his Volkswagen Microbus and Wozniak's Hewlett-Packard scientific calculator. Recalling a pleasant summer that he had spent working in the orchards of Oregon, he christened the new computer Apple. He looked around for capital and they eventually agreed to take on another partner, a former marketing manager of a computer company who not only knew something about running a business but also put in $250,000 of his own money and helped arrange other finance, including a credit line with the Bank of America.

Sales in 1977 were $2.7 million. By 1980 they had soared to $200 million and Apple went public. Jobs was chairman of the board and, at twenty-six, a wealthy man. Wozniak, incredibly, decided to go back to Berkeley to finish his studies!

The runaway progress continued: in 1981, revenue was close to $331 million, heading towards $1 billion and beyond. It was one of the great American success stories. With the computer selling so well, Jobs and his colleagues decided to create a new product, one that could get a foothold in the increasingly important office market. Jobs called it Lisa, after one of his ex-girlfriends. The importance of the Lisa project guaranteed that the new division was where the action was going to be. He naturally wanted to be in charge of it. Much to his surprise, however, his business partners turned him down. Their reasons were that he was too young and inexperienced to manage an organization as large and complex as the Lisa division was bound to become.

The real problem with Jobs, as perceived by the others, was that his personality didn't fit easily into a big organization. He was enthusiastic, hard-working and full of ideas. But he was also restless, easily bored and blunt to the point of tactlessness. He frequently told subordinates that their plans were 'dogshit' and expected everyone to work a ninety-hour week, as he did. In short, he was what one Apple executive described as 'a royal pain in the butt'.

The job of running the Lisa division went to a former Hewlett-Packard man who brought in other people from HP

The real problem with Jobs, as perceived by the others, was that his personality didn't fit easily into a big organization.

to build the machine. Jobs became increasingly agitated over the shape it was taking but, because he did not have financial control of the company, could do nothing about it. His judgment was later proved correct: Lisa turned out to be an expensive fiasco. Meanwhile, he decided to build a computer that, as he saw it, would save Apple from itself. His colleagues agreed to let him have a go, and he started work on a machine he called the Macintosh. With the Macintosh project, Jobs was attempting to recapture those glorious days when he and Wozniak were alone, dreaming their dream, in a garage. 'The metaphysical garage,' he called the venture. He even moved the Mac group into its own 'garage', a building away from the rest of Apple, and fostered a culture in which the Mac people thought they were somehow divorced from the company that paid their salaries.

When the new computer was unveiled at the annual stockholders' meeting in January 1984 it was greeted with a standing ovation that lasted for a full five minutes. Jobs later called it the greatest day of his life. He said it was an intense experience – 'I think I know what it must be like to watch the birth of your child.' But the Macintosh did not create the revolution that the original Apple computer had done. The company eventually merged the Lisa division with the Macintosh division, and put Jobs in charge. But he couldn't change his style: he was simply not cut out to be the manager of a large enterprise in which people led normal lives. By the spring of 1985, Apple was about to announce its first quarterly loss ever, and the board of directors decided that Jobs would have to leave. The power struggle lasted for three weeks. It was bitter and very public, and it ended in defeat for the man who had created the business.

Jobs was worth $150 million or so, and could easily have chosen to lead a life of leisure. He tried it for a while, reading and travelling. He toyed with the idea of going back to university, or even getting into politics. But he was only thirty, and he missed the challenge which Apple had provided – and he missed the work. Then, one day in late August 1985, he had lunch with Paul Berg, Stanford's Nobel Prize-winning biochemist. The conversation turned to the subject of recombinant DNA, on which he had been reading up. Why, he asked Berg, weren't scientists speeding up the lengthy, arduous DNA

With the Macintosh project, Jobs was attempting to recapture those glorious days when he and Wozniak were alone, dreaming their dream, in a garage. 'The metaphysical garage,' he called the venture.

experiments by simulating them on a computer? Because, Berg replied, any hardware powerful enough to simulate such experiments cost close to $100,000; and the software didn't exist at all. Jobs immediately became enthused: he had to build the computer that Berg – and every other scientist and professor and student in America – was waiting for. He had a purpose again.

Within weeks of that lunch, Jobs was talking excitedly to the press about his new dream: to build the first personal computer specifically designed for universities – a machine for learning, a machine at least three times faster, ten times more powerful, than any personal computer ever made. Precise enough for science professors to re-create DNA experiments. Powerful enough to allow pre-med students to simulate the mechanics of the nervous system. Inexpensive enough for both students and professors to buy them 'by the millions'.

He put up $7 million of his own money, hired people who had worked with him at Apple and who had left when he did, and launched a new company, called NeXT Inc. He rented office space: small, cramped quarters at first – 'to get back to the purity of the garage' – and then larger offices as NeXT grew. 'We are going to take the technology to the next level,' he told an interviewer in 1986.

It is still too early to tell whether the venture will succeed. Jobs has also bought a controlling interest in another company, Pixar, the computer graphics division of George Lucas's Lucasfilm. As chairman, he is overseeing the development of the Pixar, a machine that he says will generate some of the world's finest photographic-quality computer images. Jobs, typically, envisions yet another machine that will change the world. Doctors will use the Pixar to read CAT scans; engineers for computer-aided design; and oil companies for analyzing seismic soundings. Even defence contractors, interpreting data beamed from satellites, will, Jobs hopes, find the Pixar indispensable.

There are, of course, plenty of people who would like to see him fail. Men like Jobs invariably make enemies – partly because of their behaviour but also because there is a natural tendency to envy those who make a lot of money early in life. Time will tell whether the management of Apple was right to drop him, but one can't help admiring his enthusiasm and dedication to whatever tasks he decided to tackle.

John H. Johnson

b. 1918

Black America's publisher

The founder of *Ebony* magazine can justly claim to have done more than anyone else to make America aware of the aspirations – and achievements – of the country's black businessmen. Until he came on the scene, little attention was paid to them. Big business was the province of whites. There were no blacks in the top echelons of the major industries, and the many small enterprises run by blacks were hardly known. Yet, as Johnson recognized, blacks also had their dreams of success and wealth. They represented a large potential audience for a magazine which set out to provide encouragement by publishing the stories of blacks who were doing well. That insight laid the foundation for a media empire which has made Johnson himself the richest and most powerful black businessman in the United States.

Johnson was born in Arkansas City, the only son of a sawmill worker who was killed when John was still a child. His mother married another mill hand, and the family lived a life of rural poverty. John attended a segregated school, where he was a good student; in 1933 they moved to Chicago, where John went to another segregated school. After being manager of the school newspaper and business editor of the yearbook, he decided to seek a career in publishing. It was easier said than done. Eventually, an opportunity opened up when he interviewed the president of a black insurance company for the paper. The president was impressed with the young man and offered him a job. Among his duties he helped to publish the company newsletter, which was distributed among black

Chicagoans. It brought him into contact with leaders of the black community, and made him think about the possibility of launching a general-interest magazine which contained the kind of stories printed in the newsletter. He decided to create a publication patterned after *Reader's Digest*, to be called the *Negro Digest*. In 1942, he borrowed $500 by using his mother's furniture as collateral and formed the Johnson Publishing Company.

The *Negro Digest* did well enough to convince him that there was scope for other publications. He reckoned that, if a magazine based on the *Reader's Digest* could attract a sizeable circulation, he might fare even better with one based on the format of *Life*. So he launched *Ebony*, a glossy picture magazine with articles on black middle-class life.

The first issue appeared in November 1945 and was quickly sold out. The market was clearly there, but Johnson knew that he needed substantial advertising revenue as well as income from sales if his new magazine was to survive. It wasn't too difficult to get small ads from black-owned enterprises. The real task was to persuade large corporations that there was a sizeable market for their goods and services which had to be

Yet, as Johnson recognized, blacks also had their dreams of success and wealth. They represented a large potential audience. . . .

approached differently from that of white America. It was hard work, but he succeeded.

Other magazines followed. *Tan*, launched in 1950, was originally modelled on *True Confessions* but quickly expanded into other subjects. *Jet*, which made its debut the following year, was a pocket-size picture magazine. Then Johnson started to publish books dealing with the black experience. He became involved in the cosmetics industry, using his subscription list and advertising to get customers. He also gained control of the insurance company which had given him his start.

In recent years Johnson has moved into radio, television programming and cable television. *Ebony* remains his principal publication, with a monthly circulation of more than 1½ million. All together, Johnson's magazines reach more than 60 per cent of the adult population.

Ebony has published vigorous articles on the civil rights movement, but it is still essentially a magazine devoted to success stories and visions of the Good Life, with lots of pictures of glamorous black men and women. Every year Johnson publishes lists of the largest black-owned and -operated companies.

Critics say that it doesn't reflect the real world – that even today only a small percentage of blacks are able to enjoy the advantages it publicizes. But that is equally true of glossy magazines aimed at the most affluent sector of white America, like *Town and Country*. What matters, surely, is that Johnson has given hope to millions of people by showing that colour is not necessarily a barrier to success in a country like the United States. His own remarkable career underlines the point.

John Maynard Keynes

1883–1946

The practical economist

Keynes was the most influential economist of his generation and his theories still have a worldwide following. Born in Cambridge, in the same year that Marx died, he turned to economics as a young man to prepare himself for the Civil Service examination. He was assigned to the India Office, but the job bored him and after two years he left to become a lecturer in economics at King's College, Cambridge.

During World War I Keynes was called into the Treasury, and at its close attended the peace conference as an adviser. The result was a controversial book, *The Economic Consequences of the Peace*, attacking the peace terms because they called for impossibly high reparations from Germany while depriving the defeated nation of the means of making foreign payments, and because they shattered the economic unity of a hitherto reasonably productive Europe. But the work which established him as a major economic thinker was the *General Theory of Employment, Interest and Money*, published in 1929. It came out at a time when the New Deal was in full swing in the United States and it seemed to fit the need of times.

After the Great Depression economic theorists were in disarray: classical doctrine, with its seductively logical structure, had clashed with reality and had been found wanting. Few except academic economists could understand Keynes's *General Theory*, but it was taken up by the professional economic fraternity on both sides of the Atlantic because it was obvious that something effective had to be done. It gave them a pattern of thinking which they could use in the positions of advice and responsibility to which many of them were called in government and business.

Keynes had none of the temperament of the rigid doctrinarian: he combined academic theory with practical shrewdness. If a new policy seemed desirable on pragmatic grounds, he would modify his theory to accord with what he thought ought to be done. He had already demonstrated his understanding of practical matters by acting as chairman of a successful insurance company and by managing an investment company which made a lot of money both for himself and for his college. His major contribution to economics was to adopt basic premises which were closer to existing reality than were those of his predecessors. He argued against laissez-faire, and made a strong case for government intervention to compensate for the vagaries of capitalism, even if it meant government deficits. He advocated a permanent policy of keeping interest rates low, and put heavy emphasis on the need to maintain full employment.

Hitherto the orthodox view had been that the proper role of government in fiscal matters should be neutral. Government had certain inescapable functions which cost money; it should collect the necessary money from taxpayers and pay its bills. If it ran into debt, every effort should be made to repay that debt as soon as possible. Classical theory had little to say about fluctuations of unemployment; it assumed that the laws of supply and demand would take care of it.

Keynes showed that there was a middle way between pure socialism and pure capitalism. The main stress of his doctrine was not on direct government intervention with the operation of private enterprise, but on a compensatory fiscal policy which would moderate the major flaw of the system while leaving it substantially free.

It is a measure of his success that the basic ideas he was trying to convey sound remarkably simple now. But it was in the United States, not in his native Britain, that the first attempt was made to alleviate unemployment through public works. Under Roosevelt's New Deal the administration started to spend large sums of money, over and above what it received in tax revenue, on roads, dams, harbours, irrigation and land reclamation, civic centres, public housing and many other projects. Keynes's detractors maintained that he had very little to do with this; it would have happened anyway. But his ideas were well known in the United States, and he

---

Keynes showed that there was a middle way between pure socialism and pure capitalism.

---

acquired a considerable following. There is certainly no doubt about his warm approval of Roosevelt's experiment.

'You have', he wrote in a famous open letter to the President late in 1933,

> made yourself the trustee for those in every country who seek to mend the evils of our condition by reasoned experiment, within the framework of the existing social system. If you fail, rational change will be gravely prejudiced throughout the world, leaving orthodoxy and revolution to fight it out. But if you succeed, new and bolder methods will be tried everywhere, and we may date the first chapter of a new economic era from your accession to the office.

In Britain, at this time, the emphasis was still on 'good housekeeping'; expenditure was cut and taxes increased in an attempt to get the budget into surplus, even though it involved the doubling of unemployment. By the time Keynes's views gained acceptance in official circles the country was at war again. In 1944, however, looking forward to the end of the hostilities and determined to avoid the economic disasters that had followed World War I, the British government published a White Paper committing itself for the first time to securing 'a high and stable level of employment'. The consequent Labour administrations were all 'Keynesian' and many politicians and economists still use that label to describe their approach.

In recent years, of course, it has been challenged by right-wing governments in both Europe and the United States. In their view, public spending was allowed to get out of hand, resulting not only in huge deficits but also in runaway inflation. Margaret Thatcher, in particular, has vigorously opposed the notion that Keynesian policies (as interpreted by his followers) are the best way to achieve healthy economic growth. She has paid far more attention to later economic gurus like MILTON FRIEDMAN. But even Mrs Thatcher would not dare to advocate a return to the kind of economic thinking which prevailed before Keynes arrived on the scene, even if she wanted to. Laissez-faire in the classical vein has few serious supporters these days.

Ray Kroc

b. 1902–84

Popularizer of franchising

Few people did more to popularize the concept of franchising than Ray Kroc, who built up the McDonald's hamburger chain. His only real rival was Harland Sanders, a one-time insurance salesman who found a new way to cook chicken and sold his recipe as Colonel Sanders' Kentucky Fried Chicken. Like Sanders, Kroc dropped out of school and tried various jobs: he played piano with several travelling bands, chose the music for a Chicago radio station and sold real estate in Florida. In 1937 he started a small Chicago company that distributed multimixers – machines that could make a number of milkshakes at one time. The business did reasonably well, but it didn't make him rich. Then, in 1954, he discovered that a small restaurant in California, run by Mac and Dick McDonald, was using eight of his mixers – more than anyone else. Intrigued, he went to see the McDonald operation for himself: the brothers were doing a roaring trade in hamburgers and milkshakes. When he asked why they didn't open more restaurants (he wanted to sell more mixers) they said that they were quite content to stick to the one they had. Kroc saw his chance and grabbed it. The McDonalds agreed to let him franchise their outlets anywhere in the country in exchange for ½ per cent of the gross receipts. He opened his first McDonald's, which he owned himself, in a Chicago suburb the following year and others quickly followed. In 1960 he decided to buy the name McDonald outright for $2.7 million. By the mid-seventies Kroc had franchise holders all over the world and the chain's annual turnover was several billion dollars a year. His personal fortune was estimated at $300 million.

Franchising is often said to be a 'uniquely American invention', which isn't so. The concept originated in Britain in the late eighteenth century through the brewery/tied public houses system. But it was America which made the world aware of the potential, through entrepreneurs like Kroc, and which developed business format franchising – the granting of a licence by the format creator to the franchisee, entitling the latter to sell the product or service and to utilize a package containing all the elements necessary to establish a business and run it profitably on a predetermined basis.

The main advantage to the franchise company is that it costs less to expand, and therefore it is possible to achieve more rapid growth. The company gets a dedicated and highly motivated workforce. Day-to-day administrative/staffing problems are greatly reduced. The franchisor may also gain wider buying opportunities through supplying his growing number of tied outlets, and if his business is in the service sector he will be better placed to acquire national accounts. For the franchisee, eager to run his own business, the attraction is the prospect of a hefty leg up the ladder of success. He can gain a proven product or service with an established profit record, training, financial and management advice, national advertising and sales promotion, and computerized accounts. It is an enticing alternative to toughing it out alone. That is the theory, anyway. In practice, there are all kinds of drawbacks. It doesn't take the razor-sharp brain of a banker to demonstrate that, since two parties wish to live off the proceeds, the under-

It doesn't take the razor-sharp brain of a banker to demonstrate that, since two parties wish to live off the proceeds, the underlying business idea had better be brilliant.

lying business idea had better be brilliant. It must have the potential to yield that rich double harvest. This isn't always the case.

New franchises mainly come from two sources. One is existing companies wishing to expand, and the other is an individual (or company) with an idea which, when proved, will be capable of being franchised. All too often companies are launched without sufficient homework. Some companies make the mistake of believing that because they are successful at the business in which they trade, they will naturally be successful at franchising. The fact is that franchising is a business in itself which, like any other, takes time to understand, develop and operate efficiently. Here are five of the more obvious reasons why things go wrong.

The sale of franchises based on an unproven idea. Some people try to pass off as a franchise what is little more than an unproven idea and a bad one at that. They not only want others to risk their money to see if it will work, but charge a substantial up-front fee for the so-called privilege of joining their dubious scheme. Fads are especially suspect. A franchisor should be able to show that he has made a thorough – and realistic – assessment of his product or service. In general, the younger the franchise, the higher the risks.

Limited scope for development. It isn't enough that a product or service is innovative: there must be proof of its appeal and staying power. Without that quality, the franchise is strictly a short-term venture.

Inadequate resources. This is the most common cause of failure by franchisors. Too many people, eager to cash in on what appears to be a lucrative idea, fail to make adequate funds available to support the early development of the system. The costs of setting up a properly structured franchise, and of meeting the obligations to the franchisees in the early years, when income is at its lowest, are substantial and are quite capable of putting the future of the parent company at risk. A good franchisor puts considerable effort into proving his concept. Costs in terms of preparation vary enormously, but the franchisor should be prepared to run his pilot operation (or, better still, several in tandem) for a year or more. He makes his profit from the eventual scale of the enterprise, and it will usually be some time before he has enough franchisees of the right quality to produce these profits.

Overcharging. Some franchisors use the initial fee as a means of milking or overcharging at the front end of the transaction. The result is financial problems and resentment. In normal circumstances the initial fee should not exceed 5–10 per cent of the total cost of the franchise package.

Bad choice of franchisee. Ultimately the success or failure of any business depends on the person running it. The wrong choice can cause a lot of problems; indeed, it may put the entire enterprise in jeopardy. A poor image suffered by one outlet can do irreparable damage to the franchise as a whole, and it can prove difficult to bring a lax franchisee up to a satisfactory standard. Much of McDonald's enormous success is due to Kroc's insistence that applicants must be vetted with great care and that, once accepted, they should be kept on a tight rein. This is still the company's policy. It allows little experimentation with menu or decor, and sets strict standards for everything, including grooming and dress. 'One of our main assets,' Kroc always maintained, 'is our consistency and uniformity.' Entrepreneurial flair, far from being a great asset, can actually cause chaos. The entrepreneur frequently finds the control exercised by the franchisor oppressive; he wants to do his own thing.

Having said all this, it must be acknowledged that a *good*

'One of our main assets,' Kroc always maintained, 'is our consistency and uniformity.'

franchise can work well for both parties. There are many encouraging examples, and there is no doubt that franchising will continue to grow. A number of well-established companies who have converted their branches to franchising have found that, by doing so, they have made them more profitable, with higher sales and lower management costs. And there is ample evidence that, for the franchisee, a properly constructed, visible business format franchise is considerably less risky, and often more profitable, than it would be for someone setting up a similar business of his own.

The great post-war advance in franchising has been its extension downmarket, to operations where the outlets, or some of them, are simply too small to justify the attention of a large-scale management operation but where, added together, a substantial business can be created.

The United States continues to set the pace. Fast food outlets are still way ahead of the rest of the field – there is hardly a fast food that hasn't been franchised – but the concept has taken hold in a vast range of activities. Beauty and health care, amusement and recreation facilities, and carpet cleaning/maintenance are high on the list of the fastest-growing franchises. There are franchised decorating services, day-care facilities, liquor stores, motels, maid services, car wash systems, instant printing services, pet stores, magazines, home entertainment products, delivery services, hardware stores, security systems, travel agencies, lawn maintenance services and a multitude of sports clothing and equipment outlets. There are also franchises designed to aid other people's business operations by providing management advice, financial planning, tax and accounting services and computer assistance. Even the medical profession is becoming increasingly interested in franchising as a way of reaching more people. Professional dental services and walk-in medical clinics have taken a definite hold on the market.

Ray Kroc was one of the first to see that the concept also had great overseas potential, and many others have since followed his lead. Canada continues to be the dominant market, followed by Japan, Britain and continental Europe. Moving into unfamiliar territory, of course, carries extra risks. It is all too easy to make assumptions which, although amply justified by experience at home, turn out to be wide of the mark abroad. An idea which works in one country does not necessarily work in another. Many companies have also found it difficult to maintain proper control of their foreign operations.

A well-managed business should be able to anticipate problems of this kind, and to deal with others as they arise. The really big question is whether the franchise route is, in the long run, the best method of expanding one's business. The leverage is useful in the early stages, but the advantages may become less obvious later on. The management may well ask itself why, if the idea is so brilliant, and has proved its worth, it should settle for only a share of the action. Franchisees, too, often question whether they have made the right choice. As their experience in the business develops, many feel that their success is due more to their own efforts than to the support given by the company. They believe themselves to be competent and strong enough to break free and acquire or create their own company in the field they have got to know so well.

Such considerations are, naturally, very much a matter for the people involved. Franchising has grown into a huge and complex industry, and in the process has achieved a measure of sophistication. It is one of the great inventions of western capitalism. But, as in any business, there is no guarantee of success. Everyone must make his or her own judgments.

Freddie Laker

b. 1922

Revolutionary of the aviation industry

Freddie Laker became a folk hero in the late 1970s by setting himself up as the champion of the 'forgotten man' who wanted cheap travel across the Atlantic. His bold venture eventually collapsed, but the innovative crusade had a major impact on the aviation industry.

Laker is an ebullient Englishman from a working-class background who learnt about planes as an engineer and pilot in air transport during World War II. In peacetime he dealt in aircraft spare parts and then bought some old planes from BOAC just in time to use them for the Berlin airlift of 1948. He later sold his business, which in 1960 became part of a newly formed airline called British United Airways of which he subsequently became chief executive; however five years later he had a row with the chairman and set up his own Laker Airways to cater for package holidays. He borrowed money from a bank to buy cheap planes from the big airlines, who were switching to more modern jets, and in 1969 he leased two Boeing 707s and began flying charters across the Atlantic.

Looking around for better ways to attract passengers, he

came up with the idea of the Skytrain – a basic service which would allow people to arrive at the last moment and fly cheaply on planes with 'no frills'. Inevitably he encountered vigorous opposition from the big airlines, who saw him as a 'disruptive force'. Laker, undeterred, bought two giant DC airliners from the Japanese Mitsui Bank and pressed his case for a licence. He succeeded in getting one from Britain's Civil Aviation Authority, but the equivalent body in Washington, the CAB, refused to let him go ahead; and when a new Trade Secretary took office in London he, too, ruled against Laker, revoking his licence. It was a bleak moment, but Laker had no intention of giving up. He hired an American lawyer, Bob Beckman, who was an expert on aviation law and anti-trust legislation, and together they sued the airlines for conspiring to delay the Skytrain. They also appealed against the British government's ruling. By then, the energetic Laker had found another formidable ally: the media. A shrewd publicist, he played up his role as the lone entrepreneur of the air battling against a cartel of corporations. The press found it irresistible.

Early in 1977 both London and Washington gave in, and that summer Laker started his new service amid much ballyhoo. The other airlines introduced their own bargain fares, but plenty of people were eager to try the Skytrain and he had a good year. The British government, acknowledging his popularity, gave him a knighthood and *Time* magazine put his face on the cover.

Laker promptly announced plans for further expansion. He began a service to Los Angeles and talked about flying round the world with a Globetrain. He said that he was going to buy five more DC10s, and that he also intended to place orders for ten European airbuses, to cater for Laker holidays in Europe. The following year, however, brought two serious setbacks. A DC10 (not his) crashed in Chicago, killing all 274 passengers, and every DC10 was grounded for six weeks, forcing him to cancel Skytrain. At the same time, another oil crisis pushed up his operating costs and an economic recession depressed traffic. Competition for business across the Atlantic intensified. His problems continued to mount in 1980 and 1981. The value of sterling, which provided most of his revenues, was declining, while the dollar, which accounted for most of his debts, rose sharply. By the spring of 1981 he was in deep financial trouble and had to tell the banks that he would not be able to repay the loans due at the end of the year. They agreed to a postponement and, subsequently, two of his other creditors – McDonnell Douglas and General Electric (who did not want to lose a good customer) – offered to convert debts into preference shares in Laker's company.

But the rival airlines, who had their own financial problems and sensed an opportunity to finish him off, cut fares still further and put strong pressure on McDonnell Douglas and GE to stop their support of the 'disruptive force'. Laker's revenues continued to fall and the banks decided that enough was enough: they were not going to lend him any more cash. Laker appealed to Mrs Thatcher, who had warmly praised his efforts to help the 'forgotten man', but after holding a meeting with her ministers she reluctantly concluded that it wouldn't be fair to taxpayers to bail him out. Laker had no choice but to cease

A shrewd publicist, he played up his role as the lone entrepreneur of the air battling against a cartel of corporations. The press found it irresistible.

trading. The liquidators moved in and disposed of the planes, the hangars and the equipment.

But it was not the end of the story. While a bitterly disappointed Laker was fuming in London, Bob Beckman announced that, in his view, the company had a valid claim against the big airlines for conspiring to violate the American anti-trust laws. He estimated the compensatory damages at $350 million, which under anti-trust laws could be trebled to over a billion dollars. The liquidators went ahead with the lawsuit, and a fierce battle began. The airlines strongly denied the charges, and the argument went on for quite some time. Faced with mounting legal bills, and the possibility that they might lose, they eventually offered to settle out of court. Laker personally collected several million dollars. It was enough to provide him with a comfortable living for the rest of his days, but it was certainly not what he had hoped for when he embarked on his great adventure.

There will always be some dispute about the Laker experiment. Many people agree with the big airlines that he was an opportunist who ultimately became a victim of the open market he was preaching himself. He went after the giants of the business and, like so many others who have done the same in various fields, got hurt when they hit back. He expanded too fast, at a time when it would have been more sensible to settle for a slower pace. He bought expensive planes before he had permission to fly them, which was reckless. He ignored the warnings of people who wished him well but who were disturbed by his sunny optimism.

Laker was not the first entrepreneur in the aviation business who over-reached himself, and he was certainly not the last. It has happened to others since: Donald Burr of People Express is a notable example. It is entirely possible that Laker Airways would have failed even without the alleged 'conspiracy'. But Laker, like Burr, undoubtedly helped the public to get a better deal. He reminded the airlines that it was dangerous to take their customers for granted. (See also RICHARD BRANSON.)

Edwin Land

b. 1909

Inventor of the instant camera

Dr Edwin Land is chiefly remembered as the inventor of the Polaroid camera, though he holds numerous other patents. He is both a gifted scientist and a shrewd businessman, a combination which has made him enormously wealthy.

Land's first product was a transparent plastic sheet capable of polarizing light – a type of light filter soon familiar to almost everyone in the form of sunglasses. His interest in the subject had begun when he was a seventeen-year-old freshman at Harvard; walking along Broadway in New York at night, it suddenly struck him that polarizing filters could eliminate headlight glare and thus reduce the hazards of night driving. He took leave of absence from the college and spent day after day in the New York Public Library, reading everything which might be relevant. At night he carried out experiments in a small laboratory he had set up in a rented room nearby. For the next three years college was forgotten, but when he patented his sheet polarizers Harvard not only welcomed him back but also offered him one of its laboratories. He spent the following three years there, but never got around to taking his degree: the 'Dr' attached to his name is strictly honorific.

In 1937, at the age of twenty-eight, he launched the Polaroid Corporation with the help of a group of Wall Street financiers who relished the prospect of putting his filters on every car headlight and windshield in the country. He made such an impression on them that they left Land with a majority of the voting stock and placed him in complete control of the company for ten years. But Detroit turned Polaroid down, and he had to find other uses for his invention. During World War II the company was kept busy manufacturing lenses and gun-sights for the military, but Land also spent a great deal of time in his lab trying to invent an 'instant camera'.

He later said that it was his small daughter who provided the inspiration. When he was taking pictures of her on a family holiday she asked impatiently how soon she could see them; he explained that it took time to get them developed, and then thought about what he had said. There was something basically wrong with photography if people had to wait hours, or even days, to see a picture. He started to experiment with ways of getting a finished picture directly out of the camera that took it. By 1947 he had come up with the answer, and his new sixty-second camera went on the market in the summer of 1948.

The trade was sceptical, but the public liked it. Land had the good sense to hire an outstanding general manager, J. Harold Booth, who had a great talent for promotion. He conceived the

He later said that it was his small daughter who provided the inspiration. When he was taking pictures of her on a family holiday she asked how soon she could see them; he explained that it took time to get them developed, and then thought about what he had said.

plan of offering one department store in each major city an exclusive on the product for thirty years, provided it would advertise prominently in local newspapers and give the camera intense promotion throughout the store. When it went on sale for the first time, at Jordan Marsh, the big Boston department store, it was an instant hit. Booth subsequently opened a dazzling promotion in Miami, supplying a squad of pretty girls and lifeguards with Land cameras to snap pictures at pools and beaches and give them away to astonished tourists. Within a few weeks most Miami stores had sold out their stocks – and the tourists went back home to show off their new toys. Every owner became, in effect, a Polaroid salesman.

Land later developed a simple system for instant colour photography and produced all kinds of other ideas: by 1980 he had more than four hundred patents in his own name. He played a key role in the development of cameras which can take pictures at high altitude; the cameras used in the famous U-2 espionage project, and those which detected the Soviet missiles in Cuba, were his.

Land has always maintained that the ability to create and invent was not rare; in his opinion, it was commonplace but generally uncultivated. 'My whole life', he once said, 'has been spent trying to teach people that intense concentration for hour after hour can bring out resources in people that they didn't know they had.'

William Lear

1902–78

The classic inventor-entrepreneur

William P. Lear Sr's principal claim to public fame is the creation of the Lear jet, used by highly paid corporate executives. But he did much more than that: blessed with an inventive mind and prodigious energy, he was responsible for many other significant innovations.

Lear was born in Chicago and got his first full-time job, as an auto mechanic, at the age of thirteen. He soon became fascinated with flying and radio, the two fields that were to remain lifelong interests. He became a radio engineer and was hired by Paul Galvin, a shrewd businessman whose company specialized in making batteries.

At the time, radios were all battery-powered and were rather clumsy affairs. Galvin came up with a device called the A-Eliminator, which made it possible to operate them on house current and keep them charged. But there were technical problems, and the company ran into financial trouble. Looking for ways of boosting his business, Galvin hit on the idea of placing radios in cars. It is a simple enough process these days. In the 1920s, however, the sets were bulky and required the installation of a separate battery which was the size of a fishing tackle box. The reception was poor, and car manufacturers were understandably reluctant to make space for them.

By then Lear was running his own firm, the Radio Coil and Wire Company. He had found a way to reduce radio coils to a fraction of their former size, and had formed this company to produce them. He had also designed a compact radio which would run on a car battery. Galvin obtained the manufacturing rights and demonstrated it at an auto show in 1929. The response was encouraging, and he changed the name of his business to Motorola.

Lear quickly tired of the car radio game and sold out his interests. He wanted to be in a business which would enable him to fly aeroplanes, so he moved out to Curtis Reynolds airport in Chicago and started making aircraft radios. He later took his small team to New York, but in 1934 he went broke. Lear raised badly needed cash by devising a method for building a multi-band radio in a simpler way than had been done before and selling it to RCA for $250,000.

He went on to create one of the country's major aircraft electronics-manufacturing companies. One of his most notable achievements during this period was the F-5 autopilot, which he designed and built in 1949 for US jet fighters. In the late 1950s Lear moved to Europe to start production there and learned about the P-16, a Swiss-designed ground support jet. Two prototypes had crashed, and the project had been abandoned. Lear, however, was convinced that the plane was basically sound and that he could make a success of a modified version. The board of directors of Lear Inc. strongly opposed the idea, but he was determined to go ahead. Having sold out his 23 per cent ownership in the electronics company, he charged into the jet business alone.

Lear set up a plant in Switzerland, but later moved the operation to Wichita, Kansas. The banks, who were as sceptical as his board of directors had been, refused to lend him money, so he put his entire personal fortune – some $11 million – into the project. The first Lear jet rolled off the assembly line in October 1963. It was small, but it was reliable and comparatively inexpensive. Businessmen liked it, and the new company eventually grew into a highly successful enterprise.

William Lear, who became immensely rich, was clearly an unusual man. He had no formal education, but he was creative, self-confident, stubborn and bold. Like all innovators, he loved a challenge. He was sixty when he sold his shares in the electronics group he had built up and risked everything he had by going into a field in which he had little experience.

Like all innovators, he loved a challenge. He was sixty when he sold his shares in the electronics group he had built up and risked everything he had by going into a field in which he had little experience.

Once Lear Jet was firmly established he embarked on further ventures, such as tape units for automobiles and steam-powered cars.

Lear took out more than a hundred patents during his working life, and made more than $200 million. He was a doer rather than a theorist, a man who liked to make things happen and who had little patience with corporate bureaucrats. He was a classic example of the brilliant inventor-entrepreneur.

James Joseph Ling

b. 1922

King of the conglomerateurs

James Ling was one of the boldest and most innovative of the 'conglomerateurs' who made headlines on both sides of the Atlantic in the 1960s. The word 'conglomerate' is derived from a Latin word meaning 'to roll together'. In the simple merger, the management of one company acquires another in the same line of business to expand the scope of its operations. In assembling a conglomerate, wheeler-dealers like Ling took over companies regardless of what business they were in, often not to expand their operations but to enhance the worth of their stock by showing rapidly increasing earnings. They rolled together glittering packages of totally unrelated activities – electronic firms with meat packers, insurance companies with television networks, steel manufacturing plants with real estate developers. They talked grandly about 'synergism' – a philosophy that two and two, if put together imaginatively enough, need not add up to four but to five or more.

Ling, whose deals were so complex and imaginative that he was widely hailed as a financial genius, never had any formal training. He was born in Hugo, Oklahoma, though he preferred to call himself a Texan, and had a rootless, drifting, poverty-ridden childhood. (He later claimed the German field-marshal Rommel as 'one of my teachers'.) At nineteen he arrived in Dallas and went to work as an electrician. In 1944 he joined the Navy, which sent him to electrical school. Released from service in 1946, he went back to Dallas and, with $3000 savings, set himself up in business as an electrical contractor. After several ups and downs, his little company grew to have an annual turnover of $1.5 million. In 1955 he decided to register Ling Electric as a public company. Wall Street was unenthusiastic, so he and some associates sold the stock themselves, handing out prospectuses at the Texas State Fair. They peddled 450,000 shares at $2.20 each. The success of the venture taught Ling a basic rule of the financial game: that pieces of paper can be exchanged for cash.

Armed with funds, he made his first corporate acquisition – a small West Coast firm called LM Electronics – and changed his own company's name to Ling Industries Inc. Then he sold more stock and bought United Electronics and Calidyne Company. Without waiting to consolidate these companies, Ling floated a $2.2 million issue of convertible bonds and purchased three other firms – Altec, University Loudspeakers and Continental Electronics. The name of his rapidly growing business empire was changed again, to Ling-Altec Electronics. The deals continued, and by the end of 1962 he controlled an aerospace and electronics complex (by then called Ling-Temco-Vought) capable of competing for contracts with any other in the country.

Two years later he launched his most interesting innovation, which he called Project Redeployment. It involved selling to the public shares in the companies he had acquired. He would sell off, say, a quarter of the shares of a subsidiary and keep the rest. It gave him cash, and still left him free to use Ling-Temco-Vought, now a holding company, to borrow more money than before. As Ling himself explained: 'What we do is that we acquire companies and spin them off as one or more public companies, usually keeping the majority ownership, thus redeploying the assets to best advantage.' Wall Street's judgment was that it was a way of 'getting something for nothing', but it worked.

The proceeds helped to finance a series of further acquisitions in different fields. He repeated the procedure in 1965 when, after taking over the Okonite Corporation, a wire and cable producer, he sold off 14 per cent of the common stock. After all the manipulations were completed, the mother company had fewer shares outstanding, a larger debt, and a majority stake in yet another subsidiary.

In that year, Ling-Temco-Vought was rated number 204 on the *Fortune* list of the largest US companies. But Ling was by no means content. More acquisitions were in the works, he said. He would use long- and short-term borrowing, divestures and amalgamations, and continual restructuring. The aim was to make LTV the biggest industrial company in the country.

Some Wall Street analysts were by then beginning to express doubts about his strategy, which depended heavily on the assumption that the bull market would go on and on, making the public ever more eager to buy his paper. The price of LTV common stock fell sharply. But Ling was already pursuing his next victim, Wilson & Co., which had sales of over a billion dollars, mostly in meat packing, but with important representation in drugs, soap and sporting supplies. He bought shares on the open market and then made a tender offer for the rest. In January 1967 he had over half the shares and merged the company into LTV, which moved up to number 38 in the *Fortune* ratings.

The success of the venture taught Ling a basic rule of the financial game: that pieces of paper can be exchanged for cash.

Most of the money that Ling used for the tender offer came from short-term borrowings, which he would have to repay quickly. So he offered the remaining Wilson stockholders a new convertible LTV bond in return for their stock and received most of the remaining shares that way. But he had to move quickly to obtain funds to repay his loans and prepare for payments on the bonds. He did so by breaking down Wilson into three new companies. LTV retained the majority of the stock in all three, and sold the rest to new investors. This scheme brought in $44.5 million, all of which was used to repay the short-term notes.

The following year he took over the Greatamerica Corporation, a Texas-based insurance and banking conglomerate, which also controlled Braniff Airways and National Car Rentals. It was accepted by most stockholders, at a cost to LTV of $500 million in bonds. Greatamerica had some $150 million in cash, and Ling sold off several of its banks and insurance companies to realize another $126 million. But the merger still left LTV with an uncomfortably large debt. Undaunted, Ling embarked on his most ambitious venture and the one that, along with other factors, would eventually bring about his downfall. He made a tender offer for the common stock of Jones & Laughlin, one of the country's major steel firms. By June 1968 he had more than 63 per cent of the stock, acquired at a cost of another $500 million.

It was a fantastic feat of corporation expansion: no company had grown so fast or so much in decades. Ling's moves had been stunning in their surprise. But there was an obvious weakness in his game. The merger required massive borrowings of short-term capital at high rates. A bad year, bearable by most large firms, could throw LTV into grave straits. Servicing the debt would become difficult, and he would have trouble peddling more and more paper.

This is, indeed, what happened. Jones & Laughlin produced poor earnings, and so did other LTV companies. Worse, the government decided to put a brake on the conglomerateurs. Ling had hoped to break down Jones & Laughlin into subsidiaries, as he had done with Wilson & Co., in order to obtain funds to pay off short-term borrowings. Now he was not allowed to do so. He could not even put his own representatives on the board. There could be no dealings between LTV's concerns and the steel company for ten years. Ling would have to sell his interest either in Jones & Laughlin or both Braniff Airways and the Okonite Corporation within three years. And he had to agree that he would not acquire any company with assets in excess of $100 million during the next ten years, unless he first divested himself of Jones & Laughlin.

It was a nasty blow, but more trouble was on the way. The stock market ran out of steam, as many analysts had said it would. The Dow-Jones industrial index fell from a high of 968.85 to a low of 631.16 between May 1969 and May 1970. It was the sharpest drop since 1937, and the closest that Wall Street had come to panic and failures since the crash of 1929. Money rates soared, and the cheap paper with which the conglomerateurs had taken over companies was now undesirable.

LTV suffered a bad loss in 1969. Its debts stood at $1.5 billion and everyone was howling for Ling's blood, especially when he had to eliminate its dividend on the common stock. He was ousted from the board. By 1971 he was back in the news again. Still under fifty, and as brash and bouncy as ever, he had started a new conglomerate called Alpha-Omega Inc. But the atmosphere of the early 1970s was wrong for conglomerates, and it failed to make the impact he and his friends had hoped for.

Andrew Lloyd Webber

b. 1948

Superstar among composers

Andrew Lloyd Webber got the idea for his enormously successful musical, *Cats*, when he bought a copy of T. S. Eliot's poems at London airport and read it on the plane to Los Angeles. It was such an unlikely subject that he had trouble finding backers for it: he had to mortgage his own home to help pay for the production. Today he calls *Cats* his 'pension fund'.

Many composers have made a lot of money out of musicals, but Lloyd Webber has set unprecedented box office records with his various ventures. Even those who criticize his music acknowledge that he is a remarkable showman with a shrewd business sense. The shares of his company, the Really Useful Group, are quoted on the stock exchange and he is a multi-millionaire.

Lloyd Webber grew up in an environment dominated by music. His father, Dr William Lloyd Webber, was a distinguished organist and the principal of the London College of Music. His mother was a noted piano teacher and his brother Julian is a fine cellist. But he says that the greatest influence on his showbiz evolution was his Aunt Vi, who took him to matinee performances of virtually every musical produced in London in the 1950s and who was on first-name terms with many of the stars. At the age of eight Andrew began to devise his own shows, using a model theatre he had built himself, complete with a revolving stage made from an old gramophone turntable. This enthusiasm for the stage continued right through school and at Oxford: he says that he considers himself lucky to have known, early on, what he wanted to do with his life.

While at Oxford he met Time Rice, a fellow-student who felt the same way about the theatre and who had a gift for writing lyrics. They were soon working together. Tim was older than Andrew and due to leave Oxford earlier; Andrew decided that he, too, should depart at the same time. Finishing his education, he said later, would have meant losing his partner to another composer, which simply would not do. On his father's advice, he went to the Royal College of Music to study orchestration and conducting. He and Tim also collaborated on what was to become their first real hit – the forty-minute pop oratorio, *Joseph and the Amazing Technicolour Dreamcoat*. This biblical theme, complete with catchy music, was to resurface in their later work *Jesus Christ Superstar*.

Superstar was a big international success, but the partners did not make much money out of it – chiefly, Andrew says, because they left the financial side to others. It taught them that, if they were to do better in future, they would have to set up their own management, which they did.

They also learned, some time afterwards, what it was like to have an expensive flop. *Jeeves* was a show based on the

---

It was such an unlikely subject that he had trouble finding backers for it: he had to mortgage his own home to help pay for the production. Today he calls Cats *his 'pension fund'.*

---

superior butler invented by P. G. Wodehouse. It sounded like a promising idea, but it didn't come off. Lloyd Webber now says, with disarming candour, that it was 'a bloody awful musical'. At the time, though, the failure of *Jeeves* was a massive blow to his ego.

Happily they had another hit with *Evita*, a near-opera based on the tempestuous life and times of Eva Peron. The idea was Tim's, but Andrew Lloyd Webber had the satisfaction of hearing people singing, and whistling, 'Don't Cry for Me, Argentina' wherever he went in the world. That one song along made him a fortune.

After *Evita*, the press started to compare them to that earlier partnership, Rodgers and Hammerstein. But Rice decided to go off on his own. He wrote a musical called *Blondel*, with music by Stephen Olivier. Lloyd Webber did a show called *Song and Dance*, and then came up with *Cats*. It was a courageous venture, and when it turned into a smash-hit many people were eager to finance whatever he wanted to do next. It turned out to be another concept which sounded quite bizarre when he first outlined it. *Starlight Express*, he explained, would be about a race to find the fastest engine on an old American railroad: there would be trains, and a great deal of the action would consist of people whizzing around the stage on roller skates. After *Cats*, however, he had no trouble raising the £2 million needed to turn his idea into reality. His judgment proved to be sound: the show did excellent business.

Next, Lloyd Webber took nine months off to do something entirely different. He wrote a Requiem Mass, dedicated to the memory of his father, who had died in 1982. It received its first performance at the Church of St Thomas on New York's Fifth Avenue. He realized that it was unlikely to be a lucrative venture, but as he told me at the time, 'Money isn't everything.' One of the good things about being rich, he said, was that it gave him the freedom to tackle all kinds of projects. It was 'by far and away the most individual thing I've ever done, the most personal of all my compositions'.

Another venture was his acquisition of London's Palace Theatre, the home of some of his most successful productions. He bought it partly for 'sentimental reasons', but he also reckoned that the prime location made it a good business deal. He became an impresario, putting on other West End shows (with titles like *Daisy Pulls It Off*) and in his spare time devised a board game called Calamity – 'the winner calculates the risks and ends up with the most money'.

But he was certainly not finished with musicals. In 1986 he had another London hit with *The Phantom of the Opera*, starring Michael Crawford and Andrew's new wife, singer and dancer Sarah Brightman.

How does he find time for it all? 'I have good people to help me,' he says. The Really Useful Group looks after his business affairs, and he has been able to secure the services of brilliant collaborators like the director Trevor Nunn. But Lloyd Webber remains the driving force, the innovator who makes it all happen. One of his great strengths is his enthusiasm for projects. He becomes totally absorbed in his work, and those who know him well point out that the image of the shy, introverted young man with the manner of a self-effacing student is deceptive. He is a man who knows exactly what he wants and where he is heading. He is very proud of the fact that British musicals have done so well in America: 'We have', he says, 'destroyed the myth that only Americans know how to do them.'

At thirty-nine he still has plenty of time left to embark on other ventures, and there is no doubt about his determination to do so. Each year, at his English country home, he stages a festival at which he tries out new ideas. As his shows get more complex – and, he thinks, better – they get harder to stage. 'That means you can't run off copies for all the cities of the world as we did with *Evita* and therefore the profits are a lot less.' But the shareholders seem happy enough to trust the judgment of a man whose sweet melodies have the even sweeter obbligato of ringing cash registers.

Henry Luce

1898–1967

Founder of picture magazines

Henry Luce, known to his friends as Harry, was an innovative publisher who gave America three of its greatest magazines – *Time*, *Fortune*, and *Life*. It made him both powerful and very rich.

Luce was born in a mud-walled missionary compound in China, where his father (who came from Scranton, Pennsylvania) was a Presbyterian missionary. It is said that young Henry learned to speak Chinese at the feet of his nursemaid before he spoke English. At ten he went to a tough British-run boarding school in Cheffoo, where the boys, including Henry, were frequently flogged. He later said that he hated Cheffoo and loved it at the same time. When he was fourteen he went to the United States, having won a scholarship at Hotchkiss. His classmates promptly named him 'Chink'. Throughout his life he harboured a lingering resentment over the fact that he had not been born in America. He used to say wistfully that he would give anything to be able to claim some home town in the United States; when this remark was published he was invited to become an honorary citizen of Oskaloosa, Iowa, and he accepted.

Luce showed an early talent for journalism. At Hotchkiss he was editor-in-chief of the *Literary Monthly* and assistant managing editor of its weekly newspaper. Subsequently he went to Yale. His father, who had also been to Yale, gave him $500, but beyond that he earned every dollar of the cost of his education himself. He waited on tables, ran a student eating house, became campus representative of a tailor and a dry cleaner, and in his sophomore year took on the editorship of the *Daily News*. When he graduated, in the class of 1920, he was voted 'the most brilliant student'. He went to England for a year of postgraduate study at Oxford on a scholarship grant and, on his return, found a job on the old Chicago *Daily News* at a salary of $16 a week. He later switched to the *Baltimore News*, and the idea of *Time* was born there.

Luce was twenty-four when he and a classmate, Briton Hadden, decided to go into the publishing business on their own. Luce contributed the name, after noting how frequently it was linked in advertising with mankind's common goals – time to save, time to retire, time to get well, time to travel, time to think. Much of what *Time* was to become was set out in a section of their prospectus headed 'Editorial Bias'.

> There will be no editorial page in *Time*.
>
> No article will be written to prove any special case.
>
> But the editors recognize that complete neutrality on public questions and important news is probably as undesirable as it is impossible, and are therefore ready to acknowledge that certain prejudices may in varying measure predetermine their opinions on

the news. A catalogue of these prejudices would include such phrases as:

1. A belief that the world is round and an admiration of the statesman's 'view of the world'.
2. A general distrust of the present tendency toward increasing interference by government.
3. A prejudice against the rising cost of government.
4. Faith in things which money cannot buy.
5. A respect for the old, particularly in manners.
6. An interest in the new, particularly in ideas.

But this magazine is not founded to promulgate prejudices, liberal or conservative. To keep men well-informed . . . that, first and last, is the only axe this magazine has to grind. The magazine is one of news, not argument, and verges on the controversial only where it is necessary to print out what the news means.

Luce invented what is now known as '*Time*-style'. But it was one thing to have a good idea and quite another to raise the finance necessary to make it work. It took the two young men eight months to collect $86,000 of capital, mostly by selling stock to other Yale men. The first issue was published in 1923.

Luce contributed the name, after noting how frequently it was linked in advertising with mankind's common goals – time to save, time to retire, time to get well, time to travel, time to think.

It did well, and a few years later they were able to embark on another venture, a magazine for business which Luce decided to call *Fortune*. Briton Hadden died in 1929, and Luce became the undisputed boss of Time Inc.

According to people who worked for him at the time, he was serious, determined, introspective. His talent commanded respect, but it wasn't easy to like him. *Time* was his great love, and he never saw it merely as a commercial, money-making property: he was always striving to improve on the magazine's coverage and broaden its scope. He did, however, find time for romance: in 1935, he married Clare Boothe, a beautiful woman who later developed a remarkable career of her own – as a journalist, playwright and United States ambassador in Rome.

It was Clare who persuaded him to start a picture magazine. He assigned two of his senior editors to the project and they

'To keep men well-informed . . . that, first and last, is the only axe this magazine has to grind.'

came up with a host of possible names: *Look*, *Scoop*, *Eye*, *Parade*, *Click*, *Pick* and *Flash*. Luce didn't think any of them was right for what he had in mind. He decided, instead, to buy a defunct humour magazine called *Life* for $80,000 and launched his new publication under that title.

It was an instant success – something which no one had counted on. Yet it cost Harry Luce more than $5 million before it began to show a profit. The reason was that the money received from subscriptions and news-stand sales for any magazine is never enough to meet all the costs; the advertiser fills the gap. Space is usually contracted for long in advance of the publication date, and rates are determined by the publisher's estimate of circulation. Luce based his charges on an expected circulation of 250,000, but by the end of three months demand had reached the million mark. Luce had two alternatives. He could cut the print order until the advertising rates could be increased, but if *Life* were suddenly unavailable the public might turn to something else. The other option was to absorb the loss. Luce did just that: he put in $1 million of his own cash and borrowed another $4 million, pledging his Time Inc. stock as security in order to meet the deficits. It was a wise decision: *Life* went on to even greater glories.

Clare became a regular correspondent, interviewing most of

the important leaders of Europe and travelling to the Philippines, Burma, China, India and Egypt. In 1942 she won a seat in Congress, which she kept until 1946. By then she was a well-known public figure, and when Eisenhower became President he asked her to become US ambassador to Italy. Clare liked the idea, but said that it might be difficult for the Italians to accept a woman and that she didn't want a job which would separate her too long from her husband. When she talked it over with Harry, he urged her to accept. He had an office in Rome; he could, he said, run his magazines from there just as well as from New York. He promised to spend at least six months of every year in the Italian capital, and was confident his wife could handle the assignment.

When the nomination was announced the Italian press reacted strongly, as Clare had foreseen, but the US Senate confirmed the appointment and the couple sailed for Italy in 1953. The criticism continued, but she was popular with the Italian people and when she left, three years later, even the politicians who had opposed her expressed regret. Harry, who had made good on his promise of support, said in later years that the period in Rome was one of the happiest of his life.

He died in 1967 of an acute coronary thrombosis. His estate, amounting to well over $100 million worth of Time Inc. stock and other investments, has been carefully parcelled out beforehand. Clare received a lifetime income from $30 million of Time Inc. stock, producing a before-tax return of about $300,000 a year.

Since then all sorts of criticisms have been levelled against Luce: he was, it is said, arrogant and aggressive; difficult to work for; cold and lacking a sense of humour. He may well have been all of these things, but he was also a man who was deeply devoted to his craft – and to his country – and who managed to build and retain a close relationship with a woman who was equally strong-minded and individualistic. Time Inc., the publishing empire he built, continues to flourish.

Mark H. McCormack

b. 1930

The man who marketed sportsmen

In the early 1960s Mark McCormack was working for a law firm in Cleveland, Ohio, and playing golf as often as he could, when he first recognized that there was money to be made in sport. He was an admirer of Arnold Palmer, who had won a major golf championship and who, although still comparatively unknown, seemed destined to become a great player. McCormack decided that Palmer needed a manager who could look after his financial interests, and that he was the right man for the job. So he started a management company with less than $500 in capital, and, as he claimed later in his book *What They Don't Teach You at Harvard Business School*, 'gave birth to a new industry – the sports management and sports marketing industry'.

Actually, the idea was not all that revolutionary. Actors and other performers had, after all, been using managers for years. Sports stars had appeared in Hollywood movies. But McCormack was shrewd enough to realize that in the television age a sports celebrity's name could be a useful asset to image-conscious companies. He established some lucrative licensing and promotional relationships for Palmer, and later for others. His little company grew into the International Management Group, with offices around the world and several hundred million dollars in annual revenues.

According to McCormack, what they don't teach you at Harvard is what they *can't* teach you, which is how to read people and how to use that knowledge to get what you want. Business situations, he says, almost always come down to people situations. It is a generalization which obviously contains a sizeable element of truth, especially if one is involved in selling. But he is not entirely fair to the Harvard Business School: the success of his company *has* been taught there as a case study.

McCormack's second and third clients were also golfers who had yet to establish big reputations – Gary Player and Jack Nicklaus. It says much for his judgment that he spotted their potential at such an early stage. As it turned out, the trio came to dominate the world of golf for two decades. Many companies felt that they would benefit by having these men's names associated with them, and McCormack was pleased to find that they were champions off the golf course as well as on it.

By 1966 his business had become a major presence in golf. It was making a lot of money for its clients, and taking a handsome cut. But McCormack recognized that, if he wanted his company to grow, he would have to diversify. He decided against team sports, partly because of the regionality of most team sports athletes, which restricted their marketability, but also because he felt that amateur sportsmen would more readily identify with individuals. It seemed to him to make more sense to branch out into other individual sports, preferably those with an international profile, and to sign individual stars who would benefit from the company's total management approach to representation.

Motor racing seemed an obvious choice. It had a macho image and its stars made frequent headlines. McCormack signed Jackie Stewart, who was the world's leading driver in 1966, and soon added a score of other world-class drivers. In 1968, when tennis abandoned its amateur status, he added Rod Laver and Margaret Court (then the world's leading male and female players) to his stable. That year also produced skiing's first international superstar, Jean-Claude Killy, and it wasn't hard to persuade him that he would benefit from McCormack's efforts to exploit his popularity.

Such popularity, of course, is often short-lived. You have to keep on winning, and it is harder to do so in some sports than in others. In motor racing, you run a constant risk of death or serious injury. Men and women who have made it really big in sport can generally count on being remembered for quite some time, even if new stars have replaced them, but their market value is bound to decline. It is, therefore, important to make the most of one's fame while it lasts.

McCormack did his best to ensure that his clients would have a steady income after their playing days were over, which wasn't always easy. At the same time, he and his colleagues had to keep their eyes open for new talent. They also diversified their expertise in other ways. One significant move was the setting up of a TV division, Trans World International, which later became a leading independent producer of sports programmes and the world's largest representative of television rights to international sporting events, including Wimbledon, the US Tennis Open, the National Basketball Association and most of the major golf championships.

Another new venture was a corporate consulting division,

According to McCormack, what they don't teach you at Harvard is what they can't *teach you, which is how to read people and how to use that knowledge to get what you want.*

---

which he called Merchandising Consultants International. He hired people who could go into companies and, for a fee, work with their marketing groups to develop suitable sports promotions. By the mid-1960s the division had more than one hundred corporations on its roster. This led McCormack into the business of creating sports events, and implementing them at an add-on cost or in exchange for a profit participation. He and his colleagues invented the World Championship of

Women's Golf, the Pepsi Grand Slam, the World Triathlon championship and many other tours and events.

Still more divisions followed. The company changed its mind about team sports and also started to represent clients outside the sporting field – models, television celebrities and so on. It launched a financial management division to look after the investments of its stars (today it will even do personal financial management for top executives).

McCormack's critics say that his group has managed to get a 'stranglehold' on the sports business, which gives it undue power. He is certainly in a position of considerable strength. He has the clout to sign up new stars and get them a good deal; he is an obvious choice for corporations who want to become involved in sports promotions; and he has tied up many important events. But rival companies can, and do, compete with him. His group can't afford to become complacent: what counts, in the end, is the quality of the service it provides.

As chairman, president and chief executive McCormack spends a great deal of time travelling around the world. 'The nature of my business', he says,

> makes travel absolutely essential. It's difficult to make an arrangement to represent, say, a major sporting event in Australia without going there; it's hard to sell what they have without seeing it, and having sold it it's hard to make sure it's happening the way you sold it unless you're there watching it. Our business is international, the opportunities are international, and in order to capitalize on those opportunities you have to travel.

His lively book, *What They Don't Teach You at Harvard Business School*, has enjoyed well-deserved success; it is essential reading for any young entrepreneur who hopes to do well in a service industry.

Frank McNamara

Inventor of the charge card

After entertaining his dinner guests at a downtown New York restaurant, businessman Frank McNamara reached for his wallet and found an empty pocket instead. Following some discussion, the restaurant agreed to let him pay later. Never again, McNamara thought. Suppose he had one identification card that would give him – or any business executive – credit privileges at a number of fine restaurants? In 1950 he and two business friends evolved the concept which would, over the years, substantially affect the spending habits of businessmen around the world. The concept was Diners Club.

To say that the charge card industry started modestly seems an overstatement. In the beginning there were just two hundred members whose Diners Club cards were honoured at only two hotels and twenty-seven New York area restaurants. The first 'directory' of establishments, issued in February 1950, was the size of a pocket calendar designed to fit into a businessman's wallet. Today there are cards of virtually every type and description, issued by companies who followed McNamara's lead. A simple idea, arising from a businessman's temporary embarrassment, has spawned a vast, multi-national industry.

Charge cards have long since ceased to be a status symbol, used by a privileged few. Millions of people around the world now make regular use of them – not only in hotels and restaurants but also in stores, garages and airline ticket offices, at rent-a-car counters and so on. Diners, now owned by Citicorp, remains one of the top names but American Express has grown more rapidly through aggressive marketing. It has more than 17 million cardholders in the USA alone.

Banks and others have also established a strong position with their own credit cards. The original appeal of cards issued by the banks was to give an automatic right to borrow, summed up in the slogan 'Take the waiting out of wanting'. But the lines between credit and charge cards have become distinctly blurred. Bank cards can also be used as charge cards, and companies like American Express and Diners have moved into the lending business.

Many hotel and store chains have issued in-house cards in an effort to persuade people to spend more money with them. Another innovation, in recent years, has been the 'gold card', which is supposed to be more prestigious than the 'ordinary' card. American Express has even introduced a by-invitation-only platinum card.

Technology has also changed the nature of the card itself. The most common type of plastic card, these days, is the mag strip card. There is a core of paper or another substance laminated within layers of clear plastic material. Sealed under the plastic laminate is a brown strip of magnetic recording material very similar to conventional audio recording tape. In fact, commercial audio recording methods are used to 'write' on to the strip or read from it.

The mag strip card is very cheap to produce, but many experts predict that another type – the 'smart' card – will become dominant by the mid-1990s. The 'smart' card ('smart' meaning 'clever') looks like a credit card but in many ways is more like a mini-computer. Personal information is packed into a silicon chip on the card and then read or altered by passing it through an electronic terminal. This 'computer in your wallet' means that separate cards for cash dispensers, cheque guarantee and credit use are all incorporated in a single 'chip' card.

There is also the so-called laser card, pioneered chiefly by the Drexler Corporation. The basic idea is similar to that of the laser disc. Pits are cut in a metallic medium by a laser in a pattern representing letters and numbers. Such a card has a huge memory capacity – a typical Drexler card can store up to 2 million bytes (16 million bits) of data, equivalent to about eight hundred A4 pages of typed information.

With so much going on, it is hardly surprising that people are talking of the 'plastic age' – one in which money is gradually replaced by a plastic equivalent. There are many obvious advantages to the supplier. Among other things, cards give

In the beginning there were just two hundred members whose Diners Club cards were honoured at only two hotels and twenty-seven New York area restaurants.

him a database of names, with a personal financial profile, which can be exploited in a variety of ways. The most obvious is financial services, but all kinds of other merchandise can be sold; the process is helped by the fact that a great deal is known about the potential customer.

The principal advantage to the user is much as it appeared to Frank McNamara: it is a convenient way to settle bills, with the added merit of easy credit. But the proliferation of cards has also presented problems. Social pressures have built up as a result of borrowers with limited resources being encouraged to overspend. Using a card doesn't feel like using the real stuff – though when the monthly bill arrives the reality is considerable enough. Many people take a reckless view of debt.

Fraud is another headache. Card companies have had to defend themselves against a barrage of assaults – counterfeit cards, altered cards, lost or stolen cards, and cards lost or stolen through the mail. In the United States credit card skulduggery is estimated to cost $6 billion a year.

It is comparatively easy to forge plastic cards. One measure to defeat the forgers which was adopted a few years ago involved affixing a hologram, a three-dimensional image created by using an expensive and complex technique, as a guarantee that the card was genuine. Fears were expressed that it would prove feasible for criminals to fake or copy the holograms, but in fact they have proved a reliable test of the validity of the card. They do not, however, prove that a card belongs to a particular person. It can still be abused through lack of vigilance among retailers or banks. One of the strongest arguments in favour of 'smart' cards and laser cards is that they offer greater in-built security. Another answer to the security problem is greater computer-based co-operation among suppliers, on a worldwide scale.

But many experts say that eventually we won't need even the credit card. In theory, to achieve a 'cashless society' it is only necessary to establish that the customers really are who they say they are, and that there are sufficient funds in their account to cover the cost of their purchases. For the futuristically minded, that could mean counter-top devices capable of analyzing a customer's signature, fingerprints, even smell, and comparing the result over telecommunication lines with a master record held in a computer system.

The technology to replace cash with streams of electronic messages flowing from shop counters to bank computers has been available for years. There have been many experiments in electronic fund transfer at the point of sale. Progress, though, has been patchy. The same is true of another idea: that customers will sit at home, survey the merchandise on their television screens, order their requirements and have the funds automatically transferred from their bank account to the stores. As so often happens, the experts appear to have ignored (or at least under-rated) the human factor. People have grown used to credit cards and find them convenient; but they also like to go *out* to shop. For these and other reasons it seems likely that the plastic card will be with us for quite some time to come.

Simon Marks

1888–1964

'Don't ask the price, it's a penny'

The founder of a successful business usually hopes that his offspring will continue the good work. It doesn't always happen, of course, but sometimes a son or daughter will exceed all expectations. This was certainly the case with Simon Marks, who for nearly fifty years headed Britain's largest retail chain, Marks and Spencer. He made it into one of the best-run and most admired companies in the world.

Marks and Spencer was founded in 1884 by his father, MICHAEL MARKS. Born in 1859 at Blowim, a village in what was then Byelorussia, Michael shared the poverty and hardship suffered at that time by the great majority of Jews in Poland and Russia, and he emigrated to England at the age of twenty-four. He was penniless, he had not been trained for any trade, he had no relations or acquaintances in the country and, above all, he could neither read nor write. Stockton-on-Tees was his first stop, but he did not settle there. He soon moved on to Leeds, and the North of England was to remain the centre of his activities. The main reason why he chose Leeds may have been that the city at that time already had a Jewish community of over six thousand people, mostly employed in the rapidly developing clothing trade. It was an occupation which did not require much skill and training, and among his people in Leeds he was fairly certain of finding the work and help which they were accustomed to give to all those who came from a land of persecution.

The young Marks became a pedlar, carrying his merchandise in a pack and travelling around the area. His stock consisted of buttons, mending wools, pins, needles, tapes, woollen socks and stockings. In 1884 he opened a stall in the open market in Leeds. It consisted of a trestle table four feet by six feet and displayed the same kinds of merchandise that he had previously carried on his back. He later moved to the city's covered market hall, where he introduced an innovation which was to be of fundamental importance to the development of his business. He divided his stall into two sections, and placed all those items costing a penny in one section and all those costing more in the other, where the prices were individually marked. Above the penny section hung a board with the slogan: 'Don't ask the price, it's a penny.' The fixed-price policy quickly became so popular that he adopted it on all his stalls and henceforth sold nothing that cost more than a penny. (An American, Frank Winfield Woolworth, had applied the same principle some years earlier when he offered a table of five-cent items.)

In shops at this time it was still customary to keep goods in drawers under the counter or on shelves behind it. You had to ask for everything before you even saw if it was there. This did not happen when people came to shop with Michael Marks. They could walk around his bazaar without being pestered to buy. They were at ease. Out of the psychology of this approach to selling goods were to emerge two of the most important principles of mid-twentieth-century retail distribution: self-selection and self-service for the customer.

By 1890 the young immigrant was operating five penny bazaars in different northern cities, all selling under the slogan of 'Don't ask the price, it's a penny'. The business was becoming too large for one man to manage and Marks looked around for a partner to share the responsibilities. A business contact recommended Tom Spencer, his cashier, who he thought could offer the kind of help Michael Marks was looking for. Spencer was an excellent book-keeper and the two men got on well together. In September 1894 the firm of Marks and Spencer was formed, with Spencer paying £300 for his half-share in the partnership.

The first decade of the newly formed company witnessed spectacular growth both in sales volume and in the number of bazaars. By the end of 1900 there were thirty-six branches, of which twenty-four were in market halls and twelve were in shops. Marks moved his headquarters to Manchester and appointed regional supervisors. In 1903 the firm was transformed into a private limited company. Thomas Spencer retired in the same year; he died two years later, at the age of fifty-three. Marks found himself working harder than ever. Between 1903 and 1907 another twenty-four branches were opened. It all proved too much for Marks, who died in December 1907. He was only forty-four.

Simon Marks, his only son, was nineteen years old at the time and too inexperienced to take over. In the decade that followed, the control and management of the company fell into the hands of people outside the families of the founding partners, and there were sharp disagreements about the direction in which the business should develop. It was finally resolved through legal action by the Marks family and in 1917 the young Simon Marks became, at twenty-eight, chairman of a reconstructed board.

Marks recognized that the future would have to lie in store development. Woolworth's, which had opened its first British store in Liverpool in 1909, had become a formidable competitor and he decided to make a fact-finding visit to America. As he later recalled:

> It was there that I learned many new things. It was about my first serious lesson in the chain store art. I learned the value of more imposing, more commodious premises, modern methods of administration and the statistical control of stocks in relation to sales. I learned that new accounting machines could help to reduce the time to give the necessary information to hours instead of weeks. I learned the value of counter footage, that is, that each counter foot of space had to pay wages, rent, overhead expenses, and earn a profit. There could be no blind spots on the counters in so far as goods are concerned. This meant a much more exhaustive study of the goods we were selling and the needs of the public. It

meant that the staff who were operating with me had to be re-educated and re-trained. It meant new people, new forces.

When Marks returned from the USA he made a number of crucial decisions. His own business would be transformed into a chain of what he later called 'super stores'. There would be a new price limit of five shillings, and the primary objective of his company's merchandising policy would be to secure adequate supplies of good-quality products which could be sold within that limit. This, he felt, called for a radical new approach.

Up to that time Marks and Spencer, like other retailers, still obtained the great bulk of their supplies from the wholesaler, who acted as a middle-man between them and the manufacturers. The ultimate decision of what should be produced for the market lay in the hands of the manufacturer. The new concept in the mind of Simon Marks was something very different.

... the large-scale retailer should be an interpreter to industry of the needs and tastes of the public ... the scale of the retailer's operation could be such that the orders it placed with the manufacturer would justify long, continuous production runs with consequent economies of scale.

He firmly believed that the large-scale retailer should be an interpreter to industry of the needs and tastes of the public, and that, under the chain-store system of organization, the scale of the retailer's operation could be such that the orders it placed with the manufacturer would justify long, continuous production runs with consequent economies of scale. It required a complete change in the relationship between the retailer and the manufacturer.

The first step in implementing such a policy involved the elimination of the wholesaler. Not surprisingly, this met with strong opposition. But Marks persisted. The first with which he established a direct relationship was Corah, of Leicester, which produced hosiery under the brand name St Margaret. In 1928, when Marks and Spencer registered their own brand name for goods manufactured to their orders, a number of saints' names were considered to go along with St Margaret. Simon Marks finally chose St Michael, partly because his father's name had been Michael and partly because the archangel Michael was the guardian angel and patron of the Jewish people.

Similar arrangements were made with other companies. Marks decided to concentrate on those ranges of goods which sold most easily and, in sharp contrast to other retail stores, *reduced* the range and variety of the merchandise offered for sale. By 1932, over 70 per cent of the items listed in the 1926 prospectus had disappeared from the stores. Hardware, china and earthenware had gone, and so had cutlery, stationery and boot and shoe accessories. Fancy goods were restricted to clocks, watches and travel clocks; the range of toys had been greatly reduced. But while entire departments had been eliminated, turnover rose rapidly. The reduced range of merchandise meant increased turnover and enabled larger orders to be placed with the manufacturer, who in turn benefited from a more stable and secure volume as well as the long-term continuous run which made it possible to reduce the cost of production.

The determined pursuit of this policy gave Marks and Spencer a very special position in the retail sector and was a key factor in the company's much-envied success. By the time of Simon Marks's death it had become the most important chain in Britain, with a well-merited reputation for giving value for money.

His successors have extended the range of goods on offer, notably to food. They have opened stores in countries like France and Belgium, as well as in the UK. But there is still only one brand name – St Michael. All of the products are designed either by the company or jointly with the manufacturer, and made to precise and exacting specifications. Marks and Spencer's technical staff work closely with the manufacturer, advising and monitoring such matters as choice of raw materials, choice of production processes and techniques, quality control, production engineering and so on.

Most retailers sell, essentially, the *service* of making a good range of merchandise available to their customers. Their buyers choose among the various lines which are offered by a variety of suppliers. Simon Marks boldly rejected this conventional concept. He did not ignore the service element, but decided that what customers really wanted was not 'service' as such but a range of products that were known to be of good and dependable quality, priced at a level which they could afford. To achieve this, he drew the company into many activities which may seem more closely related to production than to distribution. It was a unique approach, maintained to this day, and Marks and Spencer's remarkable growth is ample proof of its effectiveness.

Robert Maxwell

b. 1923

Autocrat of technical publishing

But for World War II, Robert Maxwell would probably be a Soviet citizen and either a powerful bureaucrat or, as he cheerfully concedes, a prisoner in a Siberian labour camp. Instead he is an immensely rich publisher and printer in Britain, a multimillionaire who is working hard to put together a global media group. He owns national newspapers and the country's largest printing company, and is involved in various other enterprises, including television. All this started, in the late 1940s, with a brilliant innovative move: Maxwell introduced the international dimension into scientific publishing.

His childhood years were grim. Born Jan Ludwig Hoch, the only son of a Czech farm labourer, he left school at ten. His father was shot by the Nazis and his mother sent to a concentration camp. The young boy joined the Underground, was captured by the Germans and sentenced to death. He managed to escape to France, and eventually joined the British Army. Technically he was a German or Hungarian at the time, which meant that, if he had been caught again, he would have been executed as a traitor. So the Army gave him a new name, or rather several new names: he was called in turn Du Maurier, Jones and Maxwell. He earned himself a battlefield commission and Field-Marshal Montgomery personally pinned the Military Cross on his chest. He still likes to remind people that he was once a British officer, and his staff refer to him as 'Captain Bob'.

When the war ended, he spent a couple of years in Berlin. He was – and is – an accomplished linguist, speaking fluent German, Russian, Hungarian and several other languages. He worked in the press department of the Foreign Office and helped to run newly launched German newspapers, which gave him a wide range of contacts in the publishing world. Among the contacts he made was Julius Springer of Springer Verlag, the top German scientific publisher. He offered Maxwell a job as an agent for his export business.

One of the spoils of World War II for the victors in Europe was a huge cache of German classified material, much of it relating to technical developments. Maxwell was asked by the British government to import these valuable research documents in his private capacity, and was given a licence to do so. He put the deal through a company called Lange, Maxwell and Springer, but before long decided to buy his own business. Springer had a 49 per cent stake in a British publishing company, and Maxwell acquired it with the help of a London merchant bank. He renamed it Pergamon Press, and began to publish scientific journals and books.

Scientists, he recognized, are not like any other breed. As he put it: 'They are not tied to any one nation because they must build on one another's knowledge. They must be open, unless they are working on classified projects, so that they can test their ideas on one another. There are not just British nuclear physicists or Russian nuclear physicists, they are part of the same community and the best of them want to communicate with one another.'

He also understood the commercial potential of such a situation. He could, in effect, create very narrow but very powerful monopolies through starting scientific journals which became the accepted forum for exchange of information in any given discipline. Because they were essential reading, he was able to charge high subscription rates. In most cases, the cost was met by the organizations who employed the scientists and their subscriptions had to be paid in advance, which gave him a healthy cash flow. The scientists themselves, moreover, were happy to contribute material for nothing or even pay him for the privilege of having their work published. Today he owns some six hundred technical journals with a worldwide readership. He has an impressive range of contacts in the communist world, including the Soviet Union and China, and Pergamon Press is hugely profitable.

But things have not always gone smoothly for the ambitious and energetic Mr Maxwell. His early efforts to get into the newspaper business ended in several much-publicized defeats, and in 1969 he embarked on an ill-fated deal with Saul Steinberg of Leasco. Steinberg had made a bid for Pergamon, and Maxwell surprised the City by accepting. He explained that his decision was based on the conviction that Pergamon could not go it alone in the information storage and retrieval field. It was certain to become one of the major growth areas of publishing, particularly on the scientific and technical side in which Pergamon was interested. There would come a time when universities and companies would get most of their technical information, now taken from journals and books, from data banks. And for a publishing company to provide this service required a substantial investment in electronics and data processing hardware and software. Leasco had thousands of computers lying idle, and he, Maxwell, had thousands of items which needed to be computerized. It was an utterly logical and natural fit.

The deal, though, soon hit a number of snags. There was, it emerged, quite a difference between British and American auditing practices, and Leasco's auditors were unhappy about Maxwell's profit forecasts. After a stormy meeting in New York, Steinberg announced that he was withdrawing his offer. But Leasco had already bought a substantial number of shares in the market, which it could not sell without incurring huge losses. Steinberg used this holding to force Maxwell off the board. He also complained to the City Take-over Panel, and the British government decided to hold an inquiry. An interim report of that inquiry dismissed Maxwell as unfit to run a public company. He promptly took the investigators to court.

Like so many self-made men, he says he is no longer motivated by money. He claims that he works as hard as he does because 'I wish to be of service.'

The judge found substantially in Maxwell's favour, but the damage had been done.

While all this was going on, Pergamon got into a mess. The people running it were not in the founder's league, and he eventually managed to regain control by buying Steinberg's shares and making a bid for the rest. Profits revived, and he ploughed them back into the computerization programme that would have been provided by Leasco.

By 1980 he was ready for another big move. He went into

the stock market and acquired 29 per cent of the ailing British Printing Corporation, the largest printer in the country. The board fought back, but the company was making heavy losses and a year later its bankers asked Maxwell to take over. He has since restored it to profitability. In 1984 he bought the Mirror Group of newspapers. He thoroughly enjoys the role of newspaper proprietor, but says that his real aim is to build up an international information-handling giant. He reckons that one

'I have no inferiority complex,' he told me when we first met in his early days, 'and I am not frightened by big-sounding names. When I am confronted by powerful people, I remind myself that all men use lavatory paper.'

day there will only be ten or so global publishing companies – and he wants his business empire to be one of them.

Maxwell and his family trust own 100 per cent of Pergamon Press, which in turn owns 77 per cent of the publicly traded British Printing and Communications Corporation. Like so many self-made men, he says he is no longer motivated by money. He claims that he works as hard as he does because 'I wish to be of service.' But that sounds rather pompous, and is certainly not the only reason. He is the poor Czech boy who made good, the foreigner who came to Britain and won fame, the entrepreneur who loves new challenges. He needs to be admired and respected, and he needs to keep proving to himself that he is smarter than anyone else. He will never be accepted by some parts of the British establishment, and he has made numerous enemies, but he is widely admired and he has a good deal of power.

At one time, he tried to make a career in politics. He became a Labour Member of Parliament, but found life on the backbenches extremely frustrating. He never gained ministerial rank, but is proud of some of the things he achieved as an ordinary MP, such as the introduction of the Clean Air Act. He no longer wants to be in government, but clearly relishes the influence he wields as a media magnate. Single-minded and persistent, he feels that he still has much to do. He has always believed in aiming high. 'I have no inferiority complex,' he told me when we first met in his early days, 'and I am not frightened by big-sounding names. When I am confronted by powerful people, I remind myself that all men use lavatory paper.' One wonders if that thought slipped into his head during meetings with successful leaders in the Kremlin, the White House and Britain's own Downing Street. It probably did: one of his more endearing qualities is a strong sense of humour.

Louis B. Mayer

1885–1957

'More stars than there are in heaven'

It is difficult to say who was the leading innovator among the founders of the movie industry. They all contributed their share; it was, and is, that kind of business.

No person can truly be said to have invented the motion picture, though for many years the credit, in America at least, was given to Thomas Edison, who had after all invented nearly everything else from the phonograph to the electric light. The best known of the early devices was Edison's kinescope, which enabled short reels of film to be viewed through a peephole, but the real breakthrough came in 1895 with the discovery of a means of projecting the film on to a screen, thus making possible the gathering of an audience, the economic basis of an industry.

The men who *built* that industry were mainly immigrants or the sons of immigrants who arrived in America from central and eastern Europe during the mass immigration of the late nineteenth century – Louis B. Mayer, Samuel Goldwyn, Carl Laemmle, Adolph Zukor, William Fox, Harry Warner. They had little prior knowledge of show business, and most lacked serious creative talent, but they were hard-working opportunists who recognized the potential of the new medium (which many others, at the time, dismissed as a novelty) and resolved to make the most of it.

For almost three decades Louis B. Mayer was the head of Hollywood's largest and most successful studio, and he played a key role in the creation of what rapidly became one of the (if not *the*) principal economic and artistic cornerstones of the business – the Star System. He had a remarkable flair for spotting talent. It was he who immediately saw the star quality in the young Greta Garbo – before she spoke a word of English – and who discovered others, like Greer Garson and Hedy Lamarr. His studio, MGM, boasted that it had 'more stars than there are in heaven'. He also founded the Academy of Motion Picture Arts and Sciences.

Born in Russia, Mayer emigrated as a child with his parents, who settled in St John's, Nova Scotia; his father worked as a scrap collector and junk dealer. His son joined him in the business at the age of eight, and at nineteen moved to Boston, where he set up his own junk business and married the daughter of a local butcher. He bought his first movie house, at Haverhill in Massachusetts, in 1907, and gradually built up in partnership a chain of cinemas and legitimate theatres that extended from Canada to Pennsylvania. He started personal production with a hired Brooklyn studio in 1918 and then moved to a studio in Los Angeles. In 1924 he became production head at MGM, after the merger with Metro and Goldwyn's companies, a position he held until he reluctantly resigned in 1951. For several years in the thirties and forties he was the highest-salaried individual in the United States.

Mayer had a reputation as a bully, which seems to have been

well deserved. He could certainly be violent. He once knocked down Charlie Chaplin in a Los Angeles hotel after Charlie had made an allegedly offensive remark about his ex-wife, Mildred Chaplin, who was then working for Mayer.

Norman Mailer has said that the Star System was 'terribly fearful and oppressive, dictatorial and mean'. Mayer expected unquestioning obedience (he told a cocky producer that 'A man must learn to crawl before he can walk') and could wreak

He told a cocky producer that 'A man must learn to crawl before he can walk.'

terrible vengeance on those who crossed him. A self-styled expert on the behaviour of the American family, he frequently tampered with the work of writers and directors. But the System worked, the pay was good, and many able people managed to get along quite well with their temperamental boss. His flair for spotting talent extended to senior executives: it was Mayer, for example, who hired Irving Thalberg, and encouraged him to develop the concept of the 'prestige picture', a film that might lose at the box office yet bring kudos and goodwill to the studio, attracting respectable talent into the company's orbit, generating confidence and giving 'dignity' to the medium.

In the early days, movies were made in 'factories'. Mayer and others later introduced the term 'studio' for the place of production and 'laboratory' for the processing departments, because they thought it sounded more impressive and would attract a better type of person. Yet the studios *were* factories, and had to be in order to meet the huge demand from a rapidly growing number of movie houses.

Mayer was dictatorial, but he was certainly not the only one to rule his empire in an autocratic way. His rivals did much the same. Harry Cohn, the brawny, aggressive head of Columbia, boasted that 'I don't have ulcers, I give them.' Sam Goldwyn, another major star-maker, closely controlled every aspect of his production and was hard on those who failed to live up to his expectations. Darryl Zanuck, the head of Twentieth Century-Fox and a power-house of energy, often came raving on to sets to settle problems and once snapped at an over-eager director: 'For God's sake don't say yes until I've finished talking.' But even the most powerful mogul could not control public taste, and he was responsible to the bankers for his studio's flops as well as its successes. It says much for Mayer's judgment and skill that, in a rough business, he remained at the top for so many years. (See also WALT DISNEY.)

Michael Milken

b. 1946

'The premier financier of his generation'

Early in 1987 *Fortune* magazine described Michael Milken as 'the premier financier of his generation'. The label seemed well justified; at forty, he could look back on a remarkable track record in the complex business of finding ways of helping US corporations to mount takeover bids. His personal net worth was estimated at $500 million, making him one of the richest men in America.

Milken majored in economics at Berkeley, and then gained a BMA degree at the University of Pennsylvania's Wharton School in Philadelphia. While there, he got a job at Drexel Burnham Lambert, the investment banking firm. As a student, Milken had done research on so-called 'junk bonds'. These are unsecured, high-interest securities which receive low ratings from credit-rating agencies and are thus called 'junk'. At Drexel, he worked hard during the 1970s to convince some of the big institutions, such as pension funds and the banks, that these 'junk bonds' were less risky than most investors thought. The firm began to issue large amounts of them.

When the takeover boom got under way in the 1980s, Milken and his colleagues pioneered the concept of combining junk-bond financing with hostile bids. It greatly widened the range of businesses which could enter the takeover game. A potential buyer could set up a shell company – one with no real assets – which then issued new junk bonds. Drexel's corporate and individual clients were then approached by the shell company and presented with letters of commitment to buy the new junk bonds that would aid in the financing of the takeover after the shell company had acquired control. Once it had won, the corporate raider could use the target firm's assets as collateral to obtain additional bank loans.

High-yield financing, as Milken preferred to call it, proved to be of immense value to aggressive bidders. Through his network, a raider organizing a high-risk takeover could raise hundreds of millions or even billions of dollars in days. In one celebrated case, Drexel helped Saul Steinberg to come up with a $1.3 billion fund so that his shell company, MMM Acquisitions Corporation, could make an offer for Walt Disney Productions. The Disney board mounted a vigorous defence and the bid did not succeed, but Steinberg walked away with a profit of more than $60 million. Drexel was also behind most of the junk-bond financing arrangements which made it possible for T. Boone Pickens, the famous Texas raider, to mount some of his spectacular deals. Others got into the act, but the firm remained the leader in the field.

Tired, feeble companies need a good shaking up, he says. Poor managers, not takeovers, endanger companies and weaken the economy.

In 1986, the Federal Reserve Board decided to make this kind of financing more difficult. Milken was also asked by the SEC to assist with its enquiries into insider dealings. But by then junk bonds had become a major feature of the corporate scene; in 1985 alone, $18 billion worth of such bonds had been issued.

Though his name is primarily associated with junk bonds, Milken has been actively involved in other ploys, such as leveraged buy-outs. These are widely used to *prevent* a company from being taken over by a hostile bidder. In a leveraged buy-out a group of investors, which usually includes the management and financial institutions, acquires the business from the public shareholders. The acquisition is financed largely by borrowing against the assets of the company. By taking the business private, the people running it ensure, with the help of their supporters, that they not only keep their jobs but become stockholders themselves. They still have to worry about repaying their debts, but they have a much greater incentive to make their company more efficient.

Leveraged buy-outs have become an effective defence against takeovers. People like Milken make money from both, earning huge fees by selling their particular brand of expertise. Drexel's revenues in 1986 were around $4 billion; Milken's operations are said to have accounted for about 25 per cent of that staggering amount.

Inevitably, he and other investment bankers are often accused of profiting from a game which, it is said, does nothing for the economy. They are players who promote corporate capitalism for their own ends. Not surprisingly, Milken rejects this view. Tired, feeble companies need a good shaking up, he says. Poor managers, not takeovers, endanger companies and weaken the economy. It is a familiar argument, and it obviously has some merit. But it is hard to see how some of the raids he has helped to finance have benefited anyone other than the people whose main interest has been to amass easy fortunes.

Rupert Murdoch

b. 1931

The first global media magnate

Rupert Murdoch is the first media magnate of truly global influence, a unique phenomenon in the industry. He is the biggest press baron in both Britain and Australia, and a major force in the USA, where he owns newspapers, magazines, television stations and Twentieth Century-Fox. He also has a key stake in Hong Kong's *China Morning Post*. It is a formidable empire, largely built by the shrewd use of OPM – Other People's Money.

Murdoch (even those who have never met him usually call him Rupert) was born in Adelaide, Australia. His father, the late Sir Keith Murdoch, ran a well-known Australian newspaper company for many years, but never owned it. When he died, all his son inherited was a small Adelaide evening paper. In 1986, Rupert had the great satisfaction of adding his father's old company – by then one of Australia's top media groups – to his other interests. It was, he said, 'an emotional moment'. His mother described the deal as 'not a financial thing . . . it's very sentimental'.

Rupert Murdoch has always regarded himself, first and foremost, as a newspaperman. He still seems to enjoy the process of actually getting down to the job of creating the next day's paper; his editors have grown accustomed to the sudden appearance of their restless, shirt-sleeved proprietor. 'Print', he insists, 'is still the premier means of communication.'

Murdoch had just finished his degree course at Oxford when his father died in 1952. He went back to Australia and took over the evening paper. But the prospect of a lifetime in staid little Adelaide did not appeal to him: he wanted to play in the big league. Bankers were willing to listen to his ideas, initially because they had respected his father, but very soon because Rupert was bright, ambitious and bold. He acquired other papers and boosted their circulation; he also launched a new national daily, the *Australian*. But even that was clearly not enough: in 1968, at the age of thirty-seven, he went back to Britain because he saw a chance to get his hands on a paper which many people regarded as an 'institution' – the *News of the World*.

The owners were trying to fight off a takeover bid from ROBERT MAXWELL of Pergamon Press. Maxwell was a Member of Parliament and holder of the Military Cross, but he had been born in Czechoslovakia and the xenophobic management was appalled by the idea that a 'foreigner' should assume control of a paper which, in the words of the editor, was 'as British as roast beef'. Murdoch offered a deal under which his company, News Limited, would put some of its assets into the *News of the World* organization in return for shares which would give him virtual control. But Maxwell still thought he could win. A fierce battle developed, with both sides hurling insults at each other. At one point, Maxwell even tried to buy up Murdoch's own group.

Murdoch eventually emerged as the victor and, in subsequent years, added other newspapers. He bought the fading *Sun* from the Mirror Group for a trifling sum and transformed it into a brash tabloid – sharply presented stories, racy features and pretty girls. The formula was a tremendous success and the profits from the *Sun* later helped him to buy the country's two most prestigious papers, *The Times* and the *Sunday Times*.

Not long after reviving the *Sun*, Murdoch turned his attention to the United States, where he bought the *New York Post* and *New York* magazine. The *Post* was doing badly, but Murdoch thought it would benefit from the *Sun* treatment and bought in journalists from Britain and Australia to popularize it. The circulation doubled, but advertisers didn't like the new readers and the paper continued to lose money. It was one of his rare mistakes.

Other deals turned out to be more lucrative. He bought the *Village Voice* in 1977 for $8 million and sold it in 1986 for $50 million. He also acquired the *Chicago Sun-Times* in 1983, and sold it three years later at a profit of $75 million. Another bold move took him into films and television. He paid $250 million for a half-share in *Twentieth Century-Fox* and within a short

---

'Print', he insists, 'is still the premier means of communication.'

---

time bought the other half from his partner, Texas oil man Marvin Davis, for $325 million.

Many people were surprised that a man who claimed to be firmly committed to print should wish to branch out into the movie business. But Murdoch already owned television stations in Australia and he had plans to set up a fourth TV network in the United States, alongside NBC, CBS and ABC. Ownership of a film company would give him a great deal of useful programming material, including the Fox film library. Next, he spent $1.55 billion for six major television stations belonging to Metromedia Inc. In order to do this he had to become an American citizen.

Meanwhile he also commuted across the Atlantic to do battle with the powerful Fleet Street labour unions. For years they had held managements to ransom by threatening to strike whenever attempts were made to introduce new technology and curb overmanning. Murdoch decided on a course of action which other proprietors, afraid of losing their circulations, had not dared to take. He provoked a strike and then sacked his print workers, announcing that production would be transferred to a new plant at Wapping, in East London, where modern technology would be used whether they liked it or not. He offered to pay substantial compensation; at one point during the dispute he even told them that they could have the old plant for nothing and, if they wished, launch their own paper. The unions refused, and during the year-long fight that followed there were ugly scenes outside 'Fortress Wapping', as it became known after Murdoch surrounded it with barbed wire. The unions eventually gave in. It was a triumph for Murdoch: his bold, innovative move saved the company some $75 million in costs.

With the British problem sorted out, he was able to concentrate once again on his American venture. But then came the call from Australia which led to the acquisition of the company which his father had once managed. Murdoch was enjoying a brief Thanksgiving holiday in Aspen, Colorado, and made his decision at once. He flew to Australia by executive jet, called an immediate meeting and offered A$1.8 billion for the Melbourne-based company, which owned radio and television stations as well as influential newspapers like the *Melbourne Herald*. But there was a hurdle. Under Australian law, foreign citizens are prohibited from controlling more than 15 per cent of radio and TV stations. Having renounced his Australian citizenship in order to become an American, Murdoch had to accept that he could not hold on to his broadcasting interests. He therefore agreed to sell them for A$842

A typical headline in a business magazine called his activities a 'debt-defying high wire act'.

---

million. The deal still left him with the largest press group in the country, controlling about two-thirds of Australia's newspaper circulation.

Murdoch is an opportunist and an operator who likes to seek out poorly run bargains and turn them round. His technique, for many years, has been to look around the part of the business he knows best for under-managed assets and to go after them with single-minded determination. He has the ability continually to expand his horizons, to look beyond a single country even if the market close at hand seems almost terrifyingly large. His gambles sometimes fail, and many of his critics predict that it will all end in disaster – that eventually he will be buried under a mountain of debt. (A typical headline in a business magazine called his activities a 'debt-defying high wire act'.) They claim that he is on a treadmill: he has to keep gobbling up new properties simply to feed the monster he has created. But he has also pulled off some spectacularly successful deals, and if things should go wrong there are plenty of assets he could sell. Apart from his formidable media empire, they include interests in such diverse fields as hotels and resorts, property development, computer software, insurance and shipping, and Australia's Ansett airline.

To some people Murdoch is an ogre – a ruthless predator whose all-consuming ambition makes him not only a dangerous opponent but also an impossible man to work for. Some of the editors he has hired – such as Harold Evans, former editor of *The Times* – have become implacable enemies. To others he is the swashbuckler from Down Under, an aggressive tycoon who relishes a fight and constantly needs to prove to himself that he is a winner. To his many admirers he is the ultimate Media Man – a visionary with a global strategy that has already made him one of the most powerful tycoons in the world and who still has a long way to go.

Alfred Nobel

1833–96

The 'mad scientist' who benefited mankind

Everyone has heard of the Nobel Prize, but not everyone remembers these days that the man who set it up also gave the world one of its most important products – dynamite. Nobel was born in southern Sweden and moved with his parents to St Petersburg, Russia, when he was nine years old. His father, Immanuel, was a brilliant man with the unique gifts of being both a scientist and a shrewd businessman. Amongst many other projects he invented new types of land and sea mines which were used by the Russians during the Crimean War. He was renowned as an industrial pioneer and built up an international network of some ninety laboratories and factories in twenty countries, including Germany, France, Italy and Sweden. The Nobels were so successful in tsarist Russia that they were dubbed 'The Russian Rockefellers'.

When Alfred was twenty he started work in one of his father's laboratories outside Stockholm, where he quickly acquired a reputation as a 'mad scientist'. When the factory blew up in 1864, killing his youngest brother Emil and four others, the Swedish government refused permission to rebuild it. Determined, Alfred moved his experiments with nitroglycerine on to a barge on a lake and invented the formula for dynamite. He was an eccentric, a nomadic recluse who never married but who was a far-thinking humanitarian and a philanthropist.

It was his hand-written will which, in 1896, left £1,706,000 (equivalent to about £60 million today) to establish the five Nobel Prizes – for literature, physics, chemistry, medicine and peace, to be conferred on those who 'during the preceding year shall have conferred the greatest benefit on mankind'. They have been awarded annually since 1901.

The home of the Nobel Foundation, which manages the fund's capital and arranges the presentation of the prizes each December on the anniversary of Nobel's death, is a handsome house in the centre of Stockholm. The spirit of Alfred Nobel dominates the house – from an imposing bust atop a tall column in the lofty entrance hall to a powerful portrait of him as a scientist at work, which presides over the board room. His will is displayed in a glass showcase.

Choosing Nobel winners is not like judging an ordinary competition. It is a lengthy and expensive task, costing as much as the prizes themselves. Nominations – several hundred for each prize – pour in from previous winners and bodies around the world; they are adjudicated by a network of Nobel committees which then make recommendations to the prize-awarding institutions. These are all Swedish except in the case of the peace prize, which is decided by a group of Norwegians because Norway and Sweden were united when the Nobel Foundation was established. The people who run the Foundation say that the awards are made strictly on merit: it doesn't

'The Nobel idea is 100 per cent international; Nobel himself was an internationalist.'

matter which country the candidates come from. 'We are against counting prizes like Olympic medals. The Nobel idea is 100 per cent international; Nobel himself was an internationalist.' All laureates except the winner of the peace prize collect their medals, diplomas and cheques from the King of Sweden in front of an audience of 1600 before attending a banquet in Stockholm's City Hall.

It strikes many people as ironic that the 'mad scientist' who invented a destructive force like dynamite, which has been responsible for the death of so many people, should also have originated the world's most famous peace prize. But, of course, dynamite has also been a force for good – among other things it has greatly reduced the need for the kind of back-breaking toil which, in earlier times, led to the death of so many workers. Nobel himself no doubt thought that he was conferring a benefit on mankind.

Ken Olson

b. 1926

The ultimate team leader

When *Fortune* magazine called him 'America's most successful entrepreneur' in an article published in 1986, many people asked: 'Ken *who*?' Olson has never courted publicity and prefers to be labelled a professional manager; he assiduously avoids the use of the first person singular, insisting that he is simply the leader of a team. But his remarkable track record undoubtedly makes him one of the country's authentic business heroes and, though his authority is exercised through a central committee, colleagues say that he is in absolute control of the company he founded in 1957 – Digital Equipment Corporation.

Olson's love of machines began early, messing about with radios in the cellar of the family home in Stratford, Connecticut. At the age of eighteen he went into the US Navy and then entered the Massachusetts Institute of Technology, graduating as an electronics engineer. He became a research worker in the MIT computer laboratory and spent a year with IBM before setting up shop, with five partners, in the corner of an old Massachusetts textile mill.

They started with virtually nothing – just $70,000, mostly borrowed from a Boston venture capital firm. They did everything themselves, from sweeping the floors to the demanding, cerebral effort of designing the world's first commercial mini-computer. The company's growth since then is the epitome of the American business dream: in 1986 it had revenues of $7.6 billion and was generally reckoned to be IBM's most formidable competitor. Olson's stock was worth well over $200 million.

DEC is the star of the middle sector of the computer market, where it has outmanoeuvred IBM with a series of innovative products. It all started with that first mini-computer, a small, robust machine designed for scientists and engineers like Olson himself. An immediate smash hit, it opened an entire new chapter in the history of the computer industry, bringing data processing power down from remote corporate eyries to the departmental levels where the engineers could use it to crack day-to-day problems. Olson says that 'We saw our mission as introducing interactive computing, a strange new concept at the time.'

Scores of start-up companies in the US computer and electronics industry have since mirrored DEC's success, but Olson and his team have stayed ahead of all of them despite some daunting setbacks. In 1982–3 the company went through a crisis when its personal computer flopped dramatically and profits plunged. It generated a flood of obituary notices in the business press: Olson was written off as a man with founders' disease, the inability to see the need for change. But he bounced back.

Far from being inactive, Olson was at that time struggling to introduce a more centralized, conventional management system. As so often happens with a rapidly growing company, DEC had been run as a free-wheeling, undisciplined organization. Many of the key people were themselves entrepreneurs, good at ad hoc, spur-of-the-moment decisions, but reluctant to work together. Olson pushed through his reforms, often against the opposition of men who had helped him to build the company. DEC also introduced a new range of machines, which met with an excellent response.

What DEC has done with its new machines is to make it possible to link various types and sizes of products in a network which spreads computer power throughout an organization. Its computers span the power range from small desk-top personal computers to the bottom end of the large mainframes. Yet because they are all designed to talk to each other without expensive adaptations, they can simply be plugged together in the way that telephones can be hooked into the public network. 'The most important thing in business', Olson told an interviewer, 'is to have an organization that works together, and the key question in computing is to be able to tie up machines easily with each other.' He reckons that DEC's 'simple, elegant solution for tying a system together' has created a much better base for substantial growth.

'The most important thing in business', Olson told an interviewer, 'is to have an organization that works together, and the key question in computing is to be able to tie up machines easily with each other.'

DEC has a lower profile that some of its smaller competitors, which clearly suits its founder. Olson shuns ostentation, driving around in a Ford Escort and still working from a corner office of the old woollen mill where it all started. He sometimes goes off to tinker with the machines. 'We believe we are a product company,' he says. Like many businessmen with his kind of background, he doesn't much care for marketing, which he habitually describes as 'selling customers something they don't want'.

Aristotle Onassis

1906–75

Inventor of flags of convenience

The public may remember him chiefly as the Greek millionaire who married President Kennedy's widow, but Onassis himself had other claims to fame. By his own account he was responsible for one of the major innovations of the post-Depression years – the systematic exploitation of flags of convenience as a way of cutting red tape and avoiding tax.

Late in 1932, according to Onassis, his ship the *Penelope* was discharging part of her cargo in Rotterdam, bound for Copenhagen with the remaining freight. She was Greek-registered for sentimental reasons. Onassis was in London when he heard that the Greek consul in Rotterdam had refused to clear the ship until a replacement was found for one crewman, an assistant cook who had been taken to the hospital. The consul had invoked Greek shipping regulations – the replacement had to be another Greek. Onassis rushed over to Holland to plead with the consul, but he was adamant: no Greek cook, no clearance. The delay threatened the *Penelope*'s carefully devised work schedule, and Onassis went into action. Cabling and telephoning throughout the night, he managed to switch the ship's registration to Panama. When he met the Greek consul the next day, Onassis greeted him with champagne and the Greek flag wrapped in brown paper. 'My friend,' he said, 'you are now aboard a Panamanian ship.'

One of his rivals, Manuel Kulukundis, later disputed the claim that Onassis had pioneered the use of this device; but he was certainly one of the first to use it. He was also a pioneer in the independent oil tanker business. In the mid-1930s tankers were still a comparatively small business. Oil accounted for only 15 per cent of the world's total energy requirements: coal was king. Onassis recognized that oil would become steadily more essential for world industry and that ships were the best way to move it from source to market. He perceived that tankers could be much bigger than anyone then considered feasible, resulting in huge economies of scale in operating costs. He had the courage to push his vision through.

He was also ahead of his rivals in the use of long-term credit. His basic conception was to circumvent the hazards of borrowing by getting the financial institutions to lend long against the security of a charter with an oil company that lasted as long as the term of the loan. In effect, the institutions were lending not to Onassis but to the oil company. The charter fee paid by the company could be 'assigned' to the bank without passing through Onassis's hands. There was little or no risk involved since the credit ratings and reputations of some of the largest and most profitable oil companies in the world were substituted for his word and ability to make payments. It was, Onassis later said, like lending money to someone who proposed to rent a house to the Rockefellers. It did not matter whether the house had holes in the roof or was gold-plated; if the Rockefellers had agreed to pay the rent, that was good enough for anyone lending money on the house.

The companies were willing to go along because they realized that bigger tanker fleets were needed but did not want to make the massive investment that was required. They preferred to invest their own capital in the area of exploration and refining. Transport, they felt, could be left to outsiders. Onassis got his first loans from the Metropolitan Life Insurance Company of New York. Like others in the insurance business, it was constantly looking for viable long terms and the board was impressed by his ideas and by his ability to get the big oil companies on his side.

Onassis was an optimist, always ready to take chances and make his own luck. Born in the Greek quarter of Smyrna (now Izmir), on the west coast of Turkey, at the age of seventeen he made his way to Argentina with a few hundred dollars in his pocket. After working for a time on a telephone exchange, he went into the tobacco business. Later he developed an interest in shipping and sailed to London, the capital of the maritime world. Ships were cheap at the time, because of the depression, and he bought six vessels for $20,000 each. When international trade began to recover he was well placed to benefit.

His business life did not always run smoothly and there were

It was, Onassis later said, like lending money to someone who proposed to rent a house to the Rockefellers. It did not matter whether the house had holes in the roof or was gold-plated; if the Rockefellers had agreed to pay the rent, that was good enough for anyone lending money on the house.

many harrowing moments. One of the worst periods came in the mid-1950s, when the oil companies turned against him and organized a worldwide boycott on new charters for the Onassis fleet. He faced disaster, but was rescued by President Nasser's decision to nationalize the Suez Canal. Almost alone among the major independent owners, Onassis had the bulk of his fleet free when the stampede began for the extra tonnage to carry oil around the Cape of Good Hope. By his own account, he made between $60 and $70 million on the spot market in the hectic six months during which the Canal remained closed.

Onassis once listed his 'secrets of success'. Here are the main points:

1. Take care of your body. Exercise and stay trim. Keep a tan even if you have to use a lamp. To most people a tan in winter means only that you have been where the sun is, and in that respect, sun is money.

2. Once you have taken care of your physical appearance, establish a successful way of life. Live in an elegant building – even if you have to take a room in the attic – where you will rub shoulders with wealthy, successful people in the corridors and on the elevators. Frequent luxury cafés even if you have to sip your drinks. Soon you will learn that many people with money are very lonely.

3. If you are short of money, borrow it. And never ask for small loans. Borrow big but always repay promptly.

4. Keep your troubles to yourself and let people believe that you are having a wonderful time.

5. Don't sleep too much or you will wake up a failure. If you sleep three hours less each night for a year, you will have an extra month and a half to succeed in.

He might have added – but didn't – that you also have to have the courage to take risks. Onassis had it in abundance, and it made him very rich.

Jeno Paulucci

b. 1918

Maverick of the grocery trade

Imaginative promoters often succeed through business ventures which others – especially executives of large corporations – reject because they seem absurd. The career of Jeno Paulucci, the founder of Chun King Foods, is a good example. He set out his philosophy in the 1960s, in a book which he called (with characteristic lack of modesty) *How It Was to Make $100 Million in a Hurry*. 'I am a maverick,' he said. 'I believe that's probably the main reason why I have succeeded. I've done things that everybody said couldn't be done, and I've done them in what everybody said was a crazy way. If any young man comes to me and asks how to make his fortune, I tell him to do the same. Don't follow everybody else. Get off the beaten track. Be a little mad.'

Luigini Paulucci (he later changed his name to Jeno) was born in a small Minnesota iron-mining town, where his father worked as a miner and later ran a small grocery store. At the age of fourteen Jeno began working after school for a large store near his home, and developed a keen interest in the food business. He then went to work as a travelling salesman for a wholesale grocery firm and soon demonstrated his skill as a promoter.

Instead of selling groceries to one store at a time in ten-case lots, he developed a technique by which he rounded up whole groups of merchants in various localities, convinced them that they'd save money by buying co-operatively in volume, and ended by selling them groceries by the carload. He increased his sales still further by persuading the merchants that they should buy in volume *now*, not next month, because the price was sure to go up. To make this pitch believable, he sent himself telegrams, ostensibly from his employers. Each telegram said something like 'Warn customers price of peas will rise.' By waving the urgent-sounding message at his customers, he was able to make them place much bigger orders than they would have done otherwise.

But Paulucci knew that he would never get rich by working for someone else, so he started his own business. After exploring various possibilities he decided to produce and sell – of all things – oriental beansprouts. He found a partner, put up his savings, and borrowed $2500. Together they converted the back of his partner's store into a hydroponic garden with rows of water-filled troughs. They hired a few Japanese as consultants and gardeners. Paulucci persuaded some food processors to buy their output of bean sprouts, pack them in cans or jars and resell them to retail stores.

His friends were sceptical: the venture, they predicted,

would be short-lived. But the beansprouts sold well enough and Paulucci felt able to expand. He gave a contract to grow sprouts to a syndicate of businessmen and arranged to have the canning, too, done on a contract basis instead of selling the sprouts to middle-men. There was a shortage of cans because of the war, so Paulucci went to Washington and talked the War Production Board into letting him have several million slightly damaged tin cans. He had them labelled with the oriental

'If any young man comes to me and asks how to make his fortune, I tell him . . . Don't follow everybody else. Get off the beaten track. Be a little mad.'

name Foo Young, which he thought sounded suitably exotic.

The business continued to grow and eventually the partners bought an old pea-canning plant, converted it and began to do all their own canning. Paulucci also decided that, by adding other vegetables to the beansprouts, he could produce a chop suey mixture. he chose a new name, Chun King, and began advertising in the press. It worked so well that the product line was extended to include chow mein and other oriental dishes, which he sold to large national market chains. The company was still operating from a small building, but Paulucci managed to give the impression that he was running a major enterprise. Sales grew rapidly, aided by his off-beat promotions. He hired satirist Stan Freberg to make a series of commercials, in defiance of the generally accepted view that humour doesn't sell products. The public thought they were great. In his autobiography, Paulucci recalled that he and Freberg made a bet: if sales didn't rise appreciably after the commercials appeared on the air, Freberg would pull Paulucci in a rickshaw along Los Angeles's La Cienega Boulevard. If they did rise, Paulucci would do the same for Freberg. When it became clear that the commercials had succeeded, Paulucci was delighted to fulfill the terms of his bet. The media turned out in force for this unusual event, and the company got a lot of valuable publicity.

Chun King eventually became the major enterprise which he had said it was. Others tried to buy their way into the business, but Paulucci rejected all offers. In 1966, though, he changed his mind and sold his stock to the R. J. Reynolds Tobacco Company for $63 million cash. Together with his other investments, including a small but growing maker of Italian food and desserts, he had a net worth well above $100 million.

One can't help wondering how Paulucci, with his unorthodox ideas, would have fared if he had joined a big corporation instead of starting his own business. Paulucci wondered, too, and during his later years at Chun King set out to find the answer. He sent away for a battery of the psychological tests which were then becoming a popular way of judging applicants for corporate jobs. A junior executive was being hired and Paulucci asked him to take the tests. He took the same tests himself, using a false name. When the results came back from the psychologist, it turned out that the junior executive was a good man and worthy of being hired. But the other fellow who had taken the test was hopeless, quite unfit for any responsible business position.

John S. Pemberton

1841–86

Coke is it!

Many people helped to make Coca-Cola one of the most famous products in the world, but Dr Pemberton merits a place in business history as the creator of the drink. He served as a major in the Confederate Army during the Civil War and, when the war ended, he went into the drug business in Atlanta. Though a qualified pharmacist he was not a conspicuous success, partly because he was always experimenting. He eventually decided to concentrate all his efforts on a soft drink, and after considerable trial and error he came up with a formula that satisfied him. The date was 8 May 1886, and he carried his newly formed syrup down to Jacob's Pharmacy where carbonated water was added to it and it was placed on sale for 5 cents a glass.

It was Dr Pemberton's partner and bookkeeper, Frank M. Robinson, who suggested the name Coca-Cola, an alliterative compound of two of the ingredients of the new drink – 'coca' (the dried leaves of a South American shrub) and 'cola' (an extract of the kola nut). Robinson also wrote the name in flowing script, substantially the same as it appears today.

Pemberton talked some of the Atlanta soda fountain owners into dispensing Coca-Cola on a trial basis. During 1886 sales averaged thirteen drinks a day – a slow beginning for the unique syrup whose production, a century later, was to reach a billion gallons a year. He never fully realized the impact of the beverage he had created and in 1888 he sold all the rights to

ASA G. CANDLER, another young Atlanta druggist, for $2300. Pemberton died soon afterwards.

Candler, who had a flair for merchandising, gave up his other business interests to devote himself full time to Coca-Cola, and by 1892 sales had increased tenfold. With his brother, John S. Candler, Frank Robinson and two other friends he formed a corporation named the Coca-Cola Company. A firm believer in advertising, he maintained a consistent and innovative promotional programme, distributing thousands of coupons to sample Coca-Cola and giving away countless novelties all depicting the trademark sign.

While Candler's efforts centred on soda fountain sales, other ideas which would lead to much wider distribution were being developed. In Vicksburg, Mississippi, Joseph A. Biederharm was so impressed by the growing demand for the drink at his soda fountain that he installed bottling machines and became the first to put it into bottles. Large-scale bottling was made possible when Benjamin F. Thomas and Joseph B. Whitehead of Chattanooga, Tennessee secured from Candler in 1899 the exclusive rights to bottle and sell Coca-Cola in almost all of the United States. They selected local businessmen to establish community bottling operations in an early form of franchising agreement (see RAY KROC) under which the individuals received an exclusive right in a defined geographical area in which to develop a market for the beverage. This was the beginning of the locally owned and operated bottling industry which has played such a significant part in the global distribution of Coca-Cola.

At the turn of the century, sales had started to grow outside the United States. Coca-Cola arrived in Europe when Howard Candler, eldest son of the founder, took a jug of syrup with him on holiday to London.

In 1919 the Coca-Cola Company was sold by the Candler interests to an investment group headed by Atlanta banker ERNEST WOODRUFF, who had a clear vision of Coca-Cola as an international institution. His leadership took the product to new heights. Concepts now commonplace in modern merchandising were revolutionary in their time. New methods included developing a distinctive glass for use at soda fountains, and the innovative six-bottle carton introduced in the early 1920s when bottle sales exceeded fountain sales for the first time. Coolers were introduced, and were later improved with refrigeration and mechanical coin control, enabling self-service in factories, offices and other institutions.

Packaging of Coca-Cola in cans began in 1955 and for several years it was only the armed forces overseas who enjoyed this form of presentation. By the end of 1959, however, test marketing was complete, and in 1960 the civilian consumer began to see the drink in 12 ounce, flat-top cans in the shop. Plastic bottles arrived in 1977.

During 1886 sales averaged thirteen drinks a day – a slow beginning for the unique syrup whose production, a century later, was to reach a billion gallons a year.

Dr Pemberton had spent just $47 in the short period before handing his invention over to Candler. His successors have spent billions in a continuous campaign to keep the trademark in the public eye. A long line of slogans has been used, beginning with the oldest, Dr Pemberton's 'Delicious and Refreshing', in 1886. Here are some of the others:

Thirst Knows No Season (1922)
It Had to Be Good to Get Where It Is (1925)
Around the Corner from Anywhere (1927)
The Pause That Refreshes (1929)
It's the Refreshing Thing to Do (1936)
Global High Sigh (1944)
Sign of Good Taste (1957)
Be Really Refreshed (1959)
Things Go Better with Coke (1959)

But it was the public, not an advertising agency, which was responsible for the nickname 'Coke'. At first the company frowned on this practice, fearing loss of identity and substitution, but when customers persisted in asking for Coke it registered the trademark and began to use it regularly. 'It's the Real Thing', first used in 1942, was revived in 1969 to support a whole new merchandising stance for Coca-Cola. In 1971 young people from around the world gathered on a hilltop to sing the memorable 'I'd Like to Buy the World a Coke', a counterpoint to the turbulent times. In 1976 the reminder that 'Coke Adds Life' was introduced. It became the foundation for 'Have a Coke and a Smile', an immensely popular run of TV commercials. It was followed by 'Coke Is It'.

Through the years, advertising for Coca-Cola has followed the trends of the times, while the overall theme has been refreshment – one of the pleasant things of life, distinctive and popular throughout the world. Diet Coca-Cola was introduced in the early 1980s in response to a growing consumer demand for diet drinks.

But the company has also had its failures. In early 1985 it made a disastrous attempt to replace its flagship product,

The secret formula for Coca-Cola is kept in a bank vault in Atlanta and the exact recipe is known only to a few individuals.

Coke Classic, with a 'new' formula product and lost its place to Pepsi as America's number one soft drink. The venture was quickly dropped. It also made an unsuccessful effort to get into wine-making in the late 1970s. Other attempts at diversification have included forays into the frozen foods business and, in 1982, the acquisition of Columbia Pictures for $700 million.

But Dr Pemberton's beverage has remained the principal product, with foreign sales playing an increasingly important role. Deals have been signed with the Soviet Union and China, both vast markets, and new outlets have been opened up in Third World countries.

The secret formula for Coca-Cola is kept in a bank vault in Atlanta and the exact recipe is known only to a few individuals. The finished product consists of these ingredients made into a syrup to which water, sugar and carbonation have been added. It is then passed through to a bottle or can filler and is automatically fed into clean, sterilized bottles or cans. The filled containers are closed and conveyed to a packing machine, to be placed in cases. It is a simple, fully automated process and it is not surprising that over the years Coca-Cola has been one of the most imitated products in the world.

Much of its success in the century since Dr Pemberton came up with his formula has been due to clever merchandising – good packaging, skilful promotion. It has made Coke into a product which is as American as the hamburger and the hot dog.

James Cash Penney

1875–1971

The man with a thousand partners

J. C. Penney has often been called 'the man with a thousand partners' because, when he decided to build up a chain of stores, he based his plans on a simple principle. A store manager could buy a one-third partnership in a new store, provided he had trained another man to manage his former store.

Penney himself started with a third share in a tiny dry goods business in Kemmerer, a frontier town in the south-west corner of Wyoming. He invested $500 of his own savings and borrowed $1500, and ran the store. He later bought out his two partners, but the partnership idea seemed to him to have great merit and he applied it, whenever possible, to his subsequent ventures. What he was looking for, he explained to the people who came to him, were 'men who are capable of assuming responsibility, men with indestructible loyalty rooted in confidence in one another'.

Penney believed that anyone and everyone has in him the latent capacity to become 'a human dynamo, capable of accomplishing anything to which he aspires'. He was born the seventh of twelve children near Hamilton, Missouri, on the mortgaged farm of his father, an unsalaried Primitive Baptist minister. He made money as a boy by raising pigs and growing watermelons, and later ran a butcher's shop that failed because he would not deal with hotels that served liquor. Flat broke, he went to work for a local store, and in 1902 opened the business in Kemmerer. Others soon followed. He called them the Golden Rule Stores, and remembering his father's admonitions undertook to deal with his customers in accordance with the biblical injunction: 'Therefore all things whatsoever ye would that men should do to you, do ye even so to them.'

In Kemmerer, at the time, nearly all local trade was on credit at stores owned by the mining companies. Penney was against debt and, as befitted his middle name, dealt only in cash. But his prices were low, the stores were the kind of places people felt at home in, and if customers were not satisfied when they got their purchases home they could return the merchandise and get their money back. By 1910 the company had fourteen stores and eight partners, all of them small-town men who had started with him as clerks. He had given up management of the Kemmerer store and set up headquarters in Salt Lake City, Utah. He opened twenty additional stores in rapid succession in eight western states and, after a trip to Europe, changed the name from the Golden Rule to the J. C. Penney Company. Around that time, too, the business was incorporated under the laws of the state of Utah. Preferred stock was issued to each of the partners in proportion to their individual store interests, and dividends were paid on the basis of the earnings of each store.

Penney did not pay high salaries – indeed, he made it a rule to offer a new executive less than he had been paid in his previous job. He took the view that if a man would not come for less he 'had no proper insight into the opportunities offered by our partnership plan'. Profit-sharing was a keystone of the operation and he never called anyone an employee – to him, they were 'associates'.

As the company grew, he decided to establish a warehouse in Salt Lake City, which seemed a convenient distribution point to all the stores. His aim was not only to warehouse goods so as to have them ready at hand when special calls for them developed, but also to employ a man with expert training and experience in the company's lines who would do the bulk

Penney . . . made it a rule to offer a new executive less than he had been paid in his previous job. He took the view that if a man would not come for less he 'had no proper insight into the opportunities offered by our partnership plan'.

of the staple buying for everyone. This, he felt, would not only reduce costs but would also leave managers free to concentrate on running their stores, and keep an eye open for new locations and for good people.

'I had learned', he said later, 'that the vitality of a business depends upon the determination to find better ways of doing business through experiments.' But his colleagues did not care for the idea; they preferred to do their own individual buying.

Penney weighed all the arguments, and then decided to go ahead with the warehouse, with his own capital and at his own risk. if it succeeded, and his associates were convinced, he would incorporate it into the company.

It didn't succeed in the short term, chiefly because his managers made little use of it. Penney refused to bring pressure on them: it would, he said, have been contrary to the basic spirit of the partner-manager principle which he had always held inviolable. But he still felt that the idea was sound. Eventually he gained the support of his associates and J. C. Penney opened its own warehouses in New York and St Louis.

By 1916 the company had 127 stores and Penney was visualizing a chain with perhaps as many as 500. A limited amount of stock was issued for public sale, and expansion went on with tremendous strides. The 500th store was opened in 1923 – it was the one which had once belonged to his first employer.

Penney remained chairman of the board until 1946, when he handed over to his chosen successor, Earl Sams, who had also begun as a clerk in the original Kemmerer store. But when Sams died in 1950 he took the post again and held it until 1958. When Penney finally retired, credit was introduced for the first time and subsequently extended to the whole chain – against the founder's wishes.

He kept an office on the forty-fifth floor of the company's New York headquarters and, right up to his death at the age of ninety-five, he had five full-time secretaries to help him with a voluminous correspondence – with Penney retirees, young people seeking his advice, and others who wrote to him in connection with his charitable and religious endeavours. By the year in which he died the company had grown into the nation's second largest retailer of general merchandise, with more than 1600 stores and profits of over $162 million. Managers could no longer expect to become one-third partners, but the company still had a profit-sharing scheme and the store manager remained the key man. He selected much of his merchandise from lists and samples sent to him by head office, but he was not required to accept anything which he considered unsuited to his climate or to his customers' tastes. He could also choose the head office training, promotion and advertising aids best fitted to his needs.

J. C. Penney left an estate of $35 million. It may not have been as large as many of the other fortunes made during his lifetime, but it was still a very respectable sum.

H. Ross Perot

b. 1930

The Texan who managed Japanese-style

Strong-willed entrepreneurs often find it difficult to fit into large organizations who have acquired their business. This is what happened to the brashly unconventional Texan, H. Ross Perot, who sold his data processing company, EDS, to the giant General Motors in 1984 for $2.5 billion. Part of the purchase price was paid in shares, and Perot joined the board. Two years later his exasperated fellow directors voted to pay him $700 million to shut up and get out. The terms of the agreement called for him to sell back his shares; they also included a provision that he could be fined up to $7.5 million if he continued to criticize the company.

Chairman Roger Smith had bought EDS primarily because of its computer expertise, but apparently he also felt that Perot's entrepreneurial drive and fighting spirit would invigorate the mammoth corporation. Perot had been all too eager to oblige: he reckoned that there was a lot wrong with General Motors and that he was the man who could put it right.

He chastised GM for its volume of rules and for not seeing that car making was the economic equivalent of war, and he made it clear that he intended to break down the corporate hierarchy. The company's greatest resource, he argued, was its people. It was essential to change the adversary relationship between labour and management, to treat workers with respect, listen to their ideas and get them involved in solving problems. The Japanese, he said, understood this far better than the Americans.

> In many of our huge corporations we treat people like commodities. And people cannot be managed. Inventories can be managed, but people must be led. When people are reacting to being treated improperly, they are not doing their best work. And when they're not doing their best work, our international competitors can beat us. That is the core of our problem. It's not robots, it's not technology, it's how we treat our people.

Perot, who drove his own car and answered his own telephone, often mingled with workers on the production line and poked around dealers' showrooms in old clothes. He also made it plain that he planned to object if the senior management paid itself the usual year-end bonuses. It was, he declared, 'totally inappropriate' at a time when the company was closing plants and laying off employees. GM's top executives talked about the need for change but balked at 'sacrificing their lush corporate lifestyle'.

Inevitably, this unorthodox approach made him a lot of highly placed enemies. What finally convinced the board that it was time to act was his insistence on breaking one of GM's most fundamental rules: never go public with criticism. Perot told workers that the management was out of touch with its employees. At a meeting for car dealers, he said that GM wasn't building the cars that customers wanted. Interviewers were told that changing GM's corporate structure was like 'teaching an elephant to tap-dance'.

Perot clearly felt that his track record and position as the largest individual shareholder entitled him to say exactly what he thought. The board should not have been taken by surprise: he had always been outspoken.

The son of a Texas horse trader, he grew up in tough times. He was breaking horses for a dollar or two apiece by the age of six: his efforts left him with a broken nose. He later went to the US Naval Academy at Annapolis, Maryland, but was frustrated by the Navy's slow-moving system of promotion. 'I have no patience for red tape and inactivity,' he recalled when he first began to attract notice as a businessman. 'I'd make a bad politician.'

'Inventories can be managed, but people must be led. . . . That is the core of our problem. It's not robots, it's not technology, it's how we treat our people.'

He joined IBM, and quickly established himself as a loner – blunt, ambitious and very successful. In his fifth year with the company he sold his entire annual quota of contracts in the first week of January. While in the job, he proposed that IBM should create a service organization that would design, install and operate electronic data processing systems on a fixed contract basis. IBM thought the idea was absurdly impractical, so in 1962 he left and founded EDS with $1000 of savings. His wife, sister and mother were charter directors. When he went public six years later EDS was brought out at $16.50 a share, representing a near-record price–earnings ratio of 118 to 1. At the close of the first trading day, the stock was selling at $23 a share. At the height of the bull market a year later, it was quoted at $150 or more. It was heady stuff for a thirty-eight-year-old supersalesman.

By the time GM made its offer, EDS had grown to a large business with fifteen thousand dedicated and competitive employees. They were expected to work hard and personal discipline was strict, with Perot imposing his own puritanical standards on everyone. (Marital infidelity brought dismissal, and the company's dress code banned short skirts, loud ties and shoes with buckles and tassels.) But EDS also provided financial incentives in the form of a merit-rise system and stocks. When two of his employees were imprisoned in a fortress in revolutionary Iran, Perot staged a commando-like rescue which was spectacularly successful.

'There is no magic to winning,' Perot told an interviewer around this time. 'Hard work and initiative will do the trick, no more, no less.' He said that Winston Churchill was his personal hero. 'Churchill knew the value of an audacious plan and he knew the value of perseverance against the odds.' Well, yes. But it is one thing to apply that kind of approach to a growing company over which one has absolute control; it is quite another to impose it on a huge bureaucratic organization with 800,000 employees and its own traditional code of behaviour. Accustomed to dominating his company through the sheer force of his personality, Perot did not have the patience required to engineer change on a massive scale.

Many of his EDS managers also found it difficult to adjust themselves to GM's ways. They saw themselves as hi-tech hotshots; GM people were bloated bureaucrats. Perot's public attacks intensified the strains. This is the human side of mergers and acquisitions – a side that is all too often forgotten when big deals are made.

Entrepreneurs are natural fighters, and they are accustomed to being in charge. Like so many of the breed, Perot believes in teamwork – as long as he is the captain. But at GM he was only one of the players on the board. It was bound to lead to trouble.

Many people agree with his basic point: that corporations can never be truly competitive unless they make better use of people. Many share his admiration of the Japanese attitude to manager-employee relationships and argue, as he does, that American industry would be stronger if management enlisted workers as equals and allies. it does not mean that they are left-wing revolutionaries: Perot himself has always been fiercely anti-communist. But, of course, every company is entitled to make up its own mind about this. Perot might have achieved his objective, in time, if he had proceeded more cautiously and had refrained from sharing his opinions with outsiders. But that is not his way. He is impetuous and abrasive – a man of action who tends to turn everything he does into a crusade. Such people should really stick to running their own ship.

Laurence J. Peter

b. 1919

Inventor of the Peter Principle

Canadian-born Dr Laurence J. Peter achieved fame in 1969 with a wickedly funny book devoted to a new science invented by him: hierarchilogy. His studies, Dr Peter declared, had led him to formulate the Peter Principle: in a hierarchy every employee tends to rise to his level of incompetence.

The term 'hierarchy' was originally used to describe the system of church government by priests graded into ranks. The contemporary meaning includes any organization whose members or employees are arranged in order of rank, grade or class. All of them, according to Dr Peter, are controlled by the Peter Principle. Many may win a promotion or two, moving from one level of competence to a higher level of competence. But this qualifies them for still another promotion. For each individual, the final promotion is from a level of competence to a level of incompetence. So, given enough time – and assuming the existence of enough ranks in the hierarchy – each employee rises to, and remains at, his level of incompetence. Work is accomplished by those employees who have not yet reached their level of incompetence.

The Peter Principle quickly became a favourite topic of

conversation in the corporate world, and still tends to be quoted whenever someone wants to score a point against an enemy. The people who do so seldom recognize, or accept, that they themselves may be proof of the Principle in action.

It is, of course, easy to dismiss it as an amusing exaggeration. But everyone who has ever worked for a big corporation knows that it contains a disturbing element of truth. We all

---

In a hierarchy every employee tends to rise to his level of incompetence.

---

know people who plainly have risen to their level of incompetence and are determined to stay there, even though they no longer make any useful contribution – or, worse, prevent others from doing so. Many are weeded out, from time to time, by the upheavals which usually take place when corporations experience serious setbacks or merge with another business. But incompetent time-servers are generally experts in the art of survival. This is even more true of those working in public administration, where people are more likely to be judged by their willingness to 'play the game' than by their managerial skills and where there is less risk of sudden, dramatic shake-ups.

Dr Peter succeeded in drawing attention to the problem, but he didn't solve it. The remedy lies in the hands of those at the top; alas, they are often prime examples of the Peter Principle at work.

Alastair Pilkington

b. 1920

Inventor of float glass

Sir Alastair Pilkington – he was honoured with a knighthood in 1970 – invented the 'float' method of glass-making which revolutionized the industry in the 1960s. He had the idea in the early 1950s, allegedly while washing up: the sight of a plate floating on water, it is said, made him think that the same principle could be applied to the manufacture of glass. But it took seven years of hard work to prove that he was right, and the cost of developing the process brought his employers close to financial ruin. Although it was announced to the public in 1959, it was not until 1962–3 that it became uninterruptedly profitable. Since then it has made a vast amount of money for Pilkington Brothers: income from licensing and technical fees is running at a rate of £30 million (about $50 million) a year.

Alastair Pilkington was educated at Sherborne School and Trinity College, Cambridge. He became an officer in the Royal Artillery just before the outbreak of World War II, and later fought in the Mediterranean, where he was taken prisoner after the fall of Crete. When the war ended, he returned to Cambridge and gained a degree in mechanical science. He joined Pilkington Brothers (there was no family connection) as a technical officer in 1947.

When he started work on his process, the target was to make, more economically, the high-quality glass essential for shop windows, cars, mirrors and other applications where distortion-free glass was necessary. At that time this quality of glass could only be made by the costly and wasteful plate process, of which Pilkington Brothers had also been the innovator. Because there was glass-to-roller contact, surfaces were marked. They had to be ground and polished to produce the parallel surfaces which bring optical perfection in the finished product. Sheet glass – glass made by drawing it vertically in a ribbon from a furnace – was cheaper than polished plate glass because it was not ground or polished, but it was unacceptable for high-quality applications because the production method imparted some distortion. It was suitable for domestic and horticultural glazing, but could not replace polished plate. Many people in the glass industry had dreamed of combining the best features of both processes. They wanted to make glass with the brilliant surfaces of sheet glass and the flat and parallel surfaces of polished plate. Float glass proved to be the answer.

In the process, a continuous ribbon of glass moves out of the melting furnace and floats along the surface of a bath of molten tin. The ribbon is held at a high enough temperature over a long enough time for the irregularities to melt and for the surfaces to become flat and parallel: because the surface of the molten tin is flat, the glass also becomes flat. The ribbon is then cooled down while still on the molten tin, until the surfaces are hard enough for it to be taken out of the bath without rollers marking the bottom surface: so a glass of uniform thickness and with bright, fire-polished surfaces is produced without the need for grinding and polishing.

Alastair Pilkington encountered numerous setbacks during his seven years of hard labour. People, he recalls, kept asking him: 'When will you succeed?' All he could say was: 'We will know the answer to that only when we have succeeded.' The cost was far higher than anyone had bargained for, and it took considerable courage for the board of directors to go on supporting him. When he finally made it, they decided to license the process, chiefly to get some income but also in order to ensure that others would not find it worthwhile to research their own technology. The first foreign licence went to the Pittsburgh Plate Glass Company in 1962, and this was quickly followed by manufacturers in Europe, Japan, Czechoslovakia, the Soviet Union and others in the USA. Today the float glass process is licensed to thirty-five companies in twenty-nine countries and the Pilkington Group itself operates fourteen plants – six in North America, three in Britain, three in Germany, one in Sweden and one in South Africa.

Under the licensing arrangement the group gets a disclosure fee, a once-and-for-all payment for each float glass plant put down, and a royalty on sales. An improvements clause which gives all manufacturers an incentive to undertake development work is built into the licence. Any improvements made by Pilkington go automatically and freely to all licensees, but any patented improvements made by any of them can be sold to other licensees – with the exception of Pilkington, who receive it free.

Pilkington glass is used in everything from shop windows to skyscrapers. The company is the world leader in supplying windshields to jet aircraft, from Boeing's fleet to the most advanced jet fighter planes. Elsewhere in aviation its glass is

Alastair Pilkington encountered numerous setbacks during his seven years of hard labour. People, he recalls, kept asking him: 'When will you succeed?' All he could say was: 'We will know the answer to that only when we have succeeded.'

used as a heatproof shield for generations of guided missiles, which puts it in the forefront of Star Wars research. It also provides submarine periscopes and the glass for NATO's Challenger tank. It makes 20 per cent of all the spectacle lenses in the world. One in five of all the cars made in the world use Pilkington glass, and the company is now developing a range of glass auto components, from engine parts to body panels, which are so tough and shatter-proof that within the next decade they could replace much of the steel used in the industry.

Alastair Pilkington's endeavours, all those years ago, *could* have led to disaster. But his persistence paid off. It is one of the most remarkable success stories in British industry.

Allan Pinkerton

1819–84

Pioneer of private security

Allan Pinkerton was one of the pioneers in what is now a vast industry – private security. He was the most famous American detective of his day, and he created a company which dominated the field of investigations for more than thirty years.

Born in Scotland, Pinkerton started his working life as an apprentice cooper; then, at the age of nineteen, he set himself up in the business of making barrels. Four years later, with a newly acquired wife, he emigrated to Canada, but changed his mind and ended up in Chicago instead. After a year as an employee, he again started his own barrel-making business. According to some accounts, while searching for trees suitable for use as barrel staves he came upon evidence of the operations of a counterfeiting gang. He made contact with the local sheriff, and was instrumental in the capture of both the counterfeiters and their printing plant. Shortly afterwards he became a deputy sheriff himself – presumably because it was more exciting, and more remunerative, than making barrels.

In 1849 Pinkerton was appointed Chicago's first detective. He showed real ability and attracted a good press. A year later he decided to start his own agency. By 1853 it had a staff of five full-time detectives (one a woman), a secretary and several clerks. The railroads, which had expanded faster than public law enforcement agencies, chose him to guard their property and rolling stock.

During the Civil War he was asked to help with intelligence work, and established the Union's spy system in the South. His wartime record and contacts proved useful when he returned to his pre-war private detective business. He opened offices in New York City in 1866 and in Philadelphia the following year. In one much-publicized case Pinkerton investigators tracked down a gang who had taken $700,000 in cash, bonds and jewels from a safe in a locked railway company car. They recovered almost all the missing valuables.

Post-war industrial expansion, fed by an increasing flow of immigrants, also helped his business. With the growth came labour unrest and movements to organize workers. In the strife that ensued, the use of private security guards became commonplace. ANDREW CARNEGIE, for example, employed Pinkerton's men in his battle with workers at the Homestead factory near Pittsburgh. But the fight got so nasty and controversial that Pinkerton said his agency would no longer engage in such activities. A congressional subcommittee which looked into the Homestead affair decided that it had no jurisdiction to legislate in matters involving labour disputes, but declared that the execution of laws should not be farmed out to private individuals in the employ of private persons or corporations. A year later Congress passed, and the President signed, a bill which became known as the 'Pinkerton law': it barred the employment of Pinkerton or similar detective agencies by the government.

But Pinkerton continued to be heavily involved in the pursuit of criminals. Regional law officers had limited jurisdiction that stopped at territorial, county or state lines. Few crimes constituted violations of federal law, under which help might be sought from the relatively small number of federal officials. Train robbery, for example, did not become a federal crime until after World War I. But the railroads, and companies like

Adams Express and Wells Fargo, needed protection against the robbers and Pinkerton was ready to provide it. His agents chased many of the people who were later featured in Hollywood movies, including Frank and Jesse James and Butch Cassidy and the Wild Bunch. Working for commercial interests whose losses were considerable, Pinkerton was able to convince his clients that the posting of substantial rewards would be in their interest. As a result, the agency set up a network of sheriffs and informants who were eager to earn some extra cash.

In an era when there was no central agency maintaining records on known criminals, Pinkerton created files that set the pattern. He not only recorded the criminal's name and physical appearance, but also included a description of his *modus operandi*. When his agents were involved in an arrest, he would insist that the police strip every prisoner, so that they could make a note of each deformity, scar and mole. He was a pioneer in the establishment of what later became known as the 'rogues' gallery' – many of the photographs used on 'Wanted' posters originated from Pinkerton's files. He is also

He was a pioneer in the establishment of what later became known as the 'rogues' gallery' – many of the photographs used on 'Wanted' posters originated from Pinkerton's files.

credited with starting the contract uniform guard business, when his agency undertook to supply six uniformed men to guard businesses in Chicago in 1860.

The press of the day was lavish in its praise of the innovative detective. Pinkerton himself added to his prestige by publishing no fewer than eighteen books. Each of them told the story of some exploit of his, or of his agents. Totalling some 3 million words, they were best-sellers in the United

States and in Britain. In 1876 Pinkerton told one of his sons that he had seven writers working on them. He would prepare an outline, and they would do the rest.

After Pinkerton's death the business continued under the management of his descendants. It changed its name to Pinkerton's Inc. in 1965, and went public in 1967.

George Mortimer Pullman

1831–97

The sleeping car king

George Pullman made a huge fortune out of a good idea – the sleeping car. He did not dream it up originally, but he came to build railroad sleeping cars in such quantities, and to operate them, that his company was a monopoly and 'Pullman' became a generic name for the product.

Pullman began his working life as a cabinetmaker in New York. He later went to Chicago, where he did well for a time as a contractor. But railroads captured his imagination, and when he heard that some inventors had patented the idea of a sleeping car he decided to get into the business. The Alton Railroad gave him two old coaches and told him to see what he could do with them. He tackled the job with enthusiasm, and in September 1858 one of the converted coaches made its first run, between Bloomington and Chicago. The Alton sleepers proved popular, and another was added.

The concept did not immediately spread to other lines, as he had hoped it would, but he persisted. In 1864 he applied for and received two patents – one for a hinged upper berth, the other for hinging the back and seat cushion so they could become a part of the lower berth. He then spent $20,000 on a sumptuous piece of rolling stock he called the Pioneer. It had plush mirrors, fancy panels and comfortable berths that could be folded up during the day. It was also a foot wider and two feet higher than other cars, and it rode on springs reinforced by solid rubber blocks.

Affluent travellers loved it, and Pullman cars were soon in use on several railroad lines. He built a combination sleeping and dining car, which he called a Pullman hotel car. A year later he designed the first diner, which he named the Delmonico. In 1870 a complete train, the Pullman Hotel Express, carried a group of Bostonians on the first transcontinental trip to San Francisco. The trip attracted enormous publicity, and Pullman's company grew rapidly. Many rich people of the day ordered their own private railroad cars, which became an important symbol of wealth. Some looked like miniature stately homes, with gilded ceilings, expensive French furniture and even pianos.

Most of the early Pullman cars were made in Palmyra, New

But its founder came under increasing attack for exploiting his twenty thousand workers. . . . Critics now called his model community 'a company-dominated serfdom operated for company profit'.

York, then in Detroit. In 1881 George Pullman founded his own satrapy, the model town of Pullman on the lake shore just south of Chicago. It was hailed as the start of a new era in the lives of working people. Pullman was by then spending more than $5 million a year in wages, and he got back a great part of this sum by renting out houses and selling his workers food, gas, water and a variety of compulsory services and conveniences at highly profitable rates.

The company was so successful that George Pullman was able to eliminate most of his rivals, by either buying them out or forcing them into bankruptcy. His town expanded. (So did Chicago, and his town in time became part of the big city.) But its founder came under increasing attack for exploiting his twenty thousand workers: the 'new era in the lives of working people' had turned out to be very different from the one which had been so optimistically expected. Critics now called his model community 'a company-dominated serfdom operated for company profit'. In 1894, after Pullman had refused to restore a recent wage cut, the men went out on strike. Thousands of federal troops were sent to 'keep order', and there was a great deal of violence. Pullman 'won' the strike, but his reputation was severely damaged. He died three years later.

It is a pity that a man who had shown such drive and imagination, and such an innovative spirit, ended up spoiling an enterprising venture with a public display of arrogance and greed. He was not the only one to do so – much the same criticism was levelled at the mining communities with their 'company stores' – but it was a foolish move which destroyed much of the goodwill he had accumulated. George Pullman made many millions, and Pullman cars retained their popularity, but the people who had helped him to make it all happen were left with bitter memories.

Mary Quant

b. 1934

The symbol of Swinging London

Mary Quant became internationally famous in the 1960s for her casual clothes and spicy colours, and especially for her popularization of the mini-skirt. As the fashion director of Harrods put it: 'Before Mary Quant girls dressed like their mothers; after her they didn't.'

Born in London, Mary went to a variety of schools before enrolling at Goldsmith's College of Art. She says that even as a child she was obsessed with clothes. 'I had a tremendous sense of Me and was always making things and adapting my school uniforms.' By the age of eighteen she was determined to be a professional designer, making the sort of clothes she wanted to wear. Her parents were academics and considered fashion too risky, so they sent her to a straight art school. At twenty-one, however, she joined up with two male business partners and opened her first boutique in the King's Road, Chelsea, which was to become the heart of 'Swinging London'.

The post-war years had until then been rather drab. People were tired of austerity; the young, particularly, wanted a bit of fun. Mary Quant caught this mood at the right moment and Bazaar was an instant success. Her specific insight was that cheap, mass-produced clothes could be given the magic ingredient of Style. And she created the style, the 'look', the image, which exactly portrayed the 'Swinging London' of her time.

There had never been a shop like Bazaar. A sculptor friend made some extravagant and provocative figures for the windows, and inside the racks were full of exciting things to wear. The partners had no working capital: they had to sell the clothes to get money to buy material to make more clothes. Mary would go off to Harrods to buy fabrics. She was paid £5 a week and made the clothes and dressed the windows. The two men handled the business side. They also ran a restaurant, called Alexander's, under the shop; it soon became the smartest eating place in Chelsea. All the In Crowd came – people like Princess Grace of Monaco, Brigitte Bardot and John Osborne.

Within a few years Quant was in mass production and British girls were wearing unheard of things: plastic boots and skirts, clashing colours, coloured rights, fun furs. Mary Quant herself, with her Vidal Sassoon haircut and mini, was a national figure – a walking advertisement for her own Total Look.

More Bazaars were opened and her clothes also began to attract attention in America. J.C. PENNEY signed her to design clothes for its stores throughout the country. She staged her own shows, and in one year made twenty-two trips across the Atlantic, taking five or six models and a pop group with her. 'The business', she said later, 'filled a vacuum which was there at the time; the climate was right.' A company was launched to manufacture dresses and sportswear for worldwide distribution, and in 1966 Mary went into cosmetics. She brought out a new range that completely broke with the tradition of packaging cosmetics in soft pastels to give them 'feminine appeal', choosing instead the hard colours of black and silver. She moved away, too, from a romantic approach in her product names and advertising copy. Everything was synonymous with the new, liberated, independent mood of mini-skirted women. Her cleaner was Come Clean, her eye-shadow Jeepers Peepers.

In 1970 she came up with a Make-up to Make Love In. The idea, she explained, was to produce a range in which a girl could kiss and cuddle without looking smudged and frightful. 'Normally if a girl goes to bed in her make-up, she gets up looking a hideous mess.' Targeted at women between the ages of eighteen and thirty, the range ran for several years and established Mary Quant in the British cosmetics industry.

In 1970, too, Mary produced her first son, whom she called Orlando. She had married one of her partners, Alexander Plunket-Greene, back in 1957, but she had been 'terribly busy doing other things and didn't want to have a child and hand him to someone else to look after'. Becoming a mother, she later said, 'was quite the most important thing that happened

'Before Mary Quant girls dressed like their mothers; after her they didn't.'

to me'. She carried on working, but the pace slowed and she became a member of the fashion establishment rather than a radical innovator. She was awarded the OBE, made a member of the Design Council, a consultant to the Victoria and Albert Museum, and an adviser to the British-American Bicentennial Liaison Committee. The cosmetics business was taken over by Smith & Nephew and subsequently sold to Max Factor. She also gave her name to household products, children's clothes, hair fashion accessories, sunglasses and even stationery.

Mary Quant's great achievement was to recognize the needs of lively young people, and to cater for them at prices they could afford. She had an instinct for anticipating a mood – like the mini – which had mass appeal. She gave her generation a chance to express their individuality and, in doing so, helped to change the London scene.

Her work has been widely imitated, and today there are numerous rivals. But the name Mary Quant lives on. One of the more recent innovations is the Colour Shop, featuring co-ordinated fashion accessories displayed sympathetically in a colour-related scheme. It seems to have done particularly well in Japan, where eighty such shops have been opened.

Cecil John Rhodes

1853–1902

Imperialist visionary

To have an entire country named after him is a rare distinction for a businessman. But Cecil Rhodes, who created Rhodesia (now Zambia and Zimbabwe), was never interested in just making money – he was a visionary imperialist who regarded his considerable fortune as a means to an end. 'If there be a God,' he said, 'I think what he would like me to do is to paint as much of Africa British-red as possible.' It was his misfortune that he came upon the scene at a time when British faith in its imperial destiny was already waning, but Rhodesia survived long after his own death at the age of forty-nine. Zimbabwe did not become known by its modern name until majority rule was established in 1980. Northern Rhodesia became independent as Zambia in 1964.

Rhodes was born in a quiet English country vicarage, the third son of the Reverend Francis William Rhodes. He was brought up in the strict, pious atmosphere of a Victorian family, and his father was anxious that Cecil and all his brothers should enter the Church 'as a preliminary step to becoming angels'. But Cecil caught tuberculosis and the doctor recommended an open-air life to restore his health. in 1870 he went to South Africa to join his eldest brother Herbert, who ran a cotton farm in Natal. Herbert soon took off for the newly discovered diamond fields of Kimberley, and his letters were so enthusiastic that Cecil decided to join him.

Herbert's claims were in the original mine of Vooruitzicht, known as the De Beers through the names of the brothers who had owned it. Cecil set up his tent and started digging. The mine was already deepening fast: each claim owner worked a patch of ground thirty feet square, gouging out the yellow earth in which the diamonds were hidden. As Cecil wrote home to his mother, it was like a monumental Stilton cheese.

After a while he went into partnership with another young Englishman, Charles Rudd. He already had a profitable sideline going in renting out steam pumps to suck the water out of flooded claims. Now he told Rudd that 'The time is coming when the small man will have to go. These pits cannot be worked much deeper. We shall have to mine the ground on the largest possible scale. Now is the time to buy.'

Rhodes and Rudd concentrated their buying on the De Beers mine. They soon owned a major share of the claims and in 1880 formed the De Beers Mining Company, with a capital of £200,000. They later joined forces with Alfred Beit, a diamond buyer who had a reputation as a financial wizard, and together they took on their most formidable rival, a cheerful young cockney called Barney Barnato. A fierce battle developed, at the end of which Rhodes emerged as the victor. It gave him, at thirty-five, control of 90 per cent of the world's diamond output and, with the resources of De Beers Consolidated Mines behind him, the financial power to pursue his African ambitions.

But another step had to be taken first. Having got his hands on diamond production, Rhodes devised a way of ensuring control over prices. His conception was that the supply of rough diamonds from the mines must be constantly adjusted to match fluctuating world demand. Production and sales must be allied, so that in boom times they would get the maximum prices – and profit – whereas in lean times they could underpin price levels by cutting production or stockpiling diamonds.

He granted the sole marketing rights to a consortium formed by ten dealers, each of whom was assigned a quota. This consortium became known as the Diamond Syndicate, and, in the years that followed, Rhodes's successors ensured that it maintained its power by persuading producers who found new diamond fields that it was in their interest to enter into a marketing arrangement with De Beers, which continued to decide how many diamonds should be taken from where, and how many parcelled out to dealers.

Rhodes also perceived that the whole foundation of the diamond's worth was based on the relationship between men and women; as long as they fell in love the future of the diamond was assured. He even calculated that four million diamonds

'If there be a God, I think what he would like me to do is to paint as much of Africa British-red as possible.'

were needed every year for engagement rings. This was later to be followed up by Sir Ernest Oppenheimer and his son, Harry, in a worldwide advertising campaign under the slogan 'Diamonds are Forever'.

While forming the syndicate, Rhodes also ran for the Cape Parliament and built the base for a political party that made him Prime Minister of the Cape Colony. He used both his money and his power to further his dream of a British Empire that would embrace the whole continent of Africa. He looked northward from South Africa and saw that the territory of the Mashonas and the Matabeles, between the Limpopo and the Zambesi, was ripe for the British touch. He induced King Lobengula of Matabeleland, who held some sort of sway over both the Mashonas and the Matabeles, to grant him a mining concession in those areas and then persuaded the British government to allow him a royal charter, authorizing him to govern and administer them. He formed a charter company, the British South Africa Company, to occupy the country, and in 1890 he sent a column of pioneers northwards into Mashonaland. When they got there, they were disbanded and set loose as settlers.

Under its charter, the British South Africa Company could acquire territory, make treaties, administer laws, levy taxes and custom duties, coin money and maintain its own armed forces. It laid its own railways, built its own roads, established courts and was served by its own district officers and telegraph services. Every immigrant was bound by its laws and required to defend its possessions if called upon to do so. In return the company helped to settle him, supplied stock at reduced terms, distributed free seed and undertook to buy crops. Before long, the company's territory was known as Rhodesia.

But it was not enough for the ambitious Englishman. As Prime Minister of the Cape he annexed Pongoland, to the east of the colony's borders, and set out to acquire other territories. All that stood in his way were the prickly little Boer republic of the Orange Free State, and President Paul Kruger's South African Republic over the Vaal. They turned out to be a tougher proposition than he – or anyone else – had bargained for. In the aftermath of a crude attempt to seize the government of the Transvaal, Rhodes was forced to resign his premiership of the Cape and leave the company's board. By the time he died in 1902 his fortune had been reduced through political spending

Rhodes also perceived that the whole foundation of the diamond's worth was based on the relationship between men and women; as long as they fell in love the future of the diamond was assured.

and inattention to about $5 million, which he left to establish the Rhodes scholarships at Oxford.

It is easy now to condemn him as an opportunistic adventurer, a man whose messianic vision led him to ride roughshod over the rights of others. But this was how the British Empire had been built: Rhodes was merely following the example of the East India Company, the Hudson's Bay Company, the Levant Company and similar enterprises. It took courage, as well as money and vision, to pursue his dreams.

At his death his coffin was taken to Rhodesia, and on the way the mourners passed several thousand Matabele tribesmen from all parts of the country. The Matabele had known Rhodes as Mla'mlakunzi, Separator of the Fighting Bulls, the man whose personal bravery at the time of the Matabele Rebellion had saved them from destruction at the hands of the white man. Now they gave him their royal salute: 'Bayete'. Never before had they honoured an outsider in this way: only Umziligazi, the founder of their nation, and their great chief Lobengula, had been given this accolade. He was buried in a rock cave, close to the cave in which Umziligazi himself was entombed. A plain brass plate was riveted upon the face of the rock: 'Here Lie the Remains of Cecil John Rhodes', as directed in his will.

Anita Roddick

b. 1942

'Common sense sells'

Anita Roddick says she got the idea for her business – the Body Shop – during a year-long trip around the world at the age of twenty-five. She learned how women in unsophisticated societies cleansed and moisturized their skin and hair, and thought that products made from their natural recipes might also have considerable appeal in her native England. The potential turned out to be far greater than she had expected: today there is a worldwide network of more than 250 Body Shops.

But two years went by before Anita was able to turn her idea into reality. When she returned from her trip she met and fell in love with Gordon Roddick, a Scot who had also done a considerable amount of travelling. They bought an old Victorian house and converted it into a hotel; they also ran a restaurant. It was hard work, and it didn't seem to be getting anywhere. It was then that Anita told Gordon about her project, and he agreed that she should have a go. They sold the restaurant and put a friend in charge of the hotel. Anita got a modest loan from the bank and found a small shop in Brighton.

Out of five basic ingredients a local herbalist mixed twenty-five different lotions, shampoos and bath oils. Anita overcome the problem of trying to fill a whole shop with twenty-five products by selling five sizes of each; any spaces left were filled with green plants. An art student designed the logo and Anita hand-wrote the labels herself. Gordon decided that he wasn't really needed and went off on a trip to South America; by the time he got back she had opened a second shop, in Chichester.

Anita was born into an Italian immigrant family. She is an enthusiast who believes in retailing as 'theatre'. Her concept is very different from the traditional department store counter brands of cosmetics. Each of her shops is designed to be an Aladdin's cave of bright colours, warm and tantalizing smells, and intriguing products to care for one's body – such as the pink Peppermint Foot Lotion introduced in response to foot damage suffered by a customer who had taken part in the London Marathon; Elderflower Eye Gel, which was concocted to meet a specific request from VDU operators complaining of eye strain; and a sapphire blue shampoo with menthol to slow hair loss. Traditional herbal wisdom is combined with startlingly imaginative marketing ideas. 'The Body Shop', says Anita, 'fosters a spirit of experimentation and a creative climate in which we produce new products out of old ingredients. We are not afraid to reach into the past, or look at the practices of other cultures, in order to improve what we have here and now – and in the future. The past is our prologue.'

According to her, the remarkable properties of natural organic and herbal substances which had been used for thousands of years without side effects had been ignored by the industry until she came along. During her travels, she says, she saw primitive societies using unrefined vegetable products 'with spectacular results'. When smoothed into the body, cocoa butter gives a beautiful sheen, moisturizes, protects and prevents stretch marks; when rubbed over the skin the flesh of the pineapple actually exfoliates the dead skin, leaving the surface clear and clean by the action of an enzyme called bromelin; almond oil, beeswax and rosewater have been used

'We are not afraid to reach into the past, or look at the practices of other cultures, in order to improve what we have here and now – and in the future. The past is our prologue.'

to make cleansers and moisturizers since the days of ancient Greece.

The Body Shop now sells more than three hundred products, about 30 per cent of which are manufactured by the company. Suppliers of the rest make them to Anita Roddick's formulas and sign a declaration that the ingredients have not been tested on animals in the past five years. This is very much part of the idealism which, she says, makes her operation different from others. 'I firmly believe that it is wrong to do laboratory testing of products when the end result is for our vanity.' She talks a great deal about her concern with 'environmental and social issues', which has undoubtedly added to the appeal of her enterprise, especially among the young.

A meeting of UK franchisees was told: 'We cannot go into the 1990s thinking that the Body Shop is merely a machine for grinding out profits. We have to ask ourselves essential questions: what will be the most important social issues facing ourselves and our management, or indeed British management, by 1990? We must judge ourselves by our ideals, but in the full knowledge that our staff and the public will judge us by our actions.'

Anita's actions to date have included the setting up of an Environmental Projects Department, which has joined forces with Greenpeace in the fight to save the great whales, 'which are still being hunted by some countries and whose oil is still being used in toiletries and cosmetics'. Ecological considerations, Anita says, are of prime importance to the Body Shop. Products are bio-degradable so that they will not pollute the earth, and a refill service operates in the shops so that bottles can be reused.

Much of the company's rapid growth has been achieved through franchising. Anita travels constantly around the world, visiting shops, giving advice and helping with publicity. She reckons that the overseas potential is 'enormous' and hopes to open up a thousand shops. Gordon, now chairman, is responsible for most of the financial decisions. The company went public in 1984, and since then has built a new factory and warehouse in England. Anita has also introduced a range of colour cosmetics, and a new skin and hair care range called Mostly Men. 'We have', she said in her announcement, 'turned our attention to men because we feel that they need it, although some of them may not know it yet.' There would not, she pledged, be any 'seductive or misleading names – the names of our products are simply descriptive. Those macho names beloved by the conventional men's range producers, like Bull or Thrust or Club, have no place in the Body Shop, nor do names that sound like exotic lagers, or conjugations of French or Italian verbs.' Her aim for the Body Shop, she said, was to 'continue doing what we're good at – and to do it better – that is to research, educate and innovate.' It was not in the business of marketing hopes and dreams; its maxim was 'common sense sells'.

Well, yes. But as the fast-talking, plain-speaking and enthusiastic chief executive never ceases to remind her followers, a little 'theatre' most certainly helps.

Yan Rokotov

1922–76

Wheeler-dealer of the Eastern Bloc

In the West, successful wheeler-dealers make millions. If they break the law, they may end up in jail. In the Soviet Union, they are liable to be shot. This was the ultimate fate of Yan Rokotov, one of the entrepreneurial types who flourished in the days of Khrushchev and Brezhnev, much to the disgust of the present ruler of the Kremlin, Mikhail Gorbachov, who doesn't seem to mind small-scale private enterprise but who is strongly opposed to the capitalist view that people are entitled to make a fortune, if they can.

Rokotov, who was alleged to have made the equivalent of $16 million before the KGB caught up with him, got his start when foreign tourists first began to arrive in large numbers during the late 1950s. He offered to buy their clothes, watches, cigarettes and other personal belongings at high prices, knowing that these precious items would fetch far more when he subsequently sold them to his fellow Muscovites. (Many of the tourists were dismayed to find, after the transactions had been concluded, that there was little they could buy for their roubles.)

His next move was into the lucrative 'hard currency' business. Moscow and other cities had special stores where one could buy goods not available to the proletariat – Scotch whisky, French perfumes, American cigarettes, Japanese stereo sets. These stores existed for the benefit of tourists and the Soviet elite; prices were given in dollars. Rokotov soon had a small army of touts who accosted foreigners and offered to exchange their dollars, marks, francs or pounds at double the official rate. The queue outside the Lenin Museum was a favourite mark.

Rokotov also traded in gold, after making the acquaintance of some Egyptian Arabs who were students at a nearby Soviet military academy. They were able to fly in and out of the country through special military airports, where their luggage was not examined, and they agreed to use his dollars to buy gold in Cairo. It was a highly profitable game for all concerned, but it turned out to be his undoing. A Russian plane carrying the Egyptians crashed outside Kiev and every passenger was killed. Investigators sifting through the wreckage found hundreds of gold coins and reported their discovery to the KGB, who soon established the link with Rokotov.

He had, it emerged, escaped earlier detection by systematically bribing top officials. A month after his arrest the KGB picked up three of them, including Moscow's Deputy Police Commissioner. Rokotov was sentenced to death; the officials got lengthy prison sentences but were released after three years.

The KGB has a special section dealing with 'economic crime', and Gorbachov has greatly strengthened it. Many of the people who did well under Brezhnev's rule, including some of his relatives, have been brought to trial.

Even Brezhnev occasionally felt compelled to punish some of the more blatant would-be capitalists. Rokotov was one. Another was OTAR LAZEISHVILI, a notorious Georgian 'underground millionaire' who did absolutely nothing to conceal his wealth. He had two luxurious villas, gave fabulous evening balls, ran four limousines and had half a dozen mistresses. The KGB knew all about him but for a long time did not dare to act because he was a close friend of Vasily Mzhavanadze, the party leader of Georgia, candidate member of the Politburo and personal chum of Khrushchev. Lazeishvili gave lavish gifts, including diamonds, to the party leader's fun-loving wife. It was not until Khrushchev's downfall, and the subsequent removal of Mzhavanadze from all his government posts, that the KGB made its move, with Brezhnev's approval. Lazeishvili was sent before a firing squad and his associates were dispatched to labour camps.

Lazeishvili had been the silent owner of three large factories and twenty-eight co-operatives. Officially they made goods called for by the state plan, which appeared on the books and were distributed through the usual channels; unofficially, they also produced substantial quantities of goods not registered in any documents – easily saleable merchandise like fashionable

---

He had, it emerged, escaped earlier detection by systematically bribing top officials. . . . Rokotov was sentenced to death; the officials got lengthy prison sentences but were released after three years.

---

raincoats and sweaters, ladies' underwear and leather jackets. Unaccounted for, they were known – in underground jargon – as 'left-hand goods'. They were made on the same machines, operated and supervised by the same personnel, as the official merchandise, but the supplies needed for their manufacture, as well as the labour costs, were paid for by Lazeishvili. In other words, private enterprise co-existed under the same roof, and the same name, as a state factory.

One can't help wondering how people like Rokotov and Lazeishvili would have fared if they had been born in New York or London, or if they had left the Soviet Union when it was still comparatively easy to do so. My guess is that they would have done quite well; they would certainly have lived to enjoy the benefits.

Helena Rubinstein

1872–1965

A life for beauty

According to her autobiography, *My Life for Beauty*, Helena Rubinstein embarked on her extraordinary career in the cosmetics business because she was shocked by the dry, rough skins of Australian women. Born in Cracow, Poland, she went at eighteen to visit relatives in Australia. Many of the women she met there admired her complexion and asked if they could try some of the creams she had brought with her. When her supply ran out she sent home for more; eventually she borrowed £250 (then about $1000) from an English friend and set up business in a room at 274 Collins Street, in the heart of Melbourne.

The venture did well, and more rooms were added, but in 1908 she decided to return to Europe, partly because she knew that she had a lot to learn but also because the potential was so much greater there. But she did not go back to Poland: leaving the Melbourne business in the hands of two of her sisters, she went to London, where she studied dermatology and, later, opened a salon in fashionable Mayfair. A salon in Paris followed. She also got married – to an American journalist of Polish extraction, Edward J. Titus. They had two sons.

The fact that her husband was American may well have influenced her decision, in 1914, to tackle the US market, though the desire to keep her family safe as war threatened in Europe no doubt had something to do with it. As in Australia, she declared that she was shocked by the women's complexions and opened beauty salons across the country, which not only sold her various beauty preparations but also offered clients skin analyses with their jars of cream. It was the beginning of a long competitive struggle with another determined businesswoman, ELIZABETH ARDEN. They never referred to each other by name: it was always 'that woman' or 'the other one'.

Like Arden, Rubinstein was responsible for a number of innovations. In Europe, no one before her had put colour into foundation and face powder. In America, she was the first to realize that dry skins and oily skins should not be treated with the same product – and being a shrewd businesswoman, she capitalized on the fact. And, although not the first to introduce mascara, Helena Rubinstein did claim to have been the first to introduce the waterproof variety. She took on the French, who dominated the American perfume market, by launching her own products, which she called Heaven Scent.

All this, plus a great deal of travelling, kept her extremely busy, and inevitably her family life suffered. She was dismayed when, in 1928, Edward told her that he had fallen in love with a younger woman. Her response was entirely out of character: she sold her American corporation to Lehman Brothers, a New York banking firm, for more than $7 million. It was done, she later wrote in her autobiography, for one reason only – to save her marriage. Edward left her all the same.

Lehman Brothers knew little about cosmetics and very soon things began to go wrong. Without publicizing the fact, Helena Rubinstein, now based in Paris, began to buy back some of the stock on the open market, until she eventually had one-third of it. Then, as a substantial shareholder, she wrote to the bankers complaining about the way they were running the company. For a while they ignored her, even though the business was diminishing and the stock continued to fall in price. She circulated a letter to all the stockholders, informing them that she felt the Rubinstein business was being jeopardized and urging them to join their complaints to hers. Then came the Wall Street crash, and the value of the Rubinstein stock fell from $60 to $3 per share. By this time Lehman Brothers were anxious to get it off their hands at all cost, and they sold the controlling interest back to her for a fraction of what they had paid her a year previously. She was one of the few people for whom the great crash actually proved to be a blessing.

Once back at the helm, she tackled the formidable task of restoring the company's fortunes with her usual vigour. 'I desperately needed an interest to keep me occupied so that I would have no time for anything else,' she later wrote in her autobiography. 'Besides, I knew in my heart that no one else could run the business as I could.' Her efforts paid off, as they had done before.

'I knew in my heart that no one else could run the business as I could.'

The Rubinstein cosmetics ran into hundreds of items. At one point a count showed 629 items: 62 creams, 46 perfumes and colognes, 69 lotions, 67 powders and 115 lipsticks, along with a number of soaps, rouges, eye shadows and the like. Her staff told customers that such a large selection was necessary so that exactly the right product would be available for every woman's particular beauty needs. Another reason, though, was that Helena Rubinstein – Madame – was constantly competing with Elizabeth Arden. She also opened a smart body shop on New York's Fifth Avenue, where women could come in for a morning of stretching, vibrating, massage, heat rays, sweating in hot blankets and a bath in milk.

Madame led a peripatetic existence, continually rushing from one country to another. She built up a superb art collection – miniatures, Greek sculpture, African art and so on. She also got married again – like Arden, she chose a prince, which impressed both her friends and her customers. Prince Gourielli and Madame were together for more than twenty years, until his death in 1956. During that time she formed the House of Gourielli, to sell a line of preparations for men, but the venture lost money and she closed it down when he died.

Helena Rubinstein lived out her last decade presiding over far-flung interests, restlessly travelling between a network of homes that were sometimes called 'Rubinstein Hiltons'. In the 1950s, her business was grossing $22 million a year. Theoretically it was publicly owned, although she held a controlling interest and owned all the foreign interests except the company in Britain.

She was no beauty herself, and admitted, in her book, that she had 'always been a bit short of patience where my appearance was concerned'. Small and imperious, she liked to wear a bowler hat, like a man. She was, however, very fond of jewellery.

Madame died at the age of ninety-three, leaving a personal fortune of more than $100 million. Foy Valentine Titus, her eldest son, had been a vice-president of the company during his mother's lifetime but he failed to take on her mantle. In 1973 it was bought by Colgate-Palmolive for $143 million, but, like Lehman Brothers all those years before, the new owners came to regret their decision. In 1980 it was sold again, for a mere $20 million. Madame would not have been surprised: she always believed that a cosmetics company, like a fashion business, should be run as a personal enterprise and that no one could ever truly take her place.

Maurice and Charles Saatchi

b. 1945 and 1943

Revolutionaries of the advertising world

It really is impossible to write about one Saatchi brother and not the other, because they are very much a team, a fact reflected in the name they chose for the company they started in 1970 – Saatchi & Saatchi. Together they have built up what is now the largest advertising agency in the world, and in the process have rewritten some of the ad game's most basic rules.

Born into a well-off family of Sephardic Jews in North London (their surname means 'watchmaker' in Iraqi Arabic), they joined forces while they were both still in their twenties. Maurice had gone to the London School of Economics and then joined Haymarket Publishing as promotions manager of *Campaign*, the British advertising industry's trade paper. Charles had left school at eighteen and moved through various agencies as a copywriter. They started their business with financial backing of £25,000, a modest sum even in those days.

At the time the industry body – the Institute of Practitioners in Advertising – had a rule that agencies should not directly solicit for each other's accounts. Saatchi & Saatchi refused to join the IPA and launched an aggressive new business drive. They persuaded some good people to join them, and soon had some useful accounts. Charles, the ideas man, planned strategy and produced striking creative work. Maurice made sure that the agency got a lot of publicity.

Saatchi & Saatchi grew rapidly in its first four years, gaining a number of major clients, including British Leyland, ICI and Dunlop. It also acquired three regional agencies. In 1975 the brothers pulled off a major coup – a reverse takeover of an old-established agency, Garland Compton, which was twice the size of Saatchi's London operation and had some excellent accounts. They ended up with 35 per cent of the merged company and effective control of what, as a result of the deal, became one of the top companies in the field. They later bought the rest of the shares and formed a holding company, in which they jointly held the largest single stake.

In 1978 they leaped into the headlines when they were chosen to handle advertising for the Conservative party in the 1979 election campaign. The Tories won, and that year Saatchi became the largest agency in Britain, overtaking J. Walter Thompson, which had held the lead for more than two decades. With new business flooding in, Maurice set out to convince London's financial community that advertising agencies could be good investments. The institutions were wary: agencies had few tangible assets and, it seemed, they could all too easily lose key personnel and important accounts. But Maurice's efforts

'We live', the report said, 'in an era of global communications. . . . There is no doubt that the world is becoming one marketplace.'

paid off. Saatchi went public and since then has raised huge sums of capital to help finance its acquisitions.

The brothers paid £5.6 million for Dorland Advertising, but they were not content with being number one in the UK. They were eager to make an impact in the much larger American market. For years, US agencies had dominated the British advertising industry through their local operations. Now Maurice and Charles set out to reverse the pattern. They again went after a company which was substantially bigger than their own. This was Compton, a logical choice because of their existing association. It cost them $29.2 million in cash, plus $27.6 million to be paid to key Compton executives over a period of ten years, conditional on profit targets being met.

At a stroke the deal advanced them to number nine in the world league. But they had not finished yet. They bought other agencies across the country, and in 1986 startled the industry by winning control of one of the top names on the New York

'The most advanced manufacturers are recognizing that there are probably more social differences between midtown Manhattan and the Bronx . . . than between midtown Manhattan and the 7th Arondissement of Paris.'

scene, Ted Bates Advertising. It made Saatchi & Saatchi, started sixteen years earlier with little money, the world's biggest agency, with combined billings of $7.5 billion.

Charles, the strategist, has always believed in the concept of the 'global marketplace'. He was one of the first to recognize what this could mean for the advertising business, and his vision of the future, shared by Maurice, has been the main reason for the company's relentless expansion. His views were spelled out in Saatchi & Saatchi's 1986 annual report. 'We live', the report said,

> in an era of global communications. Scientists and technologists have achieved what militarists and statesmen down the ages have attempted to establish but without success – the global empire. There is no doubt that the world is becoming one marketplace. Capital markets, products and services, management and manufacturing techniques have all become global in nature. As a result, companies increasingly find that they must compete all over the world – in the global marketplace.
>
> This new development is emerging at the same time as advanced

technology is transforming information and communication. The continued elimination of many different communications monopolies has created a more competitive environment and, with the ongoing development of international standards, has helped to make the same information technology available to everyone – no matter where they might be. The spread of open systems and architecture has also brought the world closer together by allowing any user to communicate with any other user, regardless of the manufacturer of the system and terminals in use. At the same time internationally compatible frameworks for the rapid transfer of information are uniting disparate regions.

The technological revolution owes its success not to objects or land but to *ideas*. Ideas now travel the globe instantaneously, unfettered by customs barriers, political systems, or historic allegiances. It is in the context of this new environment that far-sighted companies have seen the opportunity to obtain a competitive advantage. As the more astute businessmen and corporations have realised, wherever an idea takes root a product can follow.

The most advanced manufacturers are recognising that there are probably more social differences between midtown Manhattan and the Bronx, two sectors of the same city, than between midtown Manhattan and the 7th Arondissement of Paris. This means that when a manufacturer contemplates expansion in his business, consumer similarities in demography and habits rather than geographic proximity will increasingly affect his decisions. It is happening now. One can see many examples today, as marketers look to similarities across boundaries rather than differences.

It was the competitive intensity of maturing consumer markets around the world that underlined the economic logic of the global approach – a drive to seize all the possible efficiencies of scale by co-ordination of a company's global activities. This need for a global approach to the world market has since been at the heart of most successful multinationals' business strategy – one of the biggest shake-ups of management style and structure since the 'profit centre' was invented at Harvard 30 years ago.

The report went on to quote a study of the profitability of 1895 US businesses.

It found that the critical factor affecting a brand's profitability is not market share; it is market *rank*. A brand's rank order position

> in a market is the single most significant factor affecting profitability. This follows the 'Law of Dominance' which tell us that in a given market the top three brands can be profitable, but the fourth will be consistently unprofitable. In simple terms: No. 1 is wonderful; No. 2 is terrific; No. 3 is threatened; No. 4 is fatal.

Size and scope, Saatchi acknowledged, are not automatically better. 'But they can and do make increased resources and opportunities available so that we can do better. It is up to us to take advantage of the opportunities represented by the power of scale.' This, he explained,

> is not the same as economies of scale. The focus is not on how to do it cheaper, but how to do it *better*. How to get more effectiveness, not simply more efficiency. How does an advertiser benefit from his agency's power of scale? Power of scale in advertising means increased flexibility of resources, the ability to attract, reward, and retain the very best talent, superior media-buying clout and better media-panning systems. It means increased resistance to adversity, a greater willingness to accept risk and greater ability to invest in research and development. And it means improved global technological information systems, increased technological resources and increased access to a broad range of communications and consulting expertise.

Saatchi & Saatchi's strategy, therefore, was to build on the interconnection between key aspects of a client organization across frontiers and across functions. It was broadening the range of advisory services in which it had expertise.

> By bringing together leading companies in the vital management services fields, each with independent objectives but with common standards of excellence and cultural values, we aim to provide our clients with the objective and professional quality of service that allows them to pursue effectively a global approach in their management of the corporate enterprise.

Saatchi & Saatchi, said the report, was a family of business experts. Experts at advertising. Experts at promotion. Experts at advertising. Experts at promotion. Experts at direct marketing. Experts at market research. Experts at merchandising. Experts at design. Experts at public relations. Experts at management consultancy. 'We will maintain autonomy within the group. Companies within the group will maintain their independence yet will benefit from their family connections wherever appropriate. We are under no illusion as to the difficulties of executing such a strategy, but we are nonetheless dedicated to its achievement.'

This bold, innovative plan for a wide-ranging business services group, which goes far beyond the traditional role of an advertising agency, is typical of the drive and breadth of outlook which has brought the Saatchi brothers to where they are today. For most people, the leadership of a mammoth industry would be enough. For the Saatchis, it is simply a way of positioning their company for continued expansion into other marketing services and for continued growth. Saatchi & Saatchi, they say, 'sees itself as one of the world's major corporations in the year 2000 and for decades beyond'. It is an ambitious target and they may well stumble along the way. They may be under-rating protectionist sentiments and the strength of competition from established service companies and other aggressive newcomers. But there is no doubt about their determination to succeed.

Alan Sainsbury

b. 1902

'Traditionalists with a passion for innovation'

Alan Sainsbury brought the supermarket concept to Britain. He had seen the system in use during a visit to the United States, and recognized its potential. It was against all traditions and trends in the 1950s, but experimental supermarket branches in several areas led to a swift decision to convert all Sainsbury shops to the same model. His son, Sir John Sainsbury, has since diversified into hypermarkets and other new ventures: 'We are', he says, 'traditionalists with a passion for innovation.' He and his colleagues keep a close eye on developments in other countries, especially the USA. Their acquisition, some years ago, of a New England retail chain was at least partially motivated by the desire to gain early experience

---

'Our image is of quality, value, cleanliness, not coupons, stamps, music. . . . Our shops are . . . not gimmicky funfairs.'

---

in new retail techniques before transplanting them to the UK.

The Sainsbury business was started by John James Sainsbury in 1869. The founder was a man with a passion for orderliness and detail. He believed that cleanliness and freshness, combined with quality at low prices, were what most people wanted if only they had the opportunity to get them. This preoccupation has stayed with the company to the present day. Sainsbury is deeply concerned with hygiene, organizing regular inspections in which each store is scored and any manager is disciplined if he fails to meet the required standard. Sir John Sainsbury still makes a point of personally tasting every product before it is allowed on the shelves; each week, up to a dozen new items await his verdict. He also makes frequent visits to his stores, and to those of competitors.

Alan Sainsbury, who became Lord Sainsbury of Drury Lane in 1962, always welcomed ideas but hated anything which looked to him like a gimmick. He refused, for example, to have trading stamps in his stores. When the trading stamps war was at its hottest in the 1960s he was quoted as saying: 'Our image is of quality, value, cleanliness, not coupons, stamps, music, prices you can't assess because everything is twopence off, windows plastered with posters so you can't see in. Our shops are clean, tidy, hygienic to look at – not gimmicky funfairs.'

Sainsbury attached great importance to market research, and the company continues to spend vast numbers of man-hours collecting and analyzing any kind of market data that might give an edge to decision-making. A trade magazine carried this description of the Sainsbury process:

> An annual attitude survey, based on 2000 lengthy interviews in the home, helps establish where, how often and when people shop. Great weight is attached to what people think of Sainsbury's and the high street competition.
>
> By regularly taking the pulse of the high street, we understand better the shopping patterns by areas. We study what is being bought and where, how much is being spent and by whom, for every location in our trading area.
>
> Decisions of where we should try to open new branches are well grounded in market research. The profile of the potential customer, the volume of likely shoppers, the lines most likely to sell, the size of the car park, the extent of the competition and the potential turnover, are all closely examined.

Sir John reckons that this careful watch on changes in customer tastes and needs is a major reason why the company has survived healthily into the 1980s. 'Retail is detail' is one of his favourite maxims. Since he took over in 1969, growth has been impressive. Sainsbury's now has 268 supermarkets, and retails about 10 per cent of all food sold in Britain. Lucrative 'own label' merchandising accounts for two-thirds of the turnover. The range of products includes more than a hundred varieties of Sainsbury's wine: every seventh bottle of wine bought in the UK bears a Sainsbury label.

In the past decade the company has diversified into hypermarkets with SavaCentre, in partnership with British Home Stores, and into do-it-yourself outlets under the title Homebase, with Belgian partners GB-Inno-BM. The American associate, Shaw's, has also been doing well. Dividends have risen steadily since Sainsbury's was floated on the stock market in 1973. A profit-sharing scheme was launched in

1979, and about a quarter of employees have shares in the business.

Sir John readily concedes that his father's decision to introduce self-service was a crucial step: supermarketing has been good to the Sainsburys. Others, of course, followed Alan Sainsbury's lead, and today competition is fierce. But, as in the case of that other great British company, Marks and Spencer, the insistence on quality at the lowest possible price, and close supervision of suppliers, has paid off handsomely.

Sir John and his two brothers, one of whom became a Conservative Member of Parliament, are noted patrons of the arts, and the family's charitable trusts are among the most substantial in Britain. They cover a vast array of causes, including health, social welfare, education, the environment, scientific research, opera, ballet, London's National Gallery and the Sainsbury Centre for the Visual Arts at the University of East Anglia in Norwich.

Antonio Lopez Santa Anna

1794–1876

'Tell 'em quick, and tell 'em often'

What, you may well ask, is the famous Mexican general, who fought against Sam Houston in the war of 1836, doing in a book about business? The answer is that he gave America one of its best-known products: chewing gum. When he was taken prisoner he brought with him a large chunk of chicle, the dried sap of a Mexican jungle tree called sapodilla, which the Aztec

Indians liked to chew. Accounts vary as to the exact purpose he had in mind. One account states that he hoped to interest some American 'inventor' in it as a substitute for rubber; others say that he simply enjoyed chewing the stuff. In any event he did meet an inventor called JOHN ADAMS, of Jersey City, and persuaded him to experiment with chicle as a rubber substitute. It didn't work, but in the course of his meetings with the general Adams noticed that Santa Anna occasionally took some of the substance from his pocket and chewed it with great pleasure. Adams and his son Horatio mixed some chicle with hot water until it was about the consistency of putty. They rubbed, kneaded and finally rolled it into little balls and persuaded a local druggist to put it on sale.

The response encouraged Adams to invest in more chicle and to rent a Jersey City factory loft. The gum was unflavoured and was put into little boxes labelled 'Adams' New York Gum – Snapping and Stretching'. Another Adams son, a travelling salesman, took the new product to stores in other cities and the orders began to flow in. They now turned their efforts towards putting some taste into the stuff, and decided on a liquorice flavour which Adams called Black Jack. Competitors soon began to appear on the scene. One added aromatic balsam and, like Thomas, did reasonably well until 1880, when peppermint flavour was first introduced.

The real success story of chewing gum started with a popcorn salesman, WILLIAM WHITE. He discovered that corn syrup blended nicely with chicle and put the desired flavour in the syrup. His choice was peppermint, and he named his product Yucatan, after the Yucatan peninsula where most of the chicle came from. It caught on in a big way, making White a rich man.

Unlike most of his predecessors, White was an excellent promoter. On a trip to England, he managed to get himself included in a group who were to be presented to King Edward VII. White handed the startled monarch a box of Yucatan and urged him to try it. His Majesty accepted the box, but firmly declined to chew it 'right now'. White, unfazed, promptly sent off cables to American newspapers informing them of the King's 'gracious acceptance' of the gum. The resulting publicity gave a tremendous boost to business.

Another salesman who made a fortune estimated at more than $200 million out of chewing gum was WILLIAM WRIGLEY JR. When he started selling the gum which still bears his name he used every cent he had to mount the first spectacular advertising campaign in American history. A reporter who wanted to know his recipe for success was told: 'Get a good product. It's easier to run downstream than up. Then tell 'em quick, and tell 'em often . . . keep ever-lasting coming at them. Advertising is pretty much like running a train. Once you stop running, the fire goes out. The train will run on its own momentum for a while, but it will gradually slow down and come to a dead stop.'

Wrigley himself kept on stoking. As a result of one advertising contract each of the sixty-two thousand street, subway and elevated cars in America carried a Wrigley poster. His flashing electric sign in New York's Times Square cost $104,000 a year to run, but attracted the attention of millions. Along the Trento-Atlantic City highway in the New Jersey meadow he erected an outdoor chain sign half a mile long advertising his product. He also mailed sample sticks of gum to all 1.5 million subscribers then listed in America's telephone books, and every year sent more than 750,000 children two sticks of gum on their second birthday. He even published Mother Goose books, rewritten to tie chewing gum into nursery jingles and dedicated to the children of the world – 'from six to sixty'. Over a two-year period beginning in 1915 he distributed about 14 million of these. The rhymes were crude but made their point:

Jack be nimble
Jack be quick
Jack run and get your
WRIGLEY stick!

As I was going to St Ives
I met a man with seven wives
Each wife had a fine clear skin
All were fat – not one was thin
And each had a dimple in her chin:
What caused it? WRIGLEY'S!

The books, written when few people were concerned with dieting, were filled with reminders that Wrigley's gum steadied

'If Mr Wrigley has become one of the ten wealthiest millionaires in America, it is because humanity has instinctively recognised that he was helping to restore to it the lost art of chewing.'

the nerves, sweetened the breath, soothed the throat, relieved thirst, quickened the appetite and aided digestion.

By 1930 Wrigley had factories everywhere. They were producing 40 million sticks of gum a day and his little green packages were printed in thirty-seven languages. 'If Mr Wrigley has become one of the ten wealthiest millionaires in America,' one British newspaper observed at the time, 'it is because humanity has instinctively recognised that he was helping to restore to it the lost art of chewing.'

Few people who have taken up the 'lost art' over the years are aware of the debt they owe to the diminutive Mexican general who started it all. His fellow countrymen, alas, ceased to make money out of this enormously popular pastime when, during World War II, the gum industry came up with synthetic gum bases which could be successfully substituted for chicle. The synthetics are easier to control, of uniform quality, and perfectly harmless if swallowed. They have been used ever since.

E. F. Schumacher

b. 1912–77

Small is beautiful

German-born Dr Schumacher is best known as the economist who, in 1973, wrote the best-selling book *Small Is Beautiful*. Sub-titled *A Study of Economics as if People Mattered*, it covered a wide range of subjects, but the point which attracted most attention – in the business world as well as among academics – was the argument that we suffered from 'an almost universal idolatry of gigantism'.

Dr Schumacher's book was published at a time when there was much discussion about environmental issues like pollution, for which big companies were mostly blamed. Many people agreed with his view that 'Small-scale operations, no matter how numerous, are always likely to be less harmful to the environment.' This, he said, was 'because their individual force is small in relation to the recuperative forces of nature'. Although even small communities were sometimes guilty of causing serious erosion, generally as a result of ignorance, this was 'trifling in comparison with the devastations caused by greed, envy, and the lust for power'. It was, moreover, obvious that 'men organized in small units will take better care of *their* bit of land or other natural resources than anonymous companies or melagomanic governments which pretend to themselves that the whole universe is their legitimate quarry'.

But Dr Schumacher was not merely concerned with pollution and the wasteful use of resources: he also sought to make a strong case for the 'humanization of work'. He warned of the dangers to the integrity of the individual 'when he feels as nothing more than a small cog in a vast machine and when the human relationships of his daily working life become increasingly dehumanized; danger also to efficiency and productivity, stemming from ever-growing Parkinsonian bureaucracies'.

Dr Schumacher acknowledged that, although nobody really liked large-scale organizations, they were here to stay. The fundamental task, he argued, was to achieve smallness *within* large organizations by creating many semi-autonomous units, which he called quasi-firms. Each would have a large amount

'Small-scale operations, no matter how numerous, are always likely to be less harmful to the environment.'

of freedom, to give the greatest possible chance to creativity and entrepreneurship.

The idea was not new – many companies had already done just that – but Dr Schumacher's book reinforced the doubts which many people had about the fashionable view that bigger was better. The arguments in favour of mergers were familiar enough: economies of scale, saving of manpower, greater competitive strength in world markets, and so on. A good deal less was known, or said, about the disadvantages. I had tried to draw attention to them in my own book, *Merger Mania*, three years earlier but few people had been disposed to listen. Schumacher's timing was better. Another plus for him was that, unlike most economists, he had actually played a key role in putting his theories into practice as Economic Adviser to Britain's state-owned National Coal Board, then one of the largest enterprises in Europe. Strenuous efforts had been made to evolve a structure which would maintain the unity of one big organization and at the same time create the feeling of a federation of quasi-firms. The monolith, Schumacher, said, had been transformed into 'a well co-ordinated assembly of lively, semi-autonomous units, each with its own drive and sense of achievement'.

Such a structure, of course, may not be suitable in every case. It can lead to overlap, confusion and time-wasting corporate in-fighting. The argument that 'small is beautiful' certainly finds little favour, even today, with the autocratic empire-builders who regard delegation as weakness. But there is ample evidence to back the view that people working for small companies tend to feel more highly motivated, and have a greater sense of loyalty, than those employed by big corporations which show little concern for the individual. A semi-autonomous unit *can* generate the same kind of spirit, and the intelligent chief executive would obviously do well to ask himself whether his own organization would fare better with the kind of structure advocated by Dr Schumacher and others.

The renewed merger mania of recent years has, once again, led to 'idolatry of gigantism' on both sides of the Atlantic, with the human factor very much a secondary consideration. Yet the experience of the last few decades shows that if mere size is the prime objective, a company can topple under its own weight. Mergers often produce serious problems, especially if the reasons for them have more to do with personal ambitions than with industrial logic. Many aggressive bidders proudly declare that they aim to be the biggest, and blithely assume that we will praise them for it. In reality this kind of approach to business often does more harm than good – to the employees, to the shareholders, and to the country as a whole.

Harry Gordon Selfridge

1858–1947

Mile a Minute Harry

Selfridge had one of the most innovative minds of all the merchant princes and distinguished himself in two countries, his native America and Britain. Born in Ripon, Wisconsin, he was the only son of Robert O. Selfridge, who owned a small dry goods business. At the age of fourteen he became a junior bank clerk, though his ambition was to join the Navy. His application to the Naval Academy at Annapolis, however, was turned down because he was under the required height. Apparently he took it very badly; it has even been suggested that from that time onwards Selfridge harboured an irrational hostility to men taller than himself and automatically barred them from senior executive positions. He then joined the Chicago mail order business of Field, Leiter & Co. (later Marshall Field & Co., retailers) as an apprentice clerk earning $10 a week. Soon he displayed such a flair for merchandising that he came to the attention of Marshall Field, who in 1886 made him the manager of his large department store in State Street. Four years later Field made him a junior partner.

Selfridge introduced the novel idea of holding special sales to bring the crowds in, and established a bargain basement – or budget floor, as it came to be known – which grew to become the largest single saleroom in the world. He employed brilliant show window dressers and got Field to increase the amount spent on advertising, writing much of the copy himself. He even persuaded Field to open a tea room on the third floor of his stores, arguing that it would prevent customers from curtailing their shopping and going home or elsewhere for refreshment. It was a great success.

Selfridge worked so fast that he was known to his colleagues as Mile a Minute Harry. In 1903, though, he surprised them with the announcement that he intended to retire. He was still in his early forties, but he sold his shares in Marshall Field for about $300,000 and for a time devoted his energies to travelling, entertaining and adding to his collection of orchids. As so often happens with energetic people who retire too soon, however, it was not long before he began to get interested in new business opportunities.

In 1906 Selfridge went to London for a holiday and to survey the commercial scene there. He discovered that the city lacked a department store run on American lines, and resolved to do something about it. A site in Oxford Street was found, and he commissioned a leading Chicago architect, Daniel Burnham, to design a spectacular building. In 1909 Selfridge & Co. opened its doors to the public: it had 130 departments and catered for all tastes.

Selfridge introduced many of the features which had worked so well in America, including restaurants, American-style barber shops, a library and a roof garden. His window displays were the best in London. He invested heavily in advertising and cultivated the friendship of newspaper editors. His staff were given incentives to progress within the firm, and he organized tours to the Continent and to the United States for some of the senior people to broaden their minds.

The store did well; after World War I Selfridge acquired a number of London surburban and provincial stores, and established a chain of threepence and sixpence stores, on the model of the Woolworth five and ten cent stores. But he was not a man who felt it necessary to devote all his time to business. He enjoyed the company of beautiful women, especially theatre and show business stars, and spent a lot of money on them. He also acquired fine homes – Lansdowne

House, which had once belonged to William Waldorf Astor, and Highcliffe Castle in Hampshire – and gave lavish parties.

In 1927 he sold control of the company but remained on the board of directors. By 1937, the year in which he took out British citizenship, he was heavily in debt. In 1940, when World War II was hurting trade, his fellow directors, including his son, gave him an ultimatum: either repay at once the £118,000 he owed to the company, or resign from active management and accept the honorary title of president at a small salary. He resigned, this time for good. He was eighty-two, and lived for the rest of his life in a room at the London home of his daughter.

Selfridge introduced the novel idea of holding special sales to bring the crowds in, and established a bargain basement . . . which grew to become the largest single saleroom in the world.

Selfridge was a man who enjoyed the challenges offered by the business world – in 1918 he published a book called *The Romance of Commerce* – and who had a fertile imagination. But he also relished all the other pleasures which money could buy, and he liked the more relaxed attitude to success that he found in British society. He would no doubt have made a great deal more if he had stayed with Marshall Field, and he would certainly have *left* more if he had not been so profligate. But he had a great influence on British retailing, and he knew how to make the most of life.

Run Run Shaw

b. 1907

Movie mogul of the East

The movie industry is so widely associated with the name Hollywood that it is easy to forget that there are other parts of the world where numerous films are made each year. India, for example, is not only a huge market but also has its own production companies and stars who are as famous in that fascinating country as, say, Robert Redford or Paul Newman are in the United States and Europe. The Chinese, too, are great movie fans.

Hollywood nowadays is well aware of the enormous scope for profit offered by overseas markets, and its films and TV programmes are skilfully adapted for local audiences. Dubbing has become a major business in its own right. From time to time, though, good ideas flow in the opposite direction: Western audiences are captivated by what is, for them, a novel concept which has its origins in an alien culture. A prime example is the kung-fu cult, which the West 'discovered' in the 1970s. The man behind it was Hong Kong millionaire Run Run Shaw.

Shaw (Run Run means 'square, sincere, honest' in Chinese) was born into a theatrical family in Shanghai, where his parents owned and operated one of the live theatres. In 1929 he and his brother, Runme, left for Singapore, where they bought their first cinema. Run Run went to Hong Kong in 1959 to set up 'Shaw's Movie Town'. His first film was a musical called *Kingdom and Beauty*, and it proved to be an instant success.

The Chinese film industry was in poor shape at the time.

Most films were badly made: they were shot in seven days and released only in third-rate theatres. In Hong Kong, Chinese films produced only 10 per cent of the total revenue of all the movie theatres. Shaw decided to make better films and to concentrate on all-out action. 'I am convinced', he told me when we met some years ago, 'that action pictures are what people in this part of the world want to see. In the West there was a time when biblical pictures were all the rage. Then it was the James Bond type action and the traditional Westerns boosted into modern sagas. In our case we had the sword fights and, more recently, kung-fu. They are action pictures presented in a different way. People like excitement.'

Shaw made the final decision on all the scripts, the cast and the budget. A phenomenal worker, he liked to be at his desk at 7 a.m. after spending an hour or so in bed reading scripts ('It's the best time to read scripts'). A keep-fit enthusiast, he also managed to do half an hour's shadow boxing every morning. 'I do a thousand arm swings,' he told me. 'Yes, a *thousand*. It's what kept Mao fit for so many years, did you know that? Here, let me show you. Stand with your legs slightly apart and bend your knees. Keep your body straight. Now swing your arms back and forth – thirty degrees at the front, seventy degrees at the back. Got that? Start with a hundred swings at first. You'll be amazed how good you feel after a few weeks.' When I asked him how much he knew about kung-fu, he quietly said that 'I could break every bone in your body.' I decided to take his word for it.

Shaw said his films had no purpose other than to entertain, and that Chinese audiences liked sex and violence. In his office I saw posters with typical titles: *Spirit of the Raped*, *Forbidden Past*. He also said that he made a point of sitting unobtrusively among filmgoers at the opening of every one of the forty films his studio made every year. 'This business is all guesswork. You have to keep in touch with the tastes and attitudes of ordinary people. It helps to watch an audience, to listen to their comments. Perhaps I'm lucky; I guess I listen a little better than others.'

Early on in their careers, Run Run and his brother made a deal: one would run the Hong Kong end of the business and the other would keep his base in Singapore. They would discuss everything, but they wouldn't fight. This eminently sensible arrangement enabled them to build up a formidable organization, including a chain of cinemas and theatres, amusement parks, real estate concerns, hotels, banks and insurance companies. They also got involved in charitable work, giving money to hospitals, schools and projects like Hong Kong's Arts Centre.

'You have to keep in touch with the tastes and attitudes of ordinary people. . . . I guess I listen a little better than others.'

With the Chinese government due to take over the colony in 1997, no one can be certain what the future holds. Everyone who can afford it has taken out political insurance. The Shaw family has several homes abroad, as well as substantial investments. Run Run's two sons were educated at Oxford and his daughters graduated from Bryn Mawr. Meantime, Hong Kong's millionaires have been establishing useful contacts in Peking, Shanghai and Canton. They have a vested interest in China's reforms and, like western businessmen, they are very conscious of the enticing possibilities offered by the huge and rapidly growing domestic market. They have built new hotels, supermarkets, cinemas and even golf courses. Chinese officials make regular visits to Hong Kong, which further strengthens the relationship. The Shaw interests are playing an active role in developing the film industry and, providing there isn't another Cultural Revolution, they should do very well in the years to come.

Matsutaro Shoriki

1885–1970

Press baron, politician and idealist

Matsutaro Shoriki was responsible for many innovations during his long and extraordinarily varied life. He launched Japan's first commercial TV station, pioneered the peaceful use of nuclear energy, built up one of Japan's great newspapers, and created a vast 'cultural, religious, and sporting recreational centre' which he called Yomiuriland.

He was born in a small village, the second of three sons among the ten children of an engineer. At high school he developed a keen interest in fencing and judo, and later became a high-ranking black belt. He went to the University of Tokyo and, after gaining a law degree, joined the Metropolitan Police Board as an inspector. During the next few years he solved a number of famous cases and became one of the top people in the force.

In a remarkable switch of careers, he went into the newspaper business in the early 1920s, becoming the publisher of an ailing Tokyo daily, *Yomiriu Shimbun*, when it had a circulation of only forty thousand. Shoriki revamped the paper and used numerous promotional stunts to gain new readers. In the 1930s, he helped to popularize sports like baseball, boxing and tennis by inviting professionals from other countries to demonstrate their skills in Japan. (In 1935, he was nearly killed by a sword thrust in the back from a militant member of the War God Society, on the pretext that he had defiled the Emperor Meiji's memorial stadium by staging a Japan–USA baseball match there.) Shoriki's circulation-building efforts were so successful that WILLIAM RANDOLPH HEARST, told about this innovative Japanese publisher, twice ordered studies to be made of his techniques.

After the paper was established financially he paid off his backers and later turned the business into a limited company, giving half his shares to a welfare foundation for employees. During World War II he published *Yomiuri* in an improvised plant underground in central Tokyo, and launched other papers in occupied cities. In 1945 the Americans named him a 'war criminal suspect', and he was detained in Sugamo Prison. He was never charged or tried, and managed to maintain his authority from jail. (He also studied English and practised Zen.)

Released in 1947, he left a trusted stand-in to run the paper while he embarked on various new ventures: he formed a League of Artists and Entertainers, which helped to revive the derelict entertainment industry, and built tracks for horse and motorcycle racing.

The following year he got together a consortium of newspaper owners to apply for the first commercial radio licence;

In 1935, he was nearly killed by a sword thrust in the back from a militant member of the War God Society, on the pretext that he had defiled the Emperor Meiji's memorial stadium by staging a Japan–USA baseball match there.

this led to the setting up of a company called the Tokyo Broadcasting System. He also applied for the first commercial TV licence. He alone raised the necessary capital, subscribing a substantial part himself by selling stock and getting the rest from other newspapers, several top steel companies, six paper manufacturers, two breweries, two film producers and banks. His company, Nippon Television Network, began broadcasting in August 1953.

The commercial attractions of TV were not as obvious, at the time, as they are today. There were many sceptics. But Shoriki recognized the potential and he regarded radio and TV as natural allies of the press, not its enemies. The new station did well, and other companies soon appeared on the scene. It gave a considerable boost to the growing electronics industry.

Shoriki used his political influence to help bring about a merger between Japan's two conservative parties, arguing that 'meaningless family strife' benefited only the socialists. He stood as an Independent in his native district and was elected.

By then, he had developed a strong interest in the use of atomic energy to make up for the country's shortage of coal and oil. It was, not surprisingly, a controversial cause. After Japan's horrific first-hand experience of its awesome power, there was bound to be vigorous opposition.

Shoriki, appointed Minister of State and Commissioner to deal with this thorny matter, mounted a skilful campaign to change public opinion; among other things, he promoted a US Atoms for Peace Exhibition in Tokyo, Osaka and other cities. He became the head of a newly formed Japanese Economic Energy Commission and also created an Atomic Energy Industrial Council and the Science and Technology Agency. On his recommendation, Japan bought the world's first large (British-made) atomic reactor, which was installed in Ibaraki Prefecture, north of Tokyo.

While doing all this, he also pressed on with research into another project which had caught his imagination: colour TV. In 1960 his station became the first in Japan to broadcast in colour.

Shoriki retired from active politics in his seventy-fifth year, but he didn't lose his enthusiasm for new schemes. He established Buddhist Sunday schools throughout the country and devoted a great deal of his time to Yomiuriland – a thousand-acre complex with pavilions, pagodas, a hotel, a plastic ski jump and a roller-skating rink, an Olympic-size pool, a deep sea aquarium, an outdoor concert bowl, an underwater theatre, a TV studio and a 140-foot-high observation tower. He saw it as 'a place where the whole family can enjoy themselves and perhaps pick up some spiritual animation at the same time'. The idea was subsequently copied by American evangelist JIM BAKKER, who created a park called Heritage USA in South Carolina.

Clive Sinclair

b. 1940

The innovator who lacked business flair

Sir Clive Sinclair – he got his knighthood in 1983 – is a classic example of the inventor who has good ideas but who cannot match technical innovation with business acumen. His career has been marked by an extraordinary series of ups and downs.

Born in London, he left school at seventeen. His mother wanted him to go to university and become an academic, but Clive was far more interested in emulating his father, who ran his own business. He wasn't sure what he wanted to buy and sell, but he was keen on electronics and liked the notion of inventing new products. He had no capital, so he got himself a job as a technical journalist, which he reckoned would give him the opportunity to study the market and ask a lot of questions. He worked for *Practical Wireless* and wrote small handbooks for the electronics hobbyist. Later he said that in the process he learned more about his subjects 'than anyone who ever read the things'.

In 1962 he founded a company called Sinclair Radionics to sell amplifier kits by mail order. He designed the product (a radio amplifier), ordered the parts, and placed half-page ads in the specialist magazines, hoping that by the time he had to pay for the parts he would have enough orders to pay his suppliers. It worked, and he added hi-fis to his list.

His primary interest, though, was still in innovation. A friend agreed to look after the mail order side, and this helped to persuade Sinclair that he should concentrate on inventing and subcontract everything else. It meant a considerable saving in time and capital, but it also put him at the mercy of his subcontractors, which gave him a lot of problems as the business developed.

In 1972 he launched a cheap pocket calculator and soon became the UK market leader. From there he went on to digital watches and the world's first pocket television set. He also devised new digital metering equipment. All these projects encountered difficulties, and Sinclair Radionics slipped into the red. He was bailed out by the government-sponsored National Enterprise Board, but Sinclair did not get on with the Board's officials – they disagreed about which way the company should go – and in 1979 there was a formal parting of the ways.

Sinclair set up another company, called Sinclair Research, and brought out an inexpensive computer. The following year he produced one that cost even less – the highly successful ZX81 – and sold more than a million, worldwide, in the first eighteen months. This was followed by the equally successful Spectrum, and the more sophisticated QL. Sinclair also launched the latest version of his mini-TV, the Microvision.

But again things started to go wrong. His licensing agreement with Timex for the North American market ran into problems and was cancelled. In Britain, customers started to complain about over-long delays in meeting orders already paid for, and the company got a lot of bad publicity. Sinclair was characteristically frank. 'We are', he said, 'in the business of innovating. We're not proud of our delays and we're not at all happy that we've let people down. But as bad as we got it, we're probably better than the competition.' Inevitably, though, business was hit and in 1985 Sinclair also had to cope with a sudden downturn in the home computer market. His response was yet another innovation – the C5 electric trike, which he called a 'car' and which he said would transform in-town motoring.

The electric car was not a new idea. General Motors had tried one but couldn't make it work economically enough, and of course every golfer was familiar with battery-operated carts. Sinclair's trike was an open-topped three-wheeler with no reverse gear. Its top speed was fifteen miles an hour, it

'People are much more resistant to change than I imagined.'

needed pedals to go up hills, and it had room for just one person. But it was cheap and Sinclair thought he had a winner. He sold some of his shares in the company to raise money for the project and engaged a subcontractor, Hoover, in Merthyr Tydfil. The public, however, was distinctly unenthusiastic. Only eight thousand C5s were sold in the first three months, leaving so many in stock that production had to be cut back. Sinclair conceded that he had misjudged the market. 'People', he said, 'are much more resistant to change than I imagined.' In 1986, following staggering losses, he was forced to sell his once-thriving computer range (and his name) to arch-rival Amstrad for a paltry £5 million. But Sinclair has a remarkable capacity for coping with the most daunting setbacks. He formed a new business, the Cambridge Computer Company, and early in 1987 he launched his latest invention, the Z88, which he described as 'the first truly portable and completely comprehensive personal computer'. He also revealed that he was working on several other ideas, including a cheap portable telephone and a revolutionary wafer-scale integrated circuit which, he said, was 'potentially worth hundreds of millions of pounds'.

Sinclair's basic approach, over the years, has been to identify what people want but still can't afford: he then tries to create a product which they *can* afford. But, of course, he has not been alone in this. The NEB felt he could not stay in consumer electronics in competition with the Japanese, and one can well understand why it should have been sceptical. Creative genius is not enough: one needs volume to keep prices down, and that requires formidable skills in sales and marketing. Sinclair badly damaged his credibility by announcing innovations before they were available. He says that he did so because 'it helps to attract talent for work on the project'. But that is an attitude more suited to an inventor than to a businessman trying to serve a mass market. He has always felt that he has to move on – to keep ahead of the rest of the field. But there are obvious dangers in expanding in too many directions at the same time, especially if you are heavily dependent on the contribution of others.

Sinclair likes to work with a relatively small team of bright people who share his enthusiasms, and to remain as flexible as he can. He doesn't care for the details of management, and he is impatient. He accepts that he can't be right all the time, but reckons that making mistakes now and then is very much part of the game. He would undoubtedly be far wealthier if he had been more cautious, but he insists that money is not very important to him – 'It's just another tool.'

One of his favourite topics of conversation is the so-called fifth-generation computer, a machine that thinks and could ultimately become more intelligent than man. In 1984 he told the US Congressional Clearing House of the Future:

> I think it certain that in decades, not centuries, machines of silicon will arise first to rival and then surpass their human progenitors. Once they surpass us they will be capable of their own design. In a real sense they will be reproductive. Silicon will have ended carbon's long monopoly. And ours, too, I suppose, for we will no longer be able to deem ourselves the finest intelligence in the known universe. In principle it could be stopped; there will be those that try, but it will happen none the less. The lid of Pandora's Box is starting to open.

He has also lectured on the subject as a visiting professor at

London's Imperial College, and would clearly love to be the man who makes it all happen. But he is not the only one: numerous rival teams are working on the concept, and many have far greater resources than he does.

Isaac Merritt Singer

1811–75

Inventor of the first practical sewing machine

Singer is often said to have invented the sewing machine, which isn't so. Others got there before him, including a French tailor and a Presbyterian clergyman of Macon, Georgia. Walter Hunt, an American Quaker genius who invented the safety pin, made a machine in 1834 – sixteen years earlier than Singer – but abandoned it when his daughter told him it would throw seamstresses out of work. Elias Howe, a machinist from Cambridge, Massachusetts, was granted a patent on a sewing machine in 1846. But Singer produced the first device with which it was possible to sew continuously.

Singer's was therefore the first practical machine, but it did not prevent Howe and others from suing him. Singer hired a lawyer, Edward Clark, who soon became his partner, taking charge of finance and sales as well as legal matters. Together they ended what became known as 'the sewing machine war' by organizing the Sewing Machine Combination, America's first patent pool. Manufacture was licensed at $15 a machine. They also pioneered the use of trademarks and of instalment selling. The Singer Manufacturing Company, incorporated in 1863, became America's first multi-national corporation.

Born of poor German immigrant parents, Singer had little education and left his New York home when he was twelve years old. He was without success a farmer, a machinist, an actor in a Shakespearean troupe and an inventor of machines for excavating rock and carving wood. In 1850, at the age of thirty-nine, he borrowed $40 and went to work on a sewing machine.

The earliest machines were heavy devices for tailors and harness-makers, but by 1856 the leading companies were making lighter models for home use. They enabled housewives to do in one hour what took ten to fourteen hours by hand. The great obstacle was the fact that the average family income was less than $500 a year and the price of a sewing machine was $125 or more. Singer and Clark attacked this problem with a trade-in allowance for old machines, the barter of machines for advertising, discounts at schools and, most important, instalment selling.

Instalment selling became a bulwark of Singer sales in the United States and was soon instituted in Britain and many other overseas countries under the term 'hire purchase'. Only $5 was needed to place a new Singer machine in a home. The remainder was amortized in small monthly payments. If the purchaser failed to make payments, the machine was repossessed. The method is commonplace now, but at the time it was hailed as a brilliant new idea.

In those days Singer men had to be mechanics, collection agents, sewing teachers and versatile adventurers. They travelled mostly in well-marked buggies, but also by dugout canoe and every other form of conveyance. People lacking the co-ordination to operate the usual treadle machine were sold hand machines. When one African tribe, believing that 'Good iron makes good noise', demanded noisy machines, a Singer man obligingly loosened up his machines until they achieved the required clatter.

The manufacture of Singer machines overseas began in 1867 in Glasgow, Scotland. A Canadian plant was opened in Montreal five years later. Others followed; despite great growth in domestic business, the company was soon selling more sewing machines abroad than in the USA. Gandhi learned to sew on a Singer machine while in jail; it was, he said, 'one of the few useful things ever invented'.

Singer products were marked with the name from the first, and the bases of many spelled 'Singer' in metal. By 1870 the company had an oval trademark, which included a large 'S', crossed needles and a shuttle. About this time, the famous red

Gandhi learned to sew on a Singer machine while in jail; it was, he said, 'one of the few useful things ever invented'.

'S' with a woman at a sewing machine also began to be used.

It turned out to be a wise precaution. There had been surreptitious counterfeiting of Singer trademarks earlier, but with the expiry of the latest basic patent in 1877 imitators came out into the open. They not only copied the Singer design, but also called their machines Singers and imitated the company's trademarks. Singer filed suit. The Supreme Court eventually ruled in its favour, saying that each manufacturer should indicate who made his machine and 'unmistakably' inform the public. Imitations of the Singer product were called 'an injury to private rights and a deceit upon the public'. The deceptive practices of the defendants were 'perpetually enjoyed'. It was an important decision, upheld ever after.

Alfred P. Sloan

1875–1966

'The greatest genius ever in the auto business'

LEE IACOCCA has called Alfred P. Sloan 'the greatest genius ever in the auto business'. He certainly had an enormous influence, not only on the motor industry but on the corporate world in general. PETER DRUCKER has written of him:

> Sloan set out deliberately in the early Twenties to break the traditional pattern of business organization, business management and business leadership. To do this . . . he literally had to invent almost everything that is commonplace in business today: the concept of the big business and its organization; the very idea of a systematic management which defined responsibilities and organized means of communications and decision making; management controls. . . . Above all he had to invent a person: the professional executive who is both master and servant of his creation, the large organized institution.

Sloan was born in New Haven, Connecticut. His father was in the wholesale tea, coffee and cigar business and in 1885, when Alfred was ten years old, he moved the firm to New York City. Alfred later went to the Massachusetts Institute of Technology, where he graduated with a BS in electrical engineering, and went to work for the Hyatt Roller Bearing Company of Newark, later of Harrison, New Jersey. Hyatt was then a tiny enterprise, employing about twenty-five people. Sloan was, in his own words, 'a kind of office boy, draftsman, salesman, and general assistant to the enterprise at a salary of $50 a month'.

He did not see much future there, and soon left it to become associated with a household electric refrigerator company which seemed to offer better prospects. But after two years he heard that Hyatt was in trouble and likely to go into liquidation. His father and an associate agreed to put $5000 into the business, on the understanding that Sloan would go back for six months and see what he could do with it. He did so, and revived the company. He designed and sold bearings to the pioneers in the car industry and eventually, at the age of forty, agreed to sell Hyatt to William C. Durant, the founder of General Motors, for $13.5 million.

A substantial part of the payment was in the form of stock in a new enterprise formed by Durant, called United Motors Corporation. Sloan became president and chief operating officer of the new company, which was later acquired by General Motors. He was made president of General Motors in 1923 and chairman in 1937; in 1956 he retired, having built up the largest and in many ways the most successful industrial corporation in the world.

Durant had created the business with great entrepreneurial flair but, as so often happens, he had turned out to be a poor administrator. General Motors came close to bankruptcy in 1920, largely as a result of his incautious expansionism and central management's inability to control the various divisions. That General Motors pulled through the crisis may be attributed chiefly to the efforts of Sloan and Pierre S. du Pont, who was president at the time.

The board of directors adopted a plan of reorganization, put forward by Sloan, which subsequently became the foundation of management policy. It was based on his view that the company had to find, as he put it, 'a happy medium between the extremes of pure centralization and pure decentralization'.

Sloan himself wrote about it at length in his excellent book, *My Years with General Motors*, which still remains essential reading for every business executive. In brief, the plan presented a specific structure for the corporation as it existed at that time. It recognized the form of the divisions, each of which was a self-contained group of functions (engineering, production, sales and so on). It grouped the divisions, according to like activities, with an executive in charge of each group. It also provided for advisory staffs, which would be without line authority, and for financial staff. It distinguished policy from administration of policy, and specified the location of each in the structure. As Sloan said: 'It expressed in its way the concept that was later to be formulated as decentralized operations with co-ordinated control.'

The basic elements of financial control were cost, price, volume, and rate of return of investment. He felt very strongly that rate of return was a strategic principle of business – a point which today is an accepted part of management doctrine, but which was new then. The profit resulting from any business considered abstractly, he maintained, was no real measure of the merits of that particular business. What mattered was the relation of that profit to the real worth of invested capital within the business. 'No other financial principle with which I am acquainted', he said, 'serves better than the rate of return as an objective aid to business judgment.'

The question, though, was not simply one of maximizing the rate of return for a specific short period of time. The fundamental consideration was an average return over a long period of time. The long-term rate was to be the highest expec-

'No other financial principle with which I am acquainted serves better than the rate of return as an objective aid to business judgment.'

tation consistent with a sound growth of the business, or what he called 'the economic return attainable'.

Sloan's team worked out detailed standards, or yardsticks, and compared them with actual performance. To make this concept work, each division manager was required to submit monthly reports of his total operating results. The data from these reports was put on standard forms by the central financial office in such a way as to provide the standard basis for measuring divisional performance in terms of return of investment. These divisional return-on-investment reports were constantly studied by the top executives. If the indicated results were not satisfactory, Sloan or some other general executive would talk to the division managers about the corrective action to be taken.

Sloan also developed other techniques and laid down a product policy. He said first that the corporation should produce a line of cars in each price area, from the lowest price up to one for a strictly high-grade quantity-production car, but it would not get into the fancy-price field with small production; second, that the price steps should not leave wide gaps in the line, and yet should be great enough to keep their number within reason, so that the greatest advantage of quantity production could be secured; and third, that there should be no duplication by the corporation in the price fields or steps.

Sloan was a motivation man: he well understood the need to balance economies of scale with the motivation that small, self-sufficient organizational groups can generate. He gave individual managers within his company room to express themselves and to display leadership within a stable organizational framework. He also provided financial incentives, through stock options and bonus schemes, to ensure that GM executives could benefit personally from the success of their business. His encouragement of the entrepreneurial spirit within such a large company did much to prevent the dead hand of bureaucracy from strangling innovation, flair and the pursuit of profitable business opportunity within GM. Executives, he declared, should be placed in the same relative position, so far as possible, that they would occupy if they were conducting a business on their own account. 'This provides opportunity for the accomplishment through the exercise of individual initiative, and opportunity for economic progress commensurate with performance. In that way managerial talent is attracted and retained by the corporation.'

The GM bonus plan was introduced as early as 1918. It provided for bonuses to be paid to employees 'who have contributed to the company's success in a special degree by their inventions, ability, industry, loyalty or exceptional services'. The awards were geared to profits, but the bonus system was not a profit-sharing plan. It did not entitle any employee to any regular share in the earnings of the corporation or any of its divisions. Each employee had to earn the right to be considered for a bonus award each year by his own effort. In most cases, too, the awards were made partly or wholly in General Motors stock. This, said Sloan, had an

---

Sloan was a motivation man: he well understood the need to balance economies of scale with the motivation that small, self-sufficient organizational groups can generate.

---

important effect in creating an identity of interest between management and shareholders by creating an owner-management group. This was further strengthened, in 1957, by the introduction of a stock option plan.

Throughout his long career, Sloan stressed the importance of two factors in management: incentive compensation, and decentralization with co-ordinated control. Decentralization, he emphasized, produced initiative, responsibility, development of personnel, decisions close to the facts, flexibility – in short, all the qualities necessary for an organization to adapt to new conditions. Co-ordination produced efficiencies and economies. Incentive programmes ensured that executives became partners in the business. All this may seem obvious now, though a recent survey showed that, even today, fewer than 10 per cent of American companies give bonuses. It was certainly not obvious when Alfred Sloan took over General Motors. Iacocca may or may not have been right in his judgment that he was 'the greatest genius ever in the auto business', but the facts are plain enough: General Motors achieved tremendous growth under Sloan's leadership.

Frederick Smith

b. 1944

Mover of 'high-priority, time-sensitive' goods

The story of Fred Smith, the founder and chairman of Federal Express, is often cited as a classic example of how a young man with vision and determination can make a fortune in the service sector. His vision led him to reinvent the postal system; his determination turned the company he founded at the age of twenty-nine into one of America's great enterprises, providing a service which has become very much part of daily business life.

While still at Yale, Smith wrote a term paper which analyzed the freight services existing at the time. He suggested that there might be a market for a company that moved 'high-priority, time-sensitive' goods, such as medicines and electronic components. The system then in operation, he thought, was cumbersome and inadequate. Deliveries could and should be made overnight. This could be accomplished by setting up a 'hub-and-spokes' air freight system. A freight company could draw a circle around, say, Detroit airport. The airport would act as a 'hub'. A number of truck routes would be the 'spokes'. All day, trucks would scurry around that circle, gathering packages from businesses that wanted them to be sent quickly to another part of the United States. At the end of the business day, all spokes would lead to one aircraft waiting at the airport. Once loaded, the plane would fly off to a bigger hub somewhere in the centre of America – Memphis would be ideal: routes to Memphis from Detroit, Chicago, Los Angeles, New York, Miami, Houston and so on would be the big spokes. In Memphis, all the planes would land and be emptied.

Then all the packages would be sorted and the planes loaded again. The Detroit plane would have only Detroit parcels, the New York plane only New York parcels, etc. Then the planes would simply go back where they came from, and when they landed the same fleet of trucks would be waiting at the airport. Even before the sun was up they would again be scurrying about inside that circle, delivering the packages and gathering another batch of them for delivery the next day.

Smith's professor was unimpressed. Federal regulations, he felt, would preclude such a service and, even if one could overcome the regulatory problems, competition from the major, well-entrenched airlines would make success highly doubtful. The grade he gave him for the paper was a C. But Smith, then twenty, did not abandon the idea. He knew that the French Post Office had used it for years. It surely could be made to work in a country with a well-developed transport industry like the United States.

Some years went by before he was able to do anything about it. After graduating, he was commissioned by the Marine Corps as a lieutenant and served two tours of duty in Vietnam. When he was discharged in 1969, as a captain with six medals for bravery, he used money left to him by his father (who had made *his* fortune running bus lines through the southern states) to acquire a controlling interest in a company called Arkansas Aviation Sales, which bought and sold used corporate jets. He turned it into a profitable business, but he had no intention of spending the rest of his life as a trader. He wanted to develop the concept which he had outlined in that paper at Yale.

His first step was to commission not one but *two* market research consultants to study the feasibility of overnight delivery. Both included that, yes, customers were dissatisfied with existing services and, yes, there was scope for someone who could do better. But, they said, he would have to invest at least $20 million and it would never be anything big.

Armed with their reports, Smith set about raising funds for the venture. The consultants had said, in writing, that there was a market waiting for his concept and that the business could make money. That, as far as he was concerned, was enough. He formed a company called Federal Express, borrowed money from various banks, and hired people who shared his enthusiasm. He bought a fleet of executive jets – thirty-three of them – at a bargain price and relocated his business to the city he had chosen in that study at university, Memphis. He spent a great deal of money on advertising,

---

Smith's professor was unimpressed. Federal regulations . . . would preclude such a service and . . . competition from the major, well-entrenched airlines would make success highly doubtful. The grade he gave him for the paper was a C.

---

stressing the company's commitment to delivering packages 'absolutely, positively overnight'. Federal Express, Smith declared, was 'nothing short of being the logistics arm of a whole new society that is building up in our economy – a society that isn't built around automobile and steel production, but that is built up instead around service industries and high technology endeavours in electronics and optics and medical science. It is the movement of these support items that Federal Express is all about.'

In March 1973, the first planes flew into Memphis from all over the eastern United States, carrying a total of six packages. It was a month before Federal Express flew again, and the package count then – 186 – was hardly more encouraging. The company's first financial year, which ended in April, showed a loss of $4.4 million.

Smith still has a copy of a memo he sent to his employees in September 1973, which regretfully asked them not to cash their pay cheques for at least two weeks, pending the arrangement of another loan. The company could easily have gone under at that point, but two months later he succeeded in getting the financial support he needed – a $52 million venture capital investment in Federal Express, the largest in American business history. It was put together by a New York firm funded by the Rothschilds; two of its executives had heard about Federal Express and had decided that it was worth backing.

But Smith's problems were by no means over. The company continued to lose money and one of the backers insisted that Smith should step down as chairman, in favour of a retired Air Force general. He also fell out with his two sisters, who had become worried about his stewardship of the family's funds. He was charged with fraud. At the end of 1975 a federal jury exonerated Smith, and around that time, too, the financial situation started to improve. Smith was reinstated as head of the company. In 1976 the company had revenues of $109 million and a net income of $8 million.

From then on everything went well. De-regulation of air traffic freight in 1978 allowed him to fly bigger planes with an increased payload, and a highly effective TV advertising campaign made Federal Express far better known. By 1980 the company had earnings of $60 million on revenues of $590 million, and in 1983 turnover hit the billion mark for the first time. Three years later it was $3 billion.

Federal Express, Smith declared, was 'nothing short of being the logistics arm of a whole new society that is building up in our economy'.

Smith made it into the *Guinness Book of Records* in 1982 as the highest-paid man ever – more than $50 million, including stock options. The company now has forty-two thousand staff and an impressive fleet of trucks and planes, including DC10s and Boeing 727s. It handles more than seven hundred thousand parcels and packages a day.

Smith tried to slow the relentless march of the facsimile machine, a serious threat to the express envelope service, by developing his own electronic system. The experiment was not a success, and almost $200 million has been written off as a result. But these days Federal Express can afford such setbacks. He is also making a determined effort to expand out of the US market, where he has more than half of the air express business, into Europe. He is up against formidable competition and customs bureaucracy, but he reckons that there is considerable scope. Whatever happens, express services are bound to improve rapidly.

Axel Springer

1912–85

Press baron of post-war Germany

Axel Springer was one of the most famous – and most powerful – of the entrepreneurial German businessmen who laid the foundation for large fortunes in the years that followed the defeat of the Nazi regime. Admired and despised, loved and hated in equal measure, he created a newspaper and magazine publishing empire that today rates among the biggest in Europe.

Springer had not been conscripted for service in World War II because he suffered from a pancreas infection. The son of a publisher, he was for a time deputy editor of a newspaper in his native Hamburg until it was suppressed by the Nazis in 1941. In the remaining war years he apparently worked in one of the city's cinemas as projectionist and administrator. In 1946, when Springer was thirty-four, he moved into the publishing business on his own account, launching *Hör Zu*, a magazine that listed radio programmes and ran family interest features.

In the early post-war period, the German media were strictly controlled by the Allied occuping powers. No publication could be set up without their authority until the establishment of the Federal Republic of Germany in 1949. Springer, a great Anglophile, was judged to be the kind of man who could safely be allowed to publish magazines and newspapers.

In 1948 he started the *Hamburger Abendblatt*, an evening paper which grew into one of the largest regional papers in Germany. Four years later he launched the paper by which he is chiefly remembered, the *Bild Zeitung*. He devised it explicitly to tap the huge reservoir of Germans who read no newspaper at all. Most of the journals then on the market were worthy but dull. (They still are.) Springer's *Bild* was brash and vulgar, with racy stories, giant headlines and striking pictures. It was, as Springer had guessed, exactly what a large section of the public wanted. Traditionalists were shocked, but the newcomer quickly outpaced all its rivals. Today it is bought by more than 5 million people daily and read by 11 million – a fifth of the population of West Germany. It is by far the best-selling paper in Europe.

As the money rolled in, Springer expanded further. In 1954 he took over two highly regarded journals – the national daily *Die Welt* and its Sunday sister *Welt am Sonntag*, which had been founded by the British occupation authorities after the war. Many people feared that they, too, would be turned into sensation-hungry papers. But Springer had no intention of creating competitors for *Bild*. He wanted a major stake at both ends of the market. (RUPERT MURDOCH later followed his example in Britain when he added the *Times* and *Sunday Times* to a stable which already owned the *Sun* and the *News of the World*.)

In the next two decades Springer bought local papers and launched more specialist publications, including magazines devoted to tennis and skiing. He also acquired a book publishing house and went into the lucrative pulp fiction business. In 1984 the group made a substantial investment in the start-up of Sat-1, the German satellite television channel.

Springer was a passionate advocate of a reunited Germany. He went to Moscow in 1958 to press the cause with Khrushchev, but got nowhere; it turned him into a dedicated opponent of the Soviet regime. As a symbolic gesture he moved the headquarters of his company to Berlin, building an imposing office block right next to the infamous Wall. He also introduced four principles to which every journalist who worked for him was expected to subscribe: a reunited Germany, the market economy, reconciliation with Israel and opposition to totalitarianism in all its forms. His papers campaigned for all these causes with great vigour – inevitably leading to complaints (notably from the Left) that he had accumulated too much power.

Springer never made as much money from his serious journals as he did from his trivial *Bild* (*Die Welt* actually lost money for a long time), but he did become one of the richest men in Germany. He was a patron of the arts and a generous benefactor of the State of Israel. He had every reason to be

He ... introduced four principles to which every journalist who worked for him was expected to subscribe: a reunited Germany, the market economy, reconciliation with Israel and opposition to totalitarianism in all its forms.

pleased with his success, but tragedy struck in 1980. His eldest son and heir apparent, Axel Springer Jr, committed suicide in a fit of depression at the age of thirty-eight. It was a dreadful personal blow. In the last year of his own life Springer devoted most of his time to securing the future of his life's work. He didn't want the company to fall into the hands of outsiders, and was determined to ensure that the 'four principles' would be upheld after he was gone.

His solution was ingenious. Springer publicly floated a sizeable percentage of his group, which meant that the family would have enough cash to cover death duties and to go on expanding. The deal also included two unusual provisions. The shares held by the public were 'tied' – they could not be traded without the approval of the Springer directors, which meant that they would be in a position to fend off any unwanted bidder. And the articles of the company were changed so that an 80 per cent majority would be required to modify the 'four principles' which determined the editorial policy of his newspapers. Finally, he got his four heirs to agree that they would not break up his empire for at least thirty years.

When Springer died in 1985 Ronald Reagan – presumably acting on the advice of his ambassador in Bonn – paid tribute to him as 'a German patriot, a democrat, and a practical idealist'. In West Germany itself, leading politicians who had enjoyed his support provided equally fulsome quotes, but there were also many people who made it clear that they were delighted by his departure. That, of course, happens to every press baron who uses his papers to make propaganda as well as profits. The 'practical idealist' failed to achieve his main political objective, reunification of Germany, because it wasn't practical, and it is easy to see why the *Bild Zeitung* was – and is – so widely regarded as a cynical attempt to exploit the public's appetite for trashy sensationalism. But Springer was certainly a patriot and a democrat; he was also an innovative journalist and businessman who played an important role in the revival of his country after the trauma of the Hitler years.

Louis H. Sullivan

1856–1924

Father of modern architecture

Chicago can fairly claim to be the birthplace of modern architecture, and Sullivan was certainly one of its fathers. During his fifty-one years of practice in the city he created many fine buildings and inspired other architects who were to become famous – men like Frank Lloyd Wright (his most distinguished disciple) and Mies van der Rohe.

From the very beginning, modern architecture in Chicago was part of a search for a social philosophy as well as a search for perfection of form. Sullivan held, and others agreed, that the only architecture worth having was what he called 'democratic architecture'. This became known as 'functionalism'. The spirit of functional form was the expression of the social purpose of the building in its structure. Sullivan taught that each building must be unique. He never repeated his ornament. Each building had a 'spirit' which must be respected. The expression of this spirit was as much part of its 'utility' as the plumbing. For only when the building evoked human satisfaction determined by the form itself could it become architecture. And only when such form could be reduced to some kind of principle could it become an order, and not merely a style, of architecture.

In both his buildings and his lectures, Sullivan asked questions. What is the proper form for a democratic architecture, and what kinds of human relationships will be possible in this new architecture? He answered the first by proposing that whatever the use of a building, its form must follow its function – not a mechanical function, like a traffic flow, a circulation of air, heating, lighting and so on, but *human* function. He thought that the architect must ask himself: How can I enhance the human satisfaction of acting within my building or the communities I design? If I design a house of prayer, how do I make a prayer more significant? If I design a department store, how do I make shopping more pleasurable? If I design a factory, how do I make work healthy and pleasurable? If I design a tomb, how do I make a sorrowing family feel the serenity and peace of death as a memory of life?

Sullivan hated 'phoney' buildings. He thought a bank should look like a friendly meeting place for neighbours who had come to see each other and to talk over their problems with bank officials. A bank which looked like a fort, a great vault, a Roman temple or a Gothic cathedral enraged him. Why, he asked, does the banker not dress in a Roman toga and talk in Latin?

Architectural principles, he said, were reached by asking: What is the chief characteristic of the structure? To answer this question in respect of the tall office building, he said that the chief characteristic was its loftiness. This

> is the very organ-tone in its appeal. It must be in turn the dominant chord in the architect's expression of it, the true excitant of his imagination. It must be tall, every inch of it tall. The force and the power of altitude must be in it, the glory and pride of exaltation must be in it. It must be every inch a proud and soaring thing, rising in sheer exaltation that from bottom to top it is a unit without a single dissenting line. . . .

The deeper principle underlying the character of the soaring tower was that the outward expression, structure, 'design or whatever we may choose to call it of the tall office building should in the very nature of things follow the functions of the building'. Architectural art, Sullivan said, had failed thus far because it had not yet found a way to become truly plastic: 'It does not yield to the poet's touch.'

Sullivan's teachings had considerable influence, but sadly very little of his work survives. One wonders what he would make of today's 'soaring towers' – structures like the Hancock Building and the Sears Tower. The skyscraper made its debut about a hundred years ago, but it is very much a twentieth-century phenomenon, made possible by the development of steel frames, elevators and central heating. Chicago and New York led the way, and are still great rivals. The Sears Tower, built in the 1970s, is made up of nine rigidly interconnected tubes that rise to varying heights, the two at the centre of the cluster reaching 110 storeys and 1450 feet. The vast complex of steel, glass, aluminium and concrete is more like a mini-city than a building: it houses more than twelve thousand occupants. It is indeed a 'proud and soaring thing', but what about the 'human satisfaction' which Sullivan regarded as so important? The Sears Tower can hardly be called great visual art, and the individual can easily be overwhelmed by it all. In fairness, though, it must be recorded that the people who work in the Tower seem to like it. That, at least, was the impression I formed when I interviewed a large number of them for a BBC radio documentary in 1985.

Back in the 1950s, Frank Lloyd Wright conceived a plan for

A bank which looked like a fort, a great vault, a Roman temple or a Gothic cathedral enraged him. Why, he asked, does the banker not dress in a Roman toga and talk in Latin?

a mile-high office block in Chicago – one with a staggering 528 storeys. It has yet to be built, but technically it could be done. We may certainly see buildings of 150 floors, or more, before too long. No wonder they have already coined a new label: the super scraper.

To enthusiasts, the tall building is America's great gift to architecture, a bold symbol of economic adventurism, adding excitement to the urban scene. To detractors it is an architect's plaything, financed by a property developer's vision of big bucks and rented or bought by corporations with a macho complex. Orwellian or Olympian, it is clearly here to stay.

Gideon Sundback

1880–1949

Developer of the zip fastener

The common zipper must surely rank among the most useful items ever invented. The credit is generally given to Gideon Sundback, a Swedish-born electrical engineer who emigrated to the United States in 1905. Someone else had the original idea, but it was Sundback who invented, in all essential respects, the modern slide fastener. He also devised a machine that would satisfactorily produce it in large quantities.

The story really goes back to 1893. In that year, an American called Witcomb L. Judson patented a 'Clasp Locker or Unlocker for Shoes'. It is said that he had the idea as he bent over the tedious task of lacing and unlacing his shoes, though his application for the patent mentioned various other articles on which it could be used, such as gloves and corsets.

Judson and a business partner later produced and sold a fastener which they named the Universal. This was a metallic chain contraption made up of flat, curved hooks in the shape of battle axes, and joined together by open links. Two of these chains could be brought together and closed by progressively turning the hooks into the eyes with a slider.

A company was formed, but it proved difficult to manufacture the device by machine. In 1905 Judson designed a new fastener which could be produced more easily: instead of being linked together in a chain, the fastening elements were simply clamped about the beaded edge of a fabric tape. But the garment trade didn't think much of the device, which still had many faults and shortcomings. It had a tendency to spring open when flexed, if not used exactly right, and it would catch and tear underclothing. It also twisted everything out of shape if it wasn't removed from the dress or skirt before laundering.

Sundback was hired to develop and improve the product. He designed a new model in 1908, but it was still far from satisfactory and the trade remained sceptical. The company got close to bankruptcy; it kept going – just – by renting out the machine shop and engineering facilities for odd jobs.

Sundback, by now virtually alone, stubbornly continued with his experiments. In 1913 he came up with an entirely different approach: a fastener without hooks and eyes. Fresh capital was raised and a new company, the Hookless Fastener Co., was formed. Again, though, the new product turned out to have serious faults. Another year went by before he finally had all the answers.

The Hookless No. 2, as it was called, went on sale in October 1914. But after all the disappointments with the earlier fasteners it proved difficult to persuade people to buy it.

It is said that he had the idea as he bent over the tedious task of lacing and unlacing his shoes.

Tailors vigorously opposed it. The first real break did not come until 1917, when a New York manufacturer bought a quantity of them for use on sailors' money belts. The following year the Navy ordered ten thousand Hookless No. 2s for use on flying suits. Glove manufacturers started to take an interest in the product, and it was also tried experimentally on tobacco pouches.

The big turning point came in 1923, when the B. F. Goodrich

Company introduced rubber galoshes featuring the Hookless slide fastener. It was a Goodrich executive who came up with the word 'zipper' when he was first shown the new galoshes. They were promptly named Zipper Boots, and became very popular. Goodrich placed large orders for the fasteners and others soon did the same; Sundback's persistence had paid off at last.

Today, of course, there are numerous uses for the zipper. It seems such a simple, everyday item that it is hard to believe that years of effort went into making it work. But the same could easily be said of a great many other products which we nowadays take so much for granted. We might still be lacing up our shoes if it had not been for the impatience of one man, Judson, and the stubborn determination of another, Sundback. Neither ever won any great fame, but we clearly have reason to be grateful to them.

Robert R. Taylor

b. 1935

Creator of fads

Robert Taylor is one of those innovative businessmen who like to go out on a limb with an unusual, often untested, idea. It has made him rich: the Minnetonka Corporation, which he started in 1964 with a $3000 investment, now has assets of more than $50 million.

Taylor, a Stanford MBA, left his job as a Johnson & Johnson sales manager to launch the business. He began with a basic product – soap – but made it different. His early creations included a yellow lemon-shaped soap, a green apple-shaped soap, and cocoa butter soap wrapped in brown paper to look like a Hershey chocolate bar. He also sold sachets, fruit-scented shampoos and waxless candles. His first true breakthrough came one day when he was driving to work. He thought how ugly bar soap was, and how it usually messed up the bathroom. Why not have a high-quality liquid soap that comes in an attractive bottle?

After developing a formula for liquid soap, Minnetonka – named after the nearby town where Mr Taylor lives – ran an $8 million advertising campaign to introduce Softsoap. It was a big gamble – at the time, the company's net worth was only $8 million – but it paid off. Between 1979 and 1981 Minnetonka's sales revenues skyrocketed to $96 million.

Then the inevitable happened: other companies, including giants like Procter & Gamble, came out with their own liquid soaps and Minnetonka's market share dropped sharply. The company lost money in both 1982 and 1983. To stay afloat, Taylor laid off more than two hundred employees, reduced the size of the Softsoap bottle so that it could sell at a lower price, and introduced a bottle with new colours and floral designs. It recaptured the market lead.

Taylor's second breakthrough product, Check-Up toothpaste, had some of the same problems. It was a good idea: the first anti-plaque paste and the first in a pump dispenser. Introduced in 1984, it quickly won 4 per cent of the market. But Colgate Palmolive also started to sell toothpaste in pumps and toothpaste that fights plaque, and Minnetonka's market fell to less than 2 per cent. It has since exploited the name by selling a Check-Up anti-plaque bubble gum.

Despite his setbacks, Taylor decided to tackle another big market which already had some powerful players – the fragrance industry. He had bought Calvin Klein's cosmetics company in 1980, together with the right to use the name, and in 1985 he stunned the industry by spending $17.5 million on a massive advertising campaign for a provocative, sensual fragrance which he called Obsession.

The advertisements were erotic and caused some controversy,

but people remembered them and were intrigued by the product. Sales of Obsession reached $30 million in 1985 and double that figure in 1986. The response encouraged Taylor to expand into the international market, and to add an Obsession for Men fragrance.

'Ten per cent of the success of a new consumer product is the idea,' he told the *New York Times*. 'Ninety per cent is the execution. That means positioning the product, marketing strategy and creativity.' His rivals would certainly agree, but Taylor reckons that many large consumer products companies get caught up in structure, research and justification. 'They're always trying to do a thorough job of risk analysis. When they get all the facts together, though, they find that they can't do away with all risks and they often end up either doing nothing or moving very slowly.'

There is, obviously, a sizeable element of truth in that observation. But as they demonstrated after his earlier innovations, the big companies often move all too fast to develop a similar product and grab a share of the market.

It remains to be seen whether Obsession can continue to do well, over the years, in a fiercely competitive business. Meanwhile, Taylor has been busy with other projects. 'The philosophy at Minnetonka', the head of his research department has been quoted as saying, 'is what's happening in the marketplace, what's happening sociologically, how can we generate a product?' His team goes through hundreds of scientific journals each month to see what concerns scientists and consumers. Taylor himself spends a great deal of time looking for new ideas.

At a meeting in India, in 1985, he met a salesman from an Italian pharmaceutical company that makes Foltens, which is sold in Italy as a hair restoration agent. The company was on the verge of signing a licensing agreement with a large American group, so Taylor had to move quickly. He brought back samples for Minnetonka's laboratory to examine, and then decided to sell it as a cosmetic to protect hair through follicle stimulation and scalp massage. He also acquired a licence to sell a new Sesame Street bubble bath product for children. (When someone suggested test marketing, he said: Why bother? 'Every kid knows what Sesame Street is.')

Taylor reckons that the strength of his business lies in its ability to stay one step ahead, which means taking chances. Aggressive marketing also helps. But he is realistic enough to acknowledge that, as he learned to his cost, getting there first

When someone suggested test marketing, he said: Why bother? 'Every kid knows what Sesame Street is.'

often gives you only a temporary advantage. And there is always the risk that a bright new idea which captures the imagination of the public will prove to be just a passing fad.

In novelty-conscious America, fads can make a lot of money in a very short period of time. The hula hoop is a classic example. Others include pogo sticks, skateboards, pet rocks, platform shoes, square eggs, Rubik cubes and waterbeds. A company specializing in off-beat items cashed in on the publicity given to the energy crisis by producing a solar barbecue. Operating off sunlight, it cooked a steak in minutes and allowed the owner to talk grandly about the benefits of environmentalism and conservation.

The simplest ideas often do best. When the 'flower power' cult got under way in California during the late 1960s, a Los Angeles couple driving down a freeway were intrigued to see several cars which had been decorated with wild, bright colours. As they talked about the motivation behind this unusual touch a thought came to the husband: perhaps the world was ready for some kind of bright, good-looking, easy-to-use fun bit of madness to stick on cars and other possessions. They went home, produced some stick-on flowers and covered their own car with them. The neighbours laughed, but within a few days children started to come to their door asking if they could buy some flowers too. A week later the couple had made their first sale to a store and orders were coming in from others. During the months that followed, the fad not only caught on all over America but also found its way to such diverse places as Sweden, Japan, Germany, Mexico and Canada. The crazy little vinyl flowers even turned up on taxis in Cairo and phone booths in Tel Aviv. By the end of the following year some 180 million had been sold for more than $10 million at retail.

Sometimes a company does remarkably well by changing the format and packaging of a basic household product, as Taylor did with soap. But fads do not provide a sound base for a major corporation which intends to be around for a long time. The real challenge is to find and develop products with genuine staying power and *then* to succeed in fending off the competition.

Gilbert Trigano

b. 1920

Sun, sea, sand and learning

Trigano took a simple concept and developed it into the world's largest organized holiday travel empire – Club Med. A Belgian idealist, Gérard Blitz, thought up the idea of an inexpensive 'back to nature' holiday camp in the dreary days following World War II. The first was opened in Majorca, in 1959. But it was Trigano who, over three decades, masterminded the Club's phenomenal worldwide expansion, shrewdly exploiting the commercial potential of its idyllic 'noble savage' formula of thatched huts, Tahitian sarongs and beads used as currency. Today it manages facilities in twenty-four countries on five continents.

Trigano was born near Paris to Jewish Algerian parents, and his father was a grocer. At fifteen Gilbert left school and tried a career as an actor and songwriter. In World War II he joined the communist Resistance in the south-west and subsequently worked for the party's daily newspaper, *L'Humanité*. But he became disillusioned with Stalinism and left. He later said that

Fascinated by novelty of all kinds, he saw the Club as a 'laboratory for the new leisure era' where people could explore the new technologies.

he hated all political parties and 'isms', but still had a 'left-wing sensibility'.

After his spell in journalism, Trigano started a camping equipment firm and sold surplus American Army tents to the infant Club Med, at that time a non-profit organization. He joined Blitz in 1954 as managing director, and set about turning the company into a profit-making business. In 1955, in Greece, the hut became the first specific 'Club' dwelling. Similar to Polynesian grass huts, it helped create the Club's reputation for respecting nature – before ecology became fashionable. The basic philosophy was that people who live and work in cities need holidays in totally different surroundings. So the atmosphere of the holiday villages (never camp) that followed was kept as informal as possible. Telephones, radios, newspapers and TV were banned. Wallets and other valuables were locked away at the beginning of one's stay. The Club Med vacationer paid one price in advance, which covered everything from travel to meals and sporting activities. To cope with any extras like drinks at the bar he was given a pre-paid necklace of beads.

Guests were referred to as GMs, *gentils membres*, or 'nice

people'. The villages were run by GOs, *gentils organisateurs*, or 'nice organisers'. This approach has been maintained ever since. Each village has around a hundred GOs (one for every five guests) who mix with the GMs, teach them sports and present entertainment each night after dinner. In essence, they fill virtually all of the guest contact positions, while local employees serve as back-of-house staff.

Drawn from around the world (although a high percentage are French), the GOs are young enthusiasts who are prepared to accept low wages and long hours for a career which will last for only two or three years. They eat alongside guests at family-style meals, ensuring that each table is served properly and promptly, and generally try to make sure that GMs enjoy themselves. Although everyone is strongly encouraged to join in the activities, nothing is compulsory.

Several other distinct characteristics differentiate the Club Med villages from a normal resort hotel. For example, there are no room keys. Rooms can be locked from the inside, but not from the outside, making it absolutely essential to store all of one's valuables in the safety deposit boxes provided. At the same time, however, it allows guests to relax on the beach unconcerned with the security of their rooms or keys. The use

'The new empires are those of communications and the means of satisfying the needs and desires of men.'

of beads also has a security aspect: because they are worthless outside the resort, it is unlikely that anyone would bother to steal them.

Club Med generally seeks an isolated, scenically beautiful location where the village can become a self-contained community. It helps the GM to forget his other, 'civilized' life, while helping Club Med to control the attendance at meals and other village activities. It also gives the company tremendous leverage in negotiating for financing or tax breaks from individual countries. In many isolated locations, its resort may be the only type that could operate successfully – and it may be one of very few ways to create much-needed jobs.

Most villages are leased, rather than owned, by the Club. This reduces the political risk to the company, and also keeps debt off the balance sheet under French accounting rules. If need be, it can always threaten to pull out – and in some cases, such as Algeria, has actually done so.

The inclusion of everything, including transportation, in one price also gives the company tremendous purchasing power in its day-to-day operations. For example, the company is among the largest airline charterers in the world, allowing it to negotiate better air fares than its guests could ever hope to obtain independently. The same is true with everything from airport transfers to wind surfers. Some of the difference is passed on to the guests through a lower package price, but some also becomes reflected in the company's relatively high profit margins.

Trigano realized early on that the concept could, and should, be extended beyond the Mediterranean. He opened villages in many other parts of the world, including Morocco, the French West Indies and South America. He also built ski villages (the first began operations in Switzerland in 1956) and bought the first French seasonal time-share company, Clubhotel. He moved the Club upmarket by replacing many of the carefully 'primitive' straw hut villages with bungalow-style projects. He reduced the company's dependence on the French market by going international, which meant tailoring some of the villages specifically to an English-speaking clientele. An American subsidiary, Club Med Inc., was established to control properties in the Caribbean, South-East Asia and the Pacific. In 1973 he entered the Japanese market. North America and Japan are expected to provide much of the Club Med's future growth, so most of the extra villages are being sited within reasonable reach of those customers.

Another innovation was to give GMs a chance to learn as

well as to relax. Fascinated by novelty of all kinds, he saw the Club as a 'laboratory for the new leisure era' where people could explore the new technologies. ('We thus reduce their fear of the future.') A key element of this was the introduction of courses on how to use computers. He also pioneered the idea of 'mini-clubs' which cater exclusively for children and are designed to 'foster creativity, initiative, an opening on the world'. Trigano was so enthusiastic about this that he did not confine his efforts to Club Med. In 1982 he persuaded the French government to let him set up an August holiday camp in the Massif Central, a rough-and-ready place but with mini-computers, for 360 youngsters drawn from the 'difficult' suburbs of Lyons and Marseilles – kids of the kind ripe for delinquency. Trigano and some of his GOs lent their time and skills: the Club was not formally involved. President Mitterrand then stepped in, inviting Trigano to extend it to all-the-year centres in cities.

In 1986, Club Med announced another ambitious scheme: to build a forty-metre-high glass pyramid with a 500-room hotel attached somewhere between London and Heathrow airport. Inside the pyramid, it said, the temperature would be maintained at a subtropical 27° C, and it would house all the usual Club Med-type sporting facilities. The idea came from an Austrian businessman who had actually constructed such a complex twelve kilometres outside Vienna, but who lacked the experience and marketing skill to make it work. Club Med moved in. Trigano's son Serge, who is in charge of European operations, told reporters that the concept could be used all over the world – 'It works in hot climates as well.'

There may well be other diversification moves in the years to come, but the holiday villages are likely to remain the principal feature of the business. There are more than a hundred now; Trigano reckons the world could take another 160.

'Empires', Gilbert was quoted as saying in 1986, 'used to be conquests of territory, which is finite. The new empires are those of communications and the means of satisfying the needs and desires of men. These are infinite and always changing. I find the Club Med small compared to how it's going to be. I reckon my colleagues and successors have 150 years of work ahead of them before they can allow themselves to draw breath for a bit.'

Juan Terry Trippe

1899–1981

Emperor of the air

International air travel has changed beyond recognition since Charles Lindbergh made his historic flight across the Atlantic in 1927. Juan Trippe was one of the airline pioneers who helped to change it: he founded Pan-Am, established the first permanent service from the United States to a foreign country (carrying mail from Florida to Cuba) and pushed the western world into the jet age.

Born in New Jersey and educated at Yale, Trippe (named Juan after his step-grandfather, a rich Cuban) got interested in aviation while working for a bank. He was not romantic about it, like so many others in his day, but he saw the potential for profit and decided that this was the business he should be in. His influential Yale friends helped him to secure government mail contracts and his connections in the world of finance provided him with the necessary funds.

His first venture was a company called Long Island Airways, which bought surplus war planes to fly New York socialites to their country retreats. This was soon extended to carrying mail to various cities. Trippe raised the money to form a more ambitious company, Aviation Corporation of America, and then developed a subsidiary, Pan-American.

The airline pioneers were at the time chiefly interested in the US domestic market. Trippe decided to go for international business, starting with Latin America. He quickly gained the right to expand southwards, and hired Charles Lindbergh to publicize the scope for airlines by flying nine thousand miles through fourteen Latin American countries. By 1929, at the age of thirty, Trippe was a significant figure in the aviation industry, with a distinguished board of directors and a growing route network. He worked with local interests, but by no means all South Americans approved of his activities: some saw the airline as an adjunct of the State Department, an agent of American imperialism. Trippe pressed on, undeterred.

With government support, he also went into the Pacific market. He set up airfields on desolate islands, equipped them with radio stations and used them as refuelling bases for aircraft flying to places like Manila in the Philippines, China and Australia.

The North Atlantic route proved more difficult, not only because of the technical problems but also because rivals like Britain's Imperial Airways, backed by their own governments, were determined to keep him out. It was not until 1939, twelve years after Lindbergh's solo flight, that Pan-Am was able to start the first scheduled transatlantic flight – not to London, but via the Azores to Lisbon and on to Marseilles. Trippe used four-engined Boeing flying boats, with luxurious accommodation including sleeping berths, a dining room and five-passenger cabins. Four months later Europe was at war and Pan-Am's planes were filled with refugees, diplomats and spies. Churchill himself flew from Bermuda to Plymouth in one of the flying boats after visiting Roosevelt in 1942.

Meanwhile, Trippe continued to expand his Latin American business – he even set up a subsidiary to build twenty-five airports – and opened up a new African air route. Pan-Am became the pre-eminent world airline and Trippe was dubbed 'Emperor of the air'. Inevitably, though, his overseas monopoly was challenged by other American airlines, who had watched his impressive performance and were now eager to get in on the act. Trippe countered with an ingenious ploy: he prepared a plan to consolidate all American overseas airlines into what he called a 'Community Company'. He insisted that the company would not be controlled by any one individual, airline or group, but to his rivals it looked very much like an extension of Pan-Am and Congress failed to pass the necessary legislation. He tried again in 1947, with the help of people like Senator McCarren, who agreed that the real competition was between nations, not between companies; but the heads of other airlines testified against the bill and it never reached the floor of the Senate.

One of his strongest rivals was the formidable HOWARD HUGHES, who loved flying and had bought a controlling stake in TWA. Hughes succeeded in getting official approval to compete with Pan-Am, and ordered new planes – Boeing's four-engined Stratoliner and Lockheed's Constellation, which was capable of flying sixty passengers at 350 miles an hour. Hughes filled his inaugural flights (which he sometimes piloted himself) with Hollywood film stars and in his advertisements always stressed the romance of flying. He launched his first commercial service from New York to Paris in 1950, and other routes soon followed.

But the increasingly eccentric billionaire did not have

'Mass travel by air may prove to be more significant to world destiny than the atom bomb.'

Trippe's staying power, and eventually lost control of the airline. Trippe, who ran Pan-Am for nearly five decades, went on to play the key role in inaugurating the jet age. The Russian airline Aeroflot had first begun long-distance jet flights in 1956, but it was Trippe who saw the potential in big jets. He secretly negotiated with the major US manufacturers, pushed Boeing into building a plane which could carry 150 people across the Atlantic without a stop, and ordered forty-five of the expensive new aircraft, giving him the edge on his rivals. In 1958 a Pan-American 707 made the inaugural non-stop flight from New York to Brussels, ushering in an exciting new era in international air travel. It was, he declared (with every justification), the most important aviation development since Lindbergh's flight across the Atlantic: 'In one fell swoop we have shrunken the earth.'

Trippe was autocratic and ruthless, but he had courage and vision and his determined efforts set the pace for the others. He was an innovator who recognized the scope for international air travel at an early stage in the industry's remarkable progress and it made him, as well as numerous investors, very rich.

At the annual meeting of IATA in 1955, he explained how for years the tourist plane and the bombing plane had been racing each other. 'The tourist plane, if allowed to move forward unshackled by political boundaries and economic restrictions, will win this race between education and catastrophe. Mass travel by air may prove to be more significant to world destiny than the atom bomb.' One hopes that history will continue to prove him right.

Ted Turner

b. 1938

The maverick idealist

Ted Turner, the maverick television mogul from Atlanta, stunned the media world in 1985 when he made an audacious attempt to take over one of the giants of the American TV industry – CBS. He didn't succeed, but CBS was badly shaken and Turner established himself as a force to be reckoned with.

He had already proved himself to be a shrewd innovator by the creation of his Cable News Network and other ventures: here, clearly, was a man with great ambitions.

Turner was born in Cincinnati, where his father ran a billboard business. As a boy, Ted took up sailing and entered numerous races; he later won yachting's most coveted trophy, the America's Cup. After high school he wanted to attend the US Naval Academy at Annapolis, but his father insisted that he should join the family firm. He eventually became an account executive. But the business ran into trouble and his father decided to sell; in 1963 Ed Turner, depressed by his debts and the death of his daughter, shot himself. Ted, then twenty-four, managed to cancel the sale and went on to make a great success of the company.

At thirty, he decided to go into broadcasting. Ignoring the counsel of his financial advisers, he traded $2.5 million worth of stock in the billboard firm and bought Atlanta's Channel 17. The station was losing money, but Turner thought he had the answer. It was ingenious: he expanded the audience many times by beaming its signal via satellite to cable television systems all around the United States, a move which attracted a lot of extra advertising. He gave his venture a grandiose name: it became 'The Super Station that Serves the Nation'. By 1981 it was making a profit of $18 million and imitators appeared in New York and Chicago.

The station mostly showed re-runs, old movies and sports. Turner bought the Atlanta Braves and the Atlanta Hawks basketball teams, both of which were doing badly at the time, so that he could broadcast their games. He didn't pay much attention to news, because news-gathering was expensive, but this policy changed in 1980 when he started his Cable News Network (CNN). The newcomer soon established a loyal following. The first few years, however, were difficult financially. There was tough competition from the Satellite News Channel launched by ABC; Turner solved *that* problem by buying Satellite News for $25 million and taking it off the air. CNN has since moved solidly into the black.

When he launched his bid for CBS, many people felt that he couldn't possibly be serious. Turner Broadcasting was a dwarf compared to CBS. He would have to raise $4 or $5 billion; where would the money come from? His company had made only $10 million in 1984. But Turner *was* serious. He asked CBS stockholders to exchange their shares for some Turner Broadcasting stock and high-risk, high-yield junk bonds (see MICHAEL MILKEN) with a total value of $5.4 billion. His plan

He gave the venture a grandiose name: it became 'The Super Station that Serves the Nation'.

was to sell off substantial parts of CBS after the takeover, including all of its radio stations, one of the TV stations and the company's record division.

The CBS directors promptly rejected the offer, calling it 'grossly inadequate', and mounted a vigorous defence. One ploy was to fight Turner in the courts, charging him with misstating his company's profits in 1983 and 1984. The aim was to show that he wouldn't be able to service the debt on the securities he planned to issue. They also gained the public support of affiliates and others, who said that they liked CBS just as it was and expressed concern about Turner's motives. In June 1985, they petitioned the Federal Communications Commission to stop his bid. Turner himself also filed with the FCC, confirming that he intended to break up CBS. Finally, the directors themselves offered to buy 21 per cent of the company's stock at $150 a share. They had traded at $82 before Turner appeared on the scene, so the stockholders had good reason to be grateful to him. But it was clear that his attempt to win control would get nowhere.

Turner's next move was another stunner: he abandoned the battle and, instead, made an offer of $1.6 billion – all borrowed money – for the unprofitable MGM/United Artists entertainment group. Unlike CBS, they welcomed the bid. But in order to meet his vast debt repayments Turner later sold virtually all the pieces of the company, except its valuable library of films, back to their previous owner, financier Kirk Kekorian, and to TV producer Lorimar-Telepictures.

Meanwhile, he had come up with another idea: the Goodwill Games, a televised Olympic-style contest in Moscow meant to foster world peace, one of his obsessions. Turner signed an agreement that gave the Russians $9 million to play host; in return, he obtained the right to televise the games in the United States. They were broadcast in July 1986 and attracted a large audience, but he lost about $27 million on the deal.

Most people don't quite know what to make of Ted Turner. Some people regard him as a visionary, an idealist who cares passionately about the major issues of the day and who wants to play an active role in shaping the future. Some think he is simply a bold opportunist, someone who saw what other big players were doing and decided to join the game. Some see him as a flamboyant character whose outsize ego and ambition have put him on the road to disaster.

There is no doubt an element of truth in all these assessments – he is a complex character. On the desk in his office is a big sign: 'Either Lead, Follow, or Get Out of the Way'. One has to assume that he put it there because it represents his attitude to life. Like all innovators, Turner is a man who loves to make things happen.

Andy Warhol

1928–87

'America's most famous artist'

Whatever one may think of his paintings, there is no doubt that Andy Warhol had considerable entrepreneurial flair. He was very much aware of the value of publicity and knew how to get it; when he died early in 1987, at the age of fifty-eight, a *Newsweek* obituary called him 'America's most famous artist'. He left an estate worth $15 million, most of which he directed should go to a foundation 'for the advancement of the visual arts'.

He was born Andrew Warhola in Pittsburgh, the son of an immigrant Czech coal miner. Growing up in the grip of the Depression, he sold vegetables among other things and managed to enter the Carnegie Institute of Technology to study pictorial design. When he graduated and came to New York, he started to make the rounds of the advertising agencies; he would bring with him a bouquet from which he extracted a flower to give to each secretary. During the 1950s his work appeared in magazines like *Harper's Bazaar* and *Vogue*. But he longed for recognition as a serious artist, and the opportunity came with the Pop Movement in the early 1960s. Warhol's contribution was to find art in mass-produced images: Campbell's soup cans, stacks of Brillo soap pads, Marilyn Monroe repeated fifty times, a canvas filled edge-to-edge with images of Elizabeth Taylor, Jackie Kennedy, dollar bills or Elvis. They were designed to shock, and they succeeded. Critics lambasted Warhol, but he also attracted warm praise from people who felt that his fixation on repetition and glut was the most powerful statement ever made by an American artist on the subject of the consumer economy.

The media loved the controversy and Warhol proved to be an excellent salesman. His appearance was as bizarre as his paintings and he was always ready to pose for the photographers. He once said that, looking into a mirror, he saw 'the affectless gaze . . . the bored languor . . . the glamour rooted in despair . . . the pale, soft-spoken magical presence, the shadowy, voyeuristic, vaguely sinister aura . . . the albino-chalk skin . . . the shaggy silver-white hair. . . . I'm everything my scrapbook says I am.' He seemed to attend every party, and came up with a constant supply of attention-grabbing quotes. It was Warhol who made the immortal crack: 'In the future, everyone will be famous for fifteen minutes.'

As his own fame grew, the price of Warhols rocketed. When his soup-can pictures were first exhibited at the Ferus Gallery in Los Angeles (priced at $100) another gallery nearby put actual Campbell's soup cans in its window, advertising 'the real thing' for only 29 cents. But such ploys simply helped to get him more publicity, and his pictures soon fetched impressive prices. He went on to produce other works, including a series based on news photos of car crashes, the electric chair, race riots and the atomic bomb. He also published his own magazine, *Interview*, and made scores of underground

It was Warhol who made the immortal crack: 'In the future, everyone will be famous for fifteen minutes.'

films in which often nothing happened. (*Empire* offered eight hours of staring at the Empire State Building, while relatively action-packed *Eat* watched artist Robert Indiana eating a single mushroom for forty-five minutes.)

To his numerous detractors, Warhol was a self-publicizing fraud. To his admirers, he was a genius. Warhol himself said that art was just another job and that money was the most important thing in his life. He made far more than he could ever have done as a commercial artist working for agencies in search of novelty. The highest price ever paid for one of his works sold at auction was $385,000 – for a painting called, appropriately enough, *200 One Dollar Bills*.

According to *Newsweek*, 'His was a disquieting and unsettling art.' It unsettled one young woman so much that in 1968 she shot and gravely wounded him. Neither his health nor his talent ever fully recovered. The intensity disappeared from his work, and in the 1970s he confined himself mostly to social portraiture, liquor endorsements, and paintings of hammers and sickles. His fame still brought him commissions, but the art world no longer took him seriously. At the time of his death he was working on a series of paintings based on *The Last Supper* of Leonardo. When a critic asked Warhol: 'Does the *Last Supper* theme mean anything in particular to you?' he replied: 'No. It's a good picture.'

Warhol was a product of the 1960s – rich, clever, glib and ironic in the manner of high Manhattan fashion. He was a cynic who knew how to manipulate the media and how to titillate a youth-obsessed American culture. One could never be sure about his feelings: he displayed an emotional detachment which was seen by many as the ultimate cool. His best work magnified the icons of the day: his worst was kitsch. He made a greater impact than any other artist of his generation, but it remains to be seen whether his art will stand the test of time.

Thomas Watson Sr

1874–1956

Autocrat of computing

Thomas Watson was the creator of IBM, now one of the world's best-known corporations. For nearly four decades his influence on the business was all-pervading.

The Watson family came from Scotland and settled in New York State in the 1840s. By the age of eighteen Tom was working as a salesman. He eventually joined the National Cash Register Company and it was there, under the tutelage of its founder John Henry Patterson, that he learned the basic techniques he later used to build up IBM.

The origins of IBM lie in three companies which were merged in 1911 to form the Computing, Tabulating and Recording Company. It was then a small and unprofitable organization dealing with time clocks, weighing machines and the Hollerith calculator. Watson was appointed general manager in 1914, at the age of forty-one, and the following year he became president. He turned the company round, and in 1924 it was renamed International Business Machines. It continued to grow throughout the 1920s and the Depression, concentrating on machine rental, punch cards, a new series of calculators and a new electric typewriter. By 1937 it had over ten thousand employees, was represented in seventy countries and had an income of more than $30 million.

Like his mentor Patterson, Watson recognized the value of a disciplined workforce. Under his autocratic but benevolent leadership IBM became rather like the army, with the same kind of emphasis on neatness, sobriety and uniformity of appearance. He demanded obedience and loyalty and, in return, gave his employees job security, decent wages and fringe benefits which were better than those offered by his competitors. The IBM team was effectively organized to execute any given orders. This approach has been maintained to the present day.

Watson also applied various sales techniques which had proved effective at NCR: the Quota Sales Club, slick presentations and the use of simple, almost messianic, messages and slogans to urge on his salesmen. He developed an efficient intelligence system, to keep the company ahead of its competitors, and introduced the concept of leasing products rather than selling them.

IBM did well out of World War II, and the subsequent Cold War took it into the computer business. The first electronic computer is popularly believed to have been the ENIAC (Electrical Integrator and Numeric Calculator) developed by the Moore School of Engineering in Pennsylvania. Actually various other people, including a scientist in Nazi Germany, had hit on the idea of the electronic computer some years earlier. No one foresaw its tremendous possibilities; even the IBM management was sceptical. It was the American defence establishment which really got the computer industry under way. IBM was asked to build a large computer which could be used by defence planners, and Watson, still doubtful but willing to comply, gave his qualified approval to go ahead. Total demand was estimated at about seventeen. But it soon transpired that commercial companies were also interested in computers and IBM developed other models.

The concept of computer generations was born around this time. A generation is one in which a change in the basic components – the circuits on which computing ability rests – leads to a sizeable jump in performance. The generations were vacuum tube, transistors, MSI (or medium scale integration of circuits) and LSI (or large scale integration). All the generations after the first were essentially transistor generations.

IBM's marketing skills kept the company out in front. It had dominated the industry that preceded it – the accounting/

tabulating machine industry – and this gave it a major advantage in the conversion of users from one system to another. It was easier for IBM's salesmen to convert customers from existing equipment than it was for new entrants in the field to take away those customers. They also had an incentive to do so: their rewards were so structured that the loss of an existing account to a competitor led to a drop in the salesman's income.

Watson also applied various sales techniques which had proved effective at NCR: the Quota Sales Club, slick presentations and the use of simple, almost messianic, messages and slogans to urge on his salesmen.

Demand grew rapidly and IBM developed a new pricing technique. Computers were not to be sold or rented at prices which bore much relationship to what they cost to produce, but according to performance ability. As each computer model was a unique entity, the company could charge roughly what it liked. It did just that, and the policy contributed greatly to the company's growth.

From the early days, Watson's contract gave him both a salary and a percentage of net profit. He was already a very rich man by the mid-1930s, and in the years that followed he became richer still. He also developed some of the classic signs of megalomania. He would brook no argument, and insisted on making all decisions himself. No one dared to challenge him, even when he started to rename some of IBM's overseas subsidiaries: in countries like Sweden and Japan they were now called Watson Business Machines. Sycophants composed fulsome tributes, which he accepted as his due. They included company songs with lines like 'The name of T.J. Watson means a courage none can stem' and 'With T.J. Watson guiding us, we lead throughout the world'.

His eldest son, Tom Watson Jr, who had spent the war years flying in the US Air Force, was brought into the company and in 1952 was made president, with his father remaining chairman and chief executive officer. When the old man died he was the obvious choice to succeed him. He made many changes, setting his own stamp on the corporation, but IBM's business style remained essentially the same.

It is easy to make fun of the slogans and the company songs (now discarded), and the obsessive concern with the way its employees look. It is easier still to criticize the autocratic behaviour of its founder, which made it hard for intelligent and able people to act on their own initiative or to take decisions which they considered to be right. There are numerous stories about his capriciousness and his ruthless determination to get his own way. But that is not unusual: similar stories are told about many other self-made men. The point is that he got results. IBM is no longer a Watson fiefdom, and many things are done differently these days, but the Watsons, Senior and Junior, laid the foundations of a worldwide organization which has enjoyed remarkable success.

Index